The Least You Should Know THIRTEENTH Edition
about English

WRITING SKILLS

Paige Wilson
Pasadena City College

Teresa Ferster Glazier
Late, Western Illinois University

CENGAGE
Learning

Australia • Brazil • Mexico • Singapore • United Kingdom • United States

CENGAGE
Learning®

The Least You Should Know about English: Writing Skills, **13e**
Paige Wilson, Teresa Ferster Glazier

Product Director: Lauren Murphy

Associate Content Developer: Julie Bizzotto

Product Assistant: Chip Moreland

Senior Content Project Manager: Margaret Park Bridges

Art Director: Heather Marshall, Lumina Datamatics, Ltd.

Manufacturing Planner: Betsy Donaghey

IP Analyst: Ann Hoffman

Senior IP Project Manager: Kathryn Kucharek

Production Service: Lumina Datamatics, Ltd.

Compositor: Lumina Datamatics

Cover designer: Lumina Datamatics, Ltd.

Cover photo: © kirill_makarov/Fotolia

For product information and technology assistance, contact us at
Cengage Learning Customer & Sales Support, 1-800-354-9706

For permission to use material from this text or product, submit all requests online at **www.cengage.com/permissions.** Further permissions questions can be emailed to **permissionrequest@cengage.com.**

Library of Congress Control Number: 2016950836

Student Edition:
ISBN: 978-1-305-96094-7

Loose-leaf Edition:
ISBN: 978-1-305-95098-6

Cengage Learning
20 Channel Center Street
Boston, MA 02210
USA

Cengage Learning is a leading provider of customized learning solutions with employees residing in nearly 40 different countries and sales in more than 125 countries around the world. Find your local representative at **www.cengage.com.**

Cengage Learning products are represented in Canada by Nelson Education, Ltd.

To learn more about Cengage Learning Solutions, visit **www.cengage.com.**

Purchase any of our products at your local college store or at our preferred online store **www.cengagebrain.com.**

Printed in the United States of America
Print Number: 01 Print Year: 2016

CONTENTS

Preface   vii

Acknowledgments   viii

Getting the Most from *The Least You Should Know about English*   1

1. WORD USE   4

What Is the Least You Should Know about Word Use?   4

Word Use Preview Test   5

1. Words Often Confused (Set 1)   6
   Exercises   10

2. Words Often Confused (Set 2)   16
   Exercises   20

3. The Eight Parts of Speech   26
   Exercises   29

4. Adjectives and Adverbs   33
   Exercises   36

5. Contractions   40
   Exercises   41

6. Possessives   46
   Exercises   49

7. Consulting a Dictionary   53
   Exercises   56

Word Use Progress Test   60

Word Use Practice   61

2. SENTENCE STRUCTURE   62

What Is the Least You Should Know about Sentence Structure?   62

Sentence Structure Preview Test   64

8. Locating Prepositional Phrases   66
   Exercises   68

9. Finding Subjects and Verbs   72
   Exercises   74

10. Understanding Dependent Clauses   79
    Exercises   81

11. Correcting Fragments 89
Exercises 90

12. Correcting Run-on Sentences 95
Exercises 97
Review of Fragments and Run-on Sentences 102

13. Identifying Verb Phrases 104
Exercises 105

14. Using Standard English Verbs 110
Exercises 112

15. Using Regular and Irregular Verbs 116
Exercises 120

16. Maintaining Subject-Verb Agreement 125
Exercises 127

17. Avoiding Shifts in Time 133
Proofreading Exercises 134

18. Recognizing Verbal Phrases 136
Exercises 137

19. Correcting Misplaced or Dangling Modifiers 143
Exercises 144

20. Following Sentence Patterns 148
Exercises 150

21. Avoiding Clichés, Awkward Phrasing, and Wordiness 155
Proofreading Exercises 158

22. Correcting for Parallel Structure 160
Exercises 161

23. Using Pronouns 166
Exercises 169

24. Avoiding Shifts in Person 173
Proofreading Exercises 174

Sentence Structure Progress Test 176

Sentence Structure Practice 178

3. PUNCTUATION 179

What Is the Least You Should Know about Punctuation? 179

Punctuation Preview Test 180

25. Periods, Question Marks, Exclamation Points, Semicolons, Colons, Dashes 182
Exercises 184

26. Commas Used to Separate Elements 189
Exercises 191

27. Commas Used to Enclose Elements 197
Exercises 199
Comma Review Exercise 204

28. Quotation Marks and Italics/Underlines   205
   Exercises   206

29. Capital Letters   211
   Exercises   212

Punctuation Progress Test   217

Punctuation Practice   218

4. WRITING   219

What Is the Least You Should Know about Writing?   219
   Writing as Structure   219
   First-Person and Third-Person Approaches   220

Basic Structures   221
   30. The Paragraph   221
   Defining a Paragraph   221
   Types of Paragraphs   222
   Sample Paragraphs in an Essay   222
   Sample of a Single-Paragraph Assignment   223
   31. The Essay   224
   The Five-Paragraph Essay and Beyond   225
   Defining an Essay   225
   A Sample Professional Essay: "Wandering Home"   226

Writing Skills   228
   32. Writing in Your Own Voice   228
   Narration   230
   A Sample Student Essay: "Streetscaper"   230
   Description: "My Robot"   231
   Writing Exercises   232
      Writing Exercise 1   Narrate an Experience to Illustrate a Famous Saying   232
      Writing Exercise 2   Describe a Picture Worth 250 Words   232
   33. Finding a Topic   233
   Look to Your Interests   233
   Focused Free Writing (or Brainstorming)   234
   Clustering   234
   Talking with Other Students   235
      Writing Exercise 3   List Your Interests   235
      Writing Exercise 4   Do Some Free Writing   235
      Writing Exercise 5   Practice Clustering Ideas   235
   34. Organizing Ideas   236
   Thesis Statements   236
      Writing Exercise 6   Identify a Topic, Fact, or Thesis   237
      Writing Exercise 7   Write a Thesis Statement   237
   Organizing an Essay   237
   Topic Sentences   238
   Organizing Body Paragraphs (or Single Paragraphs)   238
   Transitional Expressions   239

Writing Exercise 8   Add Transitional Expressions 240

Writing Exercise 9   Write a Paragraph That Includes Transitions 240

35. Supporting with Details 240

Types of Support 241

A Sample Final Draft: "Drawing a Blank" 241

Writing Exercise 10   Write an Essay on One of Your Interests 243

36. Choosing and Using Quotations 244

Choosing Quotations 244

Using Quotations 245

Signal Phrases and Punctuation 245

Guidelines for Including Quotations 247

Writing Exercise 11   Write Sentences Using Signal Phrases and Quotations 247

37. Writing in Response to a Reading 248

A Sample Paragraph Response Using Quotations 248

Sample Reading Prompt 1 248

A Sample Essay Response Using Quotations: "Space Games" 249

Tips for In-Class Writing 251

Sample Reading Prompt 2 252

Writing Exercise 12   Write a Paragraph or Essay in Response to a Reading 252

38. Writing an Argument 252

Taking a Stand and Proving Your Point 252

A Sample Argument: "College at 16? I Think Not!" 253

Three Requirements of a Strong Written Argument 255

Writing Exercise 13   Write an Argument about Grades 255

39. Writing Summaries 256

A Sample Reading: "Bollywood Film Facts" 256

A Sample Summary 259

Writing Exercise 14   Write a Summary of a Reading 259

Summary Checklist 261

40. Revising, Proofreading, and Presenting Your Work 262

A Sample Rough Draft: "Drawing a Blank" 262

Writing Exercise 15   Revise a New Piece of Writing 264

Revision Checklist 264

Exchanging Papers (Peer Evaluations) 265

Proofreading Aloud 265

Presenting Your Work 265

Paper Formats 265

Titles 265

Answers 267

Index 343

Welcome to the thirteenth edition of *The Least You Should Know about English*, a text devoted to providing brief, essential explanations and deep practice with over 200 exercises to help students improve their English writing skills for the past thirty-five years.

- With a revised introduction titled "Getting the Most from *The Least You Should Know about English*," the thirteenth edition highlights key concepts of the "least you should know" approach and demonstrates their value in a world where we communicate more in writing than ever before.

- All sections in this edition are now numbered for easy reference, navigation, and syllabus preparation.

- Beginning with this edition, a Preview Test and Progress Test frame each of the first three Parts on "Word Use," "Sentence Structure," and "Punctuation." Extended answers to these tests provide full explanations with section references to help students self-manage the improvement of their sentence-level skills.

- To Part One on "Word Use," we have added a "Consulting a Dictionary" section that offers brief explanations and a full set of exercises covering eleven different uses of this often overlooked resource for writers.

- In Part Two on "Sentence Structure," we have switched the order of two existing sections so that "Locating Prepositional Phrases" precedes the related skill of "Finding Subjects and Verbs."

- Two new charts in Part Two follow the section on "Understanding Dependent Clauses" to illustrate the kinds of clauses and patterns of punctuation used to create simple, compound, complex, and compound-complex sentences.

- Continuing its thirty-five-year tradition, *The Least 13e's* clear explanations, abundant exercises, diverse topics, and complete answers encourage flexible coursework, cross-discipline reading, and self-directed learning.

- *The Least* helps student writers receive "just-in-time support" in any area, in any type of course (traditional, accelerated, stretch, or pathways), and through any delivery method (face-to-face, hybrid, or online).

In line with core standards, the updated exercises in the thirteenth edition continue to include globally relevant content from a variety of academic areas: science, art, history, film, literature, social studies, business, and the media. Students learn new, complex vocabulary as they read about both timely and timeless subjects—anything from the evolutionary reasons for our interest in video games to America's historical relationship with the number 13. Such thematic, cross-discipline exercises reinforce breadth of understanding and the need for cohesive details in students' own writing.

The Least You Should Know about English functions equally well on the go as a self-tutoring text and in the classroom (in person or online). It provides students with everything they need to progress on their own. Students who have previously felt overwhelmed by the complexities of English should, by practicing essential skills and through writing and rewriting their papers, gain the ability and confidence to fulfill all of their future writing needs.

A **Test Booklet** by Paige Wilson is available to instructors only. This supplemental booklet corresponds directly to the numbered sections of the thirteenth edition and includes both sentence-format and paragraph-format "tests" that can also act as additional exercises.

ACKNOWLEDGMENTS

First, I would like to thank the following reviewers for their insights, helpful commentary, and suggestions:

Kathleen Dorantes, *Imperial Valley College*
Jane Gamber, *Hutchinson Community College*
Kamri Goff, *Weber State University*
Victoria Hohenzy, *City Colleges of Chicago—Harry Truman*
Shuli Lamden, *Santa Fe Community College*
Becky Jean Marchant, *Weber State University*
Gay Monteverde, *Mt. Hood Community College*
Jake Patrick, *Georgia Military College*
Barbara Stanek-Salvestri, *Joliet Junior College*
Jennifer Triplett, *Santa Monica College*

I would also like to extend my gratitude to the students who have shared their writing in this thirteenth edition: Catherine Alarcon, Frances Castanar, Christine Foy, Juan Grandez, Vanessa Horta, Jessica Ovando, Adam Perez, and Maggie Wong.

As always, I am indebted to my publishing team for their expertise and hard work, especially the tireless efforts of Jacob Schott and Julie Bizzotto. And for the ongoing support and encouragement of my family, friends, students, and colleagues, I am forever grateful.

Paige Wilson
Pasadena City College

This book is dedicated to Teresa Ferster Glazier (1907–2004). In creating *The Least You Should Know about English,* she discovered a way to teach grammar and writing that students and teachers have actually enjoyed for over thirty-five years. Her original explanations and approaches have been constant sources of inspiration for this and all previous coauthored editions, as they will be for all future editions of her text.

Getting the most from
The Least You Should Know about English

Most English textbooks cover more than you need to know. This book will present the *least you should know* in order to write with clarity and confidence. Improving your writing skills doesn't require memorizing complex grammatical terms like *gerund, auxiliary verb,* or *demonstrative pronoun.* You can write well without knowing such technical labels if you understand certain key concepts—what we call "the least you should know about English." The concepts covered in the four parts of this book progress from smaller structures to larger ones but can be approached in any order.

Part One on **"Word Use"** demonstrates how words work alone and together in predictable ways to express meaning. **Part Two** on **"Sentence Structure"** explains how subjects and verbs create clauses and join other structures to form sentences. Part Two also illustrates how knowing the patterns of English can help writers avoid and correct common errors. **Part Three** on **"Punctuation"** shows how punctuation marks act as a written code to aid understanding. **Part Four** on **"Writing"** explains how paragraphs and essays present ideas and evidence on a larger scale and in a variety of ways through the process of composition. To reinforce these concepts, all four parts focus less on "rules" and more on the skills and structures that successful writers use to communicate.

The English you'll learn in this book is sometimes called Standard Written English, and it may differ slightly or greatly from the English you use when speaking. Standard Written English is the form of writing accepted in business and the professions, both online and in print. So no matter how you speak, you will communicate better in writing when you use Standard Written English. You might *say,* "That's a whole nother problem," but you would probably want to *write,* "That's a completely different problem." Knowing the difference between spoken English and Standard Written English is essential in college, in business, and in life. For example, the following sentence contains a commonly misused or misspelled word. Can you spot it?

I hope that my favorite university will except my application for admission.

The writer probably relied on the sound, not the meaning, of the word *except* to choose it. *Except* means "to exclude or leave out." The two words *except* and *accept* sound similar but have opposite meanings (see Section 1). The writer should have used the word *accept,* which means "to receive or agree to take" the application:

> I hope that my favorite university will *accept* my application for admission.

Here's another example, this time missing a comma to separate two statements joined by *and*:

> The manager fired Kevin and Chloe and I received a promotion.

Adding a comma after Chloe means that the manager fired two people:

> The manager fired Kevin and Chloe, and I received a promotion.

But perhaps Chloe received a promotion with me; then the comma should follow Kevin:

> The manager fired Kevin, and Chloe and I received a promotion.

Punctuation changes the meaning—and Chloe's life—dramatically. With the help of this text, we hope that your writing becomes so clear that no one will misunderstand it.

As you progress through the book, it's important to hold on to information because the concepts and structures of English form patterns that develop and sharpen with use. For example, knowing how subjects and verbs work will help you avoid fragments, proofread for subject-verb agreement, and use effective punctuation.

HOW TO GET THE MOST FROM THIS BOOK

1) Read the explanations within each section carefully; they're brief and full of helpful hints.

2) Do the first exercise and compare your responses with the answers. If they don't match or make sense, look at the explanations and examples again to find out why.

3) Do the second exercise and check it. If you're puzzled by even one answer, return to the explanation. You must have missed something. Be tough on yourself. Don't just think, "Maybe I'll get it next time." Review the examples, and *then* try again.

4) You may be tempted to quit after doing well on one or two exercises. Instead, encourage yourself to finish another. *Understanding* a concept or structure is just the first step; with *practice,* understanding becomes second nature.

5) Once you've explored a concept or structure fully, move on to the proofreading and writing exercises to help you apply that knowledge to sentences, paragraphs, and essays of your own.

Learning the basics of any important skill takes time. Generally, college students spend a couple of hours outside of class for each hour in class. You may want to spend more. Undoubtedly, the more you consciously explore and reinforce "the least you should know" concepts through practice, the stronger your writing skills will become.

Word Use

WHAT IS THE LEAST YOU SHOULD KNOW ABOUT WORD USE?

Words are very much like people. They mean different things and work in different ways in different locations, but these meanings and jobs are *not* random. A doctor in a white lab coat and stethoscope checking heart rates would be out of place at a pool party. But the same person, if swimming around in a bathing suit, could be a guest at a pool party. The difference is in how the person acts in different settings. Words are just the same. In the same way that we can recognize doctors when they check our heart rates and pool party guests when they paddle around in swimsuits, we can recognize nouns when they name people, places, or things and verbs when they show actions.

Just as the same person can be either a doctor or a guest at a pool party, a word can be either a noun or a verb, depending on its use in a particular sentence. For example, as a word in the sentence "Your smile brightens my day," *smile* is a noun subject that names the thing that brightens my day. But in the sentence "I smile whenever I see that video," the word *smile* is a verb, telling the action that happens when I see the video. Some words are more versatile than others. The word *back,* for instance, can be a noun, a verb, an adjective, or an adverb, depending on how it participates with the words around it: "The *back* of my car *backed* into our *back* fence, so I have to go *back* to the body shop." Our newly added section on "Consulting a Dictionary" (Section 7) helps to explain how even a common word like *back* has more than one identity and purpose. To preview the ways in which words, like people, work alone and together to create meaning, take the Word Use Preview Test.

Word Use Preview Test

Think of this preview test as an opportunity to discover how much you already know about word use, rather than as a test to be graded. You can check your answers, but first try your best. Read each of the following sentences carefully, and choose the word or term that successfully completes its meaning:

1. The height of a vehicle (affects, effects) its potential to roll over.

2. My art teacher (complemented, complimented) me on my shading skills.

3. An ambulance sped (passed, past) us and honked loudly at the intersection.

4. Allergies to nuts, especially peanuts, can be (quiet, quite) dangerous.

5. In the sentence "She left her keys *on* the dashboard," *on* is (an adverb, a preposition).

6. In the sentence "Our guests were tired, *so* the party ended early," *so* is a (pronoun, conjunction).

7. In the sentence "The twins look *identical*," *identical* is an (adjective, adverb).

8. They did not do as (good, well) as they expected on their group projects.

9. We all felt (bad, badly) about the missing backpack.

10. (Its, It's) been raining since last Saturday.

11. (Whose, Who's) the creator of Sherlock Holmes?

12. A surprise (party's, parties') success depends on secrecy.

13. The new theme park exceeded all of the (teenager's, teenagers') expectations.

14. An (eye-catching, eye catching) cover can increase book sales.

15. Last semester, we studied the history of the (internet, Internet).

1. Words Often Confused (Set 1)

To help you learn the difference between words often confused, we've divided the most commonly confused words into two sets that contain examples and helpful memory tips. Study the pairs of words in Set 1 before trying the exercises. Then move on to Set 2. If you practice each set thoroughly and check your answers along the way, your word choice skills will improve.

a, an

Use *an* before a word that begins with a vowel sound (*a, e, i,* and *o,* plus *u* when it sounds like *uh*) or silent *h.* Note that it's not the letter but the *sound* of the letter that matters.

> *an* apple, *an* essay, *an* inch, *an* onion
>
> *an* umpire, *an* ugly design (The *u*'s sound like *uh.*)
>
> *an* hour, *an* honest person (The *h*'s are silent.)

Use *a* before a word that begins with a consonant sound (all the sounds except the vowels, plus *u* or *eu* when they sound like *you*).

> *a* chart, *a* pie, *a* hat (The *h* is not silent in *hat.*)
>
> *a* union, *a* uniform, *a* unit (The *u*'s sound like *you.*)
>
> *a* European vacation, *a* euphemism (*Eu* sounds like *you.*)

accept, except

Accept means "to receive or agree to take." Think of the two *c*'s in *accept* as two hands curling up to receive something.

> I *accept* this award on my mother's behalf.

Except means "excluding" or "but." Think of the *x* in *except* as two arms crossed to block something or someone.

> The airline upgraded everyone *except* Stanley.

advise, advice

Advise is a verb. (Remember, "*Wise* people *advise.*" Note the *s* sounds like *z* in both *wise* and *advise.*)

> I *advise* you to apply for a seasonal job.

Advice is a noun. (Another rhyme helps here. You can give or take *advice* like a bowl of *rice.*)

> My math tutor gave me the best *advice.*

affect, effect   *Affect* is almost always a *verb* that means "to alter or influence someone or something." Try substituting another *verb* that starts with *a*—like *alter* or *amaze* or *astound*—to see if it works. If it does, then use this verb that starts with *a: affect*.

> All quizzes will *affect* the final grade. (All quizzes will *alter* the final grade.)

> That story *affected* everyone who heard it. (That story *amazed* everyone who heard it.)

Effect is most commonly used as a *noun* and means "a result." Focus on the *e* sound in *effect* and *result*, and try substituting *result* for *effect* as a test.

> The strong coffee had a powerful *effect*. (The strong coffee had a powerful *result*.)

> We studied the *effects* of sleep deprivation in my psychology class. (We studied the *results* . . . .)

all ready,   If you can leave out the *all* and the sentence still makes
already   sense, then *all ready* is the form to use.

> That box is *all ready* to go. ("That box is *ready* to go" makes sense.)

But if you *can't* leave out the *all,* use *already.*

> That box is *already* full. ("That box is *ready* full" does not make sense, so use *already.*)

are, our   *Are* is a present form of the verb "to be."

> We *are* going to Colorado Springs.

Our is a possessive pronoun that works as an adjective. It shows that we possess something.

> We painted *our* fence to match the house.

brake, break   *Brake* used as a verb means "to slow or stop motion." It's also the device that slows or stops motion in a *car.* Remember that both *car* and *brake* have an *a* in the middle.

> I had to *brake* quickly to avoid an accident.

> Luckily I just had the *brakes* on my car fixed.

Break used as a verb means "to shatter" or "to split." It's also the name of an interruption, as in "a coffee break."

> She never thought she would *break* a world record.

> Enjoy your spring *break*.

choose, chose The difference here is one of time. Use *choose* for present and future; use *chose* for past.

I will *choose* a new major this semester.

They *chose* the wrong time of year to travel to India.

clothes, cloths *Clothes* are garments people wear; *cloths* are pieces of material you might clean or polish something with.

I love the *clothes* that characters wear in old movies.

Workers at car washes use special *cloths* to dry the cars.

coarse, course *Coarse* describes a rough texture or quality.

I used *coarse* sandpaper to smooth the surface of the board.

Course is used for all other meanings.

Of *course* we visited the golf *course* at Pebble Beach.

complement, compliment *Complement,* spelled with an *e in* the middle, means "to complete something as a perfect pair."

Use a color wheel to find a *complement* for purple.

Juliet's personality *complements* Romeo's: she is practical, and he's a dreamer.

Compliment, spelled with an *i* in the middle, has to do with nice comments or feedback. Remember the *i* in *nice* and *compliment.*

I received a *compliment* from my new boss.

We *complimented* them on their new home.

conscious, conscience *Conscious* means "awake" or "aware."

I wasn't *conscious* during my surgery.

Conscience means "that inner voice of right and wrong." The extra *n* in *conscience* should remind you of "No," which is what your conscience often says to you.

My *conscience* told me not to keep the money I found.

dessert, desert *Dessert* is the sweet one, the one people like two helpings of. So give it two helpings of *s.* Remember also that "stressed" spelled backwards is *desserts.*

When I'm stressed, I can eat two *desserts* in a row.

The other one, *desert,* is used for all other meanings and has two pronunciations (see "Consulting a Dictionary," Section 7).

The snake slithered slowly across the *desert*.

I promise that I won't *desert* you after graduation.

do, due   *Do* is a verb, an action. You *do* something.

I *do* most of my homework on the weekends.

But a payment or a paper is *due;* it is scheduled for a certain time.

Our first essay is *due* tomorrow.

Due also comes before *to* in a phrase that means *because of.*

The outdoor concert was canceled *due to* rain.

feel, fill   *Feel* describes *feel*ings.

Whenever I stay up late, I *feel* sleepy in class.

Fill is the action of pouring into or packing something fully.

I want to *fill* my essay with memorable details.

fourth, forth   The word *fourth* has *four* in it, but *forty* does not. Remember the word *forty-fourth* to help you spell both of these words related to numbers.

This is our *fourth* quiz in *forty*-eight hours.

My grandparents celebrated their *forty-fourth* anniversary.

If you don't mean a number, use *forth*.

The ship's passengers walked back and *forth* on deck.

have, of   *Have* is a verb. Sometimes, in a contraction, it sounds like *of.* When you say *could've*, the *have* may sound like *of,* but it is not written that way. Always write *could have, would have, should have, might have.*

We should *have* planned our vacation sooner.

Then we could *have* used our coupon for a free ticket.

Use *of* in prepositional phrases. (See Section 8.)

She sent me a box *of* chocolates for my birthday.

hear, here	The last three letters of *hear* spell "ear." You *hear* with your ear.
	When I listen to a seashell, I *hear* ocean sounds.
	The other spelling *here* tells "where." Note that the three words indicating a place or pointing out something all have *here* in them: *here, there, where.*
	I'll be *here* for three more weeks.
it's, its	*It's* is a contraction of "*it is*" or "*it has*." (See Section 5.)
	"*It's* hot" means "*It is* hot."
	"*It's* been hot all week" means "*It has* been hot all week."
	Its is a possessive pronoun that works as an adjective. It means "belonging to it." Possessive pronouns such as *its, yours, hers, ours, theirs,* and *whose* do not require apostrophes. (See Section 6.)
	The jury had made *its* decision.
	The dog pulled at *its* leash.
knew, new	*Knew* has to do with *knowledge;* both start with a silent *k.*
	New means "fresh" or "recently acquired," the opposite of "old."
	Her friends *knew* that she wanted a *new* bike.
know, no	*Know* has to do with *knowledge;* both start with a silent *k.*
	By Friday, I must *know* all the state capitals.
	No means "not any" or the opposite of "yes."
	My boss has *no* patience. *No,* I am not exaggerating.

EXERCISES

Choose between the words in parentheses to successfully complete the following sentences. Check your answers after each set to make the most progress.

Exercise 1.1

1. People don't usually (choose, chose) to be right-handed or left-handed.

2. Yet (it's, its) one of the distinctions that (affects, effects) people's lives every day.

3. Left-handedness has (a, an) unpleasant connotation in almost every language, (accept, except) Greek, (do, due) to some negative qualities associated with the word *left*.

4. Lefties must (accept, except) that in Anglo-Saxon, French, Spanish, Russian, German, and Italian, *left* can mean "weak," "crude," "malicious," "sneaky," "clumsy," and "deceitful," respectively.

5. A remark that (a, an) particular person is left-handed may not be a (complement, compliment), unless (it's, its) from another lefty.

6. Luckily, lefties (all ready, already) have many left-handed celebrities to (feel, fill) proud of, including Prince William, Oprah Winfrey, Jennifer Lawrence, Morgan Freeman, Angelina Jolie, and Hugh Jackman.

7. (Here, Hear) are just a few of the objects designed for right-handed people, who make up 90 percent of the population: classic wristwatches, car ignitions, slot machines, shirt pockets, as well as certain weapons and power tools.

8. Of (course, coarse), most people are not even (conscious, conscience) of this minor snub: whenever left-handed people hold pens, pencils, crayons, spoons, forks, and other tubular utensils, their branding appears upside down.

9. One positive (affect, effect) for left-handers is that they can still function if they (break, brake) their left hand or arm because they are used to using both hands.

10. But right-handed people cannot usually (do, due) anything with their left hands if something happens to their right.

Source: The Hand Owner's Manual: A Hand Surgeon's Thirty-Year Collection of Important Information and Fascinating Facts (VBW Publishing, 2008) and http://www.mtv.com/news/2239722/left-handed-celebrities/?xrs=_s.tw_main

Exercise 1.2

1. People have (a, an) exciting (knew, new) way to buy books.

2. (It's, Its) all (do, due) to a device called the Espresso Book Machine—or EBM.

3. At bookstores and libraries, users can (choose, chose) titles from (a, an) online list and send the data directly to the EBM to be printed on the spot.

4. The EBM prints (a, an) 300-page book in only three minutes and then binds (it's, its) pages in a traditional paperback cover.

5. Many booksellers and coffee shops (all ready, already) offer the services of this new kind of "Espresso" machine.

6. Some libraries use these instant book printers to (complement, compliment) the books in their regular holdings.

7. People can also (choose, chose) to print books that they have written themselves.

8. (It's, Its) too soon to (know, no) whether readers and writers will (accept, except) the idea of instant books.

9. Once they (hear, here) about the EBM, however, most people (do, due) want to try one.

10. The cost of printing (a, an) instant book is reasonable too; (it's, its) about one penny a page.

Source: ondemandbooks.com

Exercise 1.3

1. (It's, Its) never too late to learn something (knew, new).

2. After living for nearly one hundred years without knowing how to read or write, George Dawson could (have, of) just (accepted, excepted) his life as it was.

3. But he never did (feel, fill) good about hiding his illiteracy from his children or signing his name with (a, an) X.

4. In 1996, George Dawson (choose, chose) to start school for the first time at the age of ninety-eight.

5. Dawson, who was (all ready, already) in his teens when the *Titanic* sank, worked all of his life to support his family and even outlived his (fourth, forth) wife.

6. He had enough memories to (feel, fill) a book, (accept, except) he wouldn't (have, of) been able to read it.

7. Then a man in Seattle came to (hear, here) of Dawson's long life and strong desire for (a, an) education.

8. Richard Glaubman, a teacher himself, gave Dawson the (advise, advice) to share his experiences in a book, and he helped Dawson write his autobiography.

9. In the (coarse, course) of his life as an African American man and the grandson of slaves, George Dawson witnessed and felt the (affects, effects) of racism and oppression.

10. But Dawson always believed that painful moments in life only (complemented, complimented) the joyful ones, and he titled his book *Life Is So Good.*

Source: http://www.aaregistry.org/historic_events/view/three-centuries-life-george-dawson and *Jet,* April 17, 2000

Exercise 1.4

1. If you wear any (clothes, cloths) made of polyester, you may be wearing what used to be (a, an) old movie print.

2. (Do, Due) to the huge numbers of reels of film needed to meet the demands of today's movie audiences, recycling is (a, an) necessary part of the motion picture industry.

3. Companies such as Warner Bros. and New Line Cinema (accept, except) the responsibility for film recycling.

4. Of (coarse, course), the best prints of movies are saved for the future, but there (are, our) usually thousands of leftover copies (all ready, already) to be turned into something else.

5. The recycling process begins by chopping the film into (course, coarse) pieces, then transforming the rubble into a (knew, new) substance, such as polyester fabric.

6. Movie distributors are (conscious, conscience) that collectors and other interested parties would love to get their hands on these extra movie prints.

7. Therefore, security is (a, an) essential part of the movie-recycling process.

8. Someone trying to (brake, break) into a warehouse in search of last month's hottest release would (feel, fill) very disappointed.

9. The five to six reels of each film would (have, of) (all ready, already) been separated and mixed together with other films' reels.

10. (It's, Its) (know, no) surprise that movie companies want to protect their interests.

Source: Los Angeles Times, February 17, 2003

Exercise 1.5

1. Dentists (are, our) hardworking professionals, but most of us don't want to visit them.

2. Almost all of us hate to have (are, our) teeth drilled.

3. Most of us do, however, (accept, except) the need for dental work as a part of modern life.

4. (It's, Its) surprising to learn that dentists used drills on their patients 9,000 years ago.

5. (Knew, New) scientific discoveries have brought (fourth, forth) the remains of nomads who lived in the Stone Age.

6. Amazingly, many of their teeth revealed the (affects, effects) of drilling to eliminate decay.

7. Scientists don't (know, no) exactly what substance was used to (feel, fill) the cavities.

8. (It's, Its) also unclear whether patients were given anything so that they didn't (feel, fill) pain.

9. Based on the drilling patterns, scientists believe that some Stone Age people took advantage of the holes in their teeth for a decorative (affect, effect).

10. They may have used precious stones to (feel, fill) these holes as (a, an) ancient form of "mouth bling."

Source: National Geographic News, April 4, 2006

Exercise 1.6   Proofreading Practice

Find and correct the ten errors contained in the following paragraph. All of the errors involve Words Often Confused (Set 1).

In the middle of a debate in my speech class last week, I suddenly became very self-conscience. I could fill my heart beating faster, and I didn't no what to do. I looked around to see if my nerves were having a affect on the audience. Of coarse, they could here my voice trembling. The topic that we were debating was whether to eliminate letter grades in college, and everyone else was doing really well. But for some reason, my face turned bright red, and I would of left the room if I could. After the debate, my classmates gave me lots of complements, but I new that they where just trying to be nice.

Exercise 1.7   Sentence Writing

The surest way to learn commonly confused words is to use them immediately in your own writing. Choose five pairs from Words Often Confused (Set 1). Then use each of the words correctly in new sentences of your own. You can compare your sentences with the samples in the explanations or exchange papers with another student for feedback and proofreading practice.

2. Words Often Confused (Set 2)

Study this second set of commonly confused words as carefully as you did the first. Read the short explanations, helpful hints, and sample sentences before doing the exercises. Check your answers regularly to make the most progress as you learn the pairs and word groups in Set 2.

lead, led	*Lead* is the dull metal that rhymes with *head.*
	Old paint is dangerous because it often contains *lead.*
	The past form of the verb "to lead" is *led.*
	What factors *led* to your decision?
	I *led* our school's debating team to victory last year.
	If you don't mean past time, use *lead,* which rhymes with *seed.*
	I will *lead* the debating team again this year.
loose, lose	*Loose* means "not tight." Note how *l o o s e* that word is. It has plenty of room for two *o*'s. Remember that *loose* and *tooth* both have two *o*'s in the middle.
	My sister has a *loose* tooth.
	Lose is the opposite of win. Pronounce the *s* like a *z.*
	If we *lose* the next game, we will be out for the season.
passed, past	*Passed* is a form of the verb "to pass." Use *passed* whenever it's a verb.
	Nanette easily *passed* her math test.
	The runner *passed* the baton to her teammate.
	I have *passed* your house many times before.
	Use *past* when you mean "by" or "beyond" and to refer to the time that came before the present.
	I drove *past* your house. (". . . *by* your house." The verb in this sentence is *drove.*)
	Our coach never pushes us *past* our limits. (". . . *beyond* our limits." The verb in this sentence is *pushes.*)
	It's best to learn from *past* experiences.
	In the *past,* he worked for a small company.

personal, personnel	Pronounce these two correctly, and you won't confuse them—*pérsonal, personnél.*
	She shared her *personal* views as a parent.
	Personnel means a group of employees.
	I had an appointment in the *personnel* office.
piece, peace	Remember "a *piece* of *pie*." The word meaning "a *piece*" always begins with *pie.*
	Some students asked for an extra *piece* of scratch paper.
	The other word, *peace,* is the opposite of war.
	The two sides finally signed a *peace* treaty.
principal, principle	*Principal* means "main." Both words have *a* in them: princip*a*l, m*a*in.
	The *principal* concern is safety. (m*a*in concern)
	We paid both *principal* and interest. (m*a*in amount of money)
	Also, think of a school's "princi*pal*" as your "*pal.*"
	An elementary school *principal* must be kind. (m*a*in administrator)
	A *principle* is a "rule." Both words end in *le:* princip*le*, ru*le*.
	I am proud of my *principles*. (ru*le*s of conduct)
	We value the *principle* of truth in advertising. (ru*le*)
quiet, quite	Pronounce these two correctly, and you won't confuse them. *Quiet* means "free from noise" and rhymes with *diet.*
	Golfers often ask spectators to be *quiet.*
	Quite means "very" or "really" and ends with the same three letters as *white.*
	The bleach made my towels *quite* white.
right, write	*Right* means "correct," "proper," or "the opposite of left."
	You will find your keys if you look in the *right* place, on the *right* side of the coffee table.
	It also means "in the exact location, position, or moment."
	Your keys are *right* where you left them.

Let's go *right* now.

Write means "to compose sentences, poems, essays . . . ."

I *write* in my journal every day.

than, then   *Than* is used to compare. Remember that both *than* and *compare* have an *a* in them.

I am taller *than* my sister.

Then tells when. *Then* and *when* rhyme, and both have an *e* in them.

I always write a rough draft of a paper first; *then* I revise it.

their, there, they're   *Their* is a possessive pronoun that works as an adjective. It means "belonging to them."

They read *their* essays out loud.

There points out something or points to something. Remember that the three words indicating a place or pointing out something all have *here* in them: *here, there, where.*

In Hawaii, *there* is always a rainbow in the sky.

I haven't been *there* before.

They're is a contraction of "*they are.*" (See Section 5.)

"*They're* living in Canada now" means "*They are* living in Canada now."

threw, through   *Threw* is the past form of "to throw."

The students *threw* snowballs at each other.

I *threw* away my application for a scholarship.

If you don't mean "to throw something," use *through.*

We could see our beautiful view *through* the new curtains.

They worked *through* their differences.

two, too, to   *Two* is a number.

We have written *two* papers so far in my English class.

Too means "very" or "also," and so it also has an extra *o.*

The movie was *too* long and *too* violent. (very)

They are enrolled in that biology class, *too*. (also)

Use *to* for all other meanings.

They like *to* ski. They're going *to* the mountains.

weather,
whether

Weather refers to conditions of the atmosphere.

Snowy *weather* is too cold for me.

Whether means "if."

I don't know *whether* it is snowing there or not.

were, wear,
where

These words are pronounced differently but are often confused in writing.

Were is a past form of the verb "to be."

We *were* interns at the time.

Wear usually means "to have on," as in wearing clothes.

I always *wear* a scarf in winter.

Where refers to a place. Remember that the three words indicating a place or pointing out something all have *here* in them: *here, there, where.*

Where are the teachers' mailboxes?

who's, whose

Who's is a contraction of "*who is*" or "*who has*." (See Section 5.)

"*Who's* responsible for the checks?" is asking "*Who is* responsible for the checks?"

"*Who's* been signing them?" wants to know "*Who has* been signing them?"

Whose is a possessive pronoun that works as an adjective. Words such as *whose, its, yours, hers, ours,* and *theirs* are already possessive forms and never need an apostrophe. (See Section 6.)

"*Whose* keys are these?" is asking whom the keys belong to—who possesses these keys.

woman,
women

The difference is one of number, like *man* and *men*. *Woman* refers to one adult female; wo*men* refers to two or more adult females.

I know a *woman* who has bowled a perfect game.

I bowl with a group of *women* from my work.

you're, your	*You're* is a contraction of "*you are.*" (See Section 5.)
	"*You're* as smart as I am" means "*You are* as smart as I am."
	Your is a possessive pronoun that works as an adjective. It means "belonging to you."
	I borrowed *your* lab book.

EXERCISES

Choose between the words in parentheses to successfully complete the following sentences. Check your answers after each set to make the most progress.

Exercise 2.1

1. One beautiful morning in fall, you may receive a phone call that changes (you're, your) life.

2. The caller will tell you that (you're, your) over $625,000 richer and that you don't have to do anything other (than, then) be yourself to deserve the money.

3. You might wonder (weather, whether) it is a real or a crank call.

4. Believe it or not, this wonderful (piece, peace) of news is delivered to between twenty and thirty special men and (woman, women) who receive special awards every year.

5. (Their, There, They're) unofficially called "genius grants," but (their, there, they're) actual name is MacArthur Fellowships.

6. The MacArthur Foundation awards its fellowships each year based on the (principal, principle) that forward-thinking people deserve an opportunity to pursue (their, there, they're) ideas freely and without obligation to anyone.

7. No application is necessary (two, too, to) receive the gift of $125,000 a year plus health insurance for five years, and no particular field of work receives more consideration (than, then) another.

8. The (principal, principle) characteristic that MacArthur Fellows share is (their, there, they're) creative potential—in any area.

9. Each year, the MacArthur Foundation sends about one hundred "scouts" across the country looking for people with untapped potential (two, too, to) nominate; (than, then) another anonymous group selects the year's recipients.

10. The nominees don't even know that (their, there, they're) going (threw, through) the process until the phone rings on that fateful morning in fall.

Source: http://www.macfound.org/fellows-faq/

Exercise 2.2

1. You've probably been (threw, through) this experience.

2. (You're, Your) in a movie theater or at a concert, and someone is using a smartphone to take pictures or video, ruining the live experience in the process.

3. In the (passed, past), (their, there, they're) was no way to keep this unfortunate event from happening.

4. Now (their, there, they're) is a phone-blocking sleeve that will maintain the integrity, as well as the (piece, peace) and (quiet, quite), of live events even if people still refuse to turn off (their, there, they're) smartphones.

5. This new phone-locking sleeve can keep people from getting at (their, there, they're) phones in theaters, auditoriums, classrooms, or anywhere else (their, there, they're) not wanted.

6. Of course, (their, there, they're) are people who do not want to (loose, lose) (their, there, they're) (right, write) to use these devices whenever they want.

7. One of the first performing artists (who's, whose) already required audience members (two, too, to) use a phone-locking pouch is the comedian Dave Chappelle.

8. At Chappelle's shows in Chicago in 2015, audience members received phone pouches at the door; (than, then) a phone-locking device sealed them shut.

9. When audience members walked (passed, past) the phone-locking device again to leave, the sleeves opened to allow people to remove the phones and use them again.

10. (Weather, Whether) (you're, your) for them or against them, phone-locking pouches could become popular worldwide (quiet, quite) soon.

Source: http://www.hollywoodreporter.com/news/how-dave-chappelle-is-creating-844886

Exercise 2.3

1. (Their, There, They're) is a new way to prepare children for earthquakes.

2. Researchers use current technology to put kids (threw, through) a simulated earthquake using virtual reality headphones and goggles.

3. Children in Greece have been the first (two, too, to) receive the training.

4. (Their, There, They're) very likely to experience a real earthquake, according to scientists.

5. The (personal, personnel) who teach students with special needs have seen very positive results from earthquake training.

6. In the (passed, past), children with Down syndrome, for example, would (loose, lose) control and panic during a frightening event such as an earthquake.

7. In a twist of fate, (their, there, they're) was an earthquake in Greece just a few months after some children were trained.

8. After being (lead, led) (through, threw) an artificial quake using virtual reality, the children with Down syndrome (were, wear, where) able to remain calm and follow directions.

9. In fact, all of the children who had experienced a virtual earthquake coped with the event better (than, then) those who hadn't.

10. It's unclear (weather, whether) virtual earthquake training will work as well with adults.

Source: Science News, August 5, 2006

Exercise 2.4

1. Knut is the name of a polar bear (who's, whose) early life made headlines in 2007.

2. Knut became (quiet, quite) a celebrity in Germany after being born in captivity and rejected by his mother at the Berlin Zoo.

3. The tiny abandoned polar bear was no bigger (than, then) a fat kitten when (personal, personnel) at the zoo had to make a difficult decision.

4. They had to decide (weather, whether) to let the little bear cub die naturally or to go against nature and raise him themselves.

5. At the time, some people voiced (their, there, they're) strong belief in the (principal, principle) that humans should not artificially raise wild animals.

6. As a small cub, Knut's fluffy white fur and adorable personality (lead, led) newspapers, magazines, and television stations (two, too, to) spread stories and photos of him around the world.

7. Children and adults (were, wear, where) equally impressed with Knut, and they wrote songs and books about him.

8. Companies even designed candy and other products (two, too, to) look like him.

9. Sadly, Knut (passed, past) away unexpectedly in March of 2011.

10. Although Knut lived a shorter life (than, then) most polar bears, he inspired many people (two, too, to) learn more and care more about them.

Source: http://www.dailymail.co.uk/news/article-1367921

Exercise 2.5

1. The three days following September 11, 2001, (were, wear, where) unique.

2. They offered an unprecedented opportunity to study an aspect of the (whether, weather) that could not be studied under normal conditions.

3. The situation that (lead, led) to the study was the temporary ban on nearly all airline flights over America.

4. In the (passed, past), scientists had wondered (whether, weather) the clouds produced by airplane engines affected temperatures on land.

5. These man-made clouds, called contrails, are the streaks left behind after an airplane has (passed, past) across the sky.

6. Never in the recent (passed, past) had (their, there, they're) been days when the skies were clear of contrails.

7. The absence of air traffic also produced an eerie kind of (quiet, quite).

8. Not wanting to (loose, lose) the chance to discover the effects of contrails, (two, too, to) scientists went (right, write) to work.

9. David Travis and Andrew Carleton discovered, (threw, through) comparisons of temperatures from the three days without air traffic and the same days for the (passed, past) thirty years, that the contrails may cause temperatures to cool slightly.

10. This (piece, peace) of scientific data could lead to a greater understanding of our impact on the planet's (whether, weather) overall.

Source: Discover, August 2002

Exercise 2.6   Proofreading Practice

Find and correct the ten errors in this paragraph. All errors involve Words Often Confused (Set 2).

Yesterday, we watched and discussed a short animated video in my philosophy class. The film shows office workers in a high-rise building looking down from there windows and watching pedestrians walk passed a small construction site on the street below, wear a jack hammer has broken a peace of the sidewalk. As pedestrians walk over the lose brick, several of them trip and fall but are not injured. The office personnel who are watching from above find each accident funnier then the one before until an old man with a cane approaches the dangerous site. His weak condition makes the office workers remember their principals of write and wrong, and they all try too warn the old man before he falls too. The film ends in a way that is quiet a surprise.

Source: http://creativity-online.com/work/liberty-mutual-good-vibrations/17799

Exercise 2.7   Sentence Writing

Write several sentences using any words you missed in the exercises for Words Often Confused (Set 2). Use one of the topics below or a new topic of your own.

- Something you would like to accomplish this year
- The qualities of a good friend
- A favorite game, video, series, or movie
- A place you would like to visit or know more about

3. The Eight Parts of Speech

Choosing the right word is an important aspect of writing. Some words sound alike but are spelled differently and have different meanings (*past* and *passed*, for instance), and some words are spelled the same but sound different and mean different things (*lead*, for the action of "leading," and *lead*, for the stuff inside pencils). Besides learning to use the right words, it is important to understand the roles that words play in sentences.

Just as one actor or actress can play many different parts in movies (a main character, a villain, a humorous sidekick), a single word can play many different parts in sentences (a noun, a verb, an adjective). The roles the words play are called the *eight parts of speech*, briefly defined with brief explanations and examples below:

1) **Nouns** name *people, places, things,* or *ideas* and are used as subjects and objects in sentences. **Proper nouns** that name *specific people, places, things, or ideas*—such as *Marie Curie, New York City, Kleenex,* and *Hinduism*—are capitalized and can include more than one word. (See Sections 8, 9, and 20 for more about nouns as subjects and objects. See Section 29 for more about capitalizing specific nouns.)

   Lee Frank and the other **librarians** have made many **improvements** to the **library**.

2) **Pronouns** are special words—such as *I, she, you, it, they, who, that,* and *us*—that replace nouns to avoid repeating them. Other pronouns—such as *someone, everybody, anything, all,* and *many*—stand in place of unknown people or things that we need to name. (See Section 23 and 24 for more about pronouns.)

   In fact, **we** are very proud of **them,** and **I** hope that **everyone** uses the library again.

3) **Adjectives** add description to nouns and pronouns—telling *which one, how many, what kind, color,* or *shape* they are. (See Section 4 for more about adjectives.)

   The **head** librarian helped to design **its new**, **state-of-the-art** facilities.

   The words *a, an,* and *the* are special forms of adjectives called **articles.** They always introduce a noun or a pronoun and are used so often that there is no need to label them.

4) **Verbs** show action or state of being. They can also link a subject with a description or help another verb in a verb phrase. (See Sections 9, 13–18, and 20 for more about verbs.)

   The new windows **reflect** the sky but **become** transparent after the sun **has set.**

5) Adverbs add information—such as *when, where, why,* or *how*—to verbs, adjectives, other adverbs, and whole clauses. (See Section 4 for more about adverbs.)

> The library **now** offers relaxation workshops at **highly** stressful times of year.

6) Prepositions show position in *space* and *time* and are followed by noun or pronoun objects to form prepositional phrases. (See Section 8 for more about prepositions.)

> The study rooms **on** the first floor **of** the library are full **by** 10 o'clock **in** the morning.

7) Conjunctions are connecting words that include the seven *fanboys* (*for, and, nor, but, or, yet, and so*) and the words that begin dependent clauses (such as *because, since, when, while,* and *although*). (See Sections 10 and 12 for more about conjunctions.)

> The library **and** its landscaping impress people **when** they first visit our campus.

8) Interjections begin or interrupt a sentence to convey a greeting or to show surprise or other emotions and are rarely used in Standard Written English.

> When people walk up or drive by, they say, "**Wow**, what a great building!"

To find out what parts of speech any word can play, look it up in a good, college-level dictionary. You'll find a list of definitions beginning with an abbreviated part of speech (*n, adj, prep,* and so on) that identifies its possible uses. (See Section 7 on "Consulting a Dictionary.") However, seeing how a word is used in a particular sentence is the best way to identify its part of speech. Look at these examples:

> Our **train** departs at three o'clock.
>
> (*Train* is a noun in this sentence, naming the vehicle we call a "train.")
>
> Sammy and Helen **train** new employees at Sea World.
>
> (*Train* is a verb in this example, showing the action of "training" someone.)
>
> Students can take a shuttle from the **train** station.
>
> (*Train* is an adjective here, adding to the noun *station* to say what kind it is.)

All of the words in a sentence work together to create meaning, but each one serves its own purpose by playing a part of speech. Think about how each of the words in the following sentence plays the particular part of speech labeled:

> n   prep   adj   n   adv   v   adj   n   prep   n   conj   v
> Students at community colleges often attend several classes in a day and are
>
> adv   adj   conj   pro   adv   v   adv
> very tired when they finally go home.

Below, you'll find an explanation for each label:

Students	n (*names the people* who are the subject of the sentence)
at	prep (*begins a prepositional phrase* showing position in space)
community	adj (*adds description* to the noun *colleges*, telling what kind)
colleges	n (*names the place* that is the object of the preposition *at*)
often	adv (*adds to the verb*, telling when students *attend* classes)
attend	v (*shows an action*, telling what the students do)
several	adj (*adds description* to the noun *classes*, telling how many)
classes	n (*names the things* that the students *attend*)
in	prep (*begins a prepositional phrase* showing position in time)
a	no label (an article that *points to the noun day*)
day	n (*names the thing* that is the object of the preposition *in*)
and	conj (*joins* the two verbs *attend* and *are*)
are	v (*links* the subject *students* with the descriptive word *tired*)
very	adv (*adds to the adjective* that follows, telling how *tired* the students are)
tired	adj (*describes the noun* subject *students*)
when	conj (*begins a dependent clause*)
they	pro (*replaces* the noun *students* to avoid repetition)
finally	adv (*adds to the verb*, telling when they *go* home)
go	v (*shows an action*, telling what they do)
home.	adv (*adds to the verb*, telling where they *go*)

Familiarizing yourself with the parts of speech will help you use words more correctly now and understand phrases and clauses better later. Each of the eight parts of speech has characteristics that distinguish it from the other seven, but it takes practice to learn them.

EXERCISES

Label the parts of speech above all of the words in the following sentences using the abbreviations **n**, **pro**, **adj**, **v**, **adv**, **prep**, **conj**, and **interj**. Remember that proper nouns can include more than one word and that you may ignore the words *a*, *an*, and *the*. Refer back to the definitions and examples of the parts of speech whenever necessary. When in doubt, leave a word unmarked until you check the answers after each set of ten sentences.

Exercise 3.1

1. Bette Nesmith Graham invented correction fluid in the 1950s.
2. She originally called her invention Mistake Out.
3. Later, she changed its name to Liquid Paper.
4. Originally, Graham worked as a typist, and she often made mistakes.
5. She brought white paint to work and covered her typos with it.
6. Soon everyone wanted a bottle of Graham's correction paint.
7. She mixed the product in her kitchen and bottled it like fingernail polish.
8. Single-handedly, Graham developed a product that made millions of dollars.
9. Her son, Michael Nesmith, also benefited from her success.
10. He was a member of The Monkees, a popular band in the 1960s.

Source: Invention and Technology, Fall 2009

Exercise 3.2

1. Clyde Tombaugh discovered the ninth "planet," Pluto, in 1930.
2. Tombaugh died in 1997 at the age of 90.

3. Scientists loaded Tombaugh's ashes onto New Horizons, a space probe that was launched in January of 2006.

4. New Horizons arrived near Pluto in 2015.

5. After the launch of New Horizons, astronomers deleted Pluto from the list of real planets.

6. They determined that real planets must control their own orbits.

7. Pluto is an icy ball under the influence of Neptune's orbit.

8. Astronomers put Pluto into the new category of "dwarf planet."

9. When they demoted Pluto, the official number of real planets changed to eight.

10. Yes, but recent evidence of a new planet may bring that number to nine again.

Source: Newsweek, September 4, 2006, and *http://www.space.com/16080-solar-system-planets.html*

Exercise 3.3

1. In the summer of 2005, London Zoo opened a temporary exhibit.

2. The title of the exhibit was "The Human Zoo."

3. Zoo officials selected eight human volunteers.

4. Then they put the humans on display for several days.

5. Dozens of people had applied online for the project.

6. The exhibit showcased three males and five females.

7. They dressed in fake fig leaves that covered their shorts and bikini tops.

8. With its rocky ledges and cave-like structures, the enclosure had previously housed bears.

9. The eight humans talked, played games, and received a lot of attention.

10. Outside the exhibit, the zoo posted signs about human diet, habitat, and behavior.

Source: http://news.bbc.co.uk/2/hi/uk_news/england/london/4184466.stm

Exercise 3.4

1. Wow, pigeons have a built-in compass in their brains!
2. This compass points them in the right direction as they fly.
3. Recently, pigeon experts in England conducted a study of these birds.
4. The study tracked the flights of certain pigeons for two years.
5. The results were very surprising.
6. Modern pigeons usually ignored their inner compasses.
7. They navigated by other methods instead.
8. The pigeons simply looked down and followed human highways.
9. They remembered roads from previous flights and took the same roads home again.
10. The pigeons even traced the roads' turns, curves, and roundabouts as they flew.

Source: The Daily Telegraph, February 6, 2004

Exercise 3.5

1. Some people collect rare coins and paper money.
2. The Del Monte twenty-dollar bill is very famous.
3. The mint made a mistake when it printed this bill.
4. A sticker from a banana accidentally attached itself to the paper during the printing process.
5. The round green and red sticker became a part of the bill.
6. Such mistakes usually lead to a bill's destruction.
7. This flawed note, however, left the mint with the normal twenties.
8. Experts immediately authenticated its rare status.
9. The bill first sold on eBay for $10,000.
10. Eventually, a couple from Texas paid $25,000 for this one-of-a-kind note.

Source: www.delmontenote.com

Exercise 3.6   **Paragraph Practice**

Here is a brief excerpt from the book *Fashion 101: A Crash Course in Clothing*, in which author Erika Stalder details the unique features and history of the baseball cap. Label the parts of speech above as many of the words as you can before comparing your labels with the answers in the back of the book.

BASEBALL HAT

This billed cap with a dome-shaped crown is sometimes constructed with an adjustable band or elastic in back for a customized fit. The hat obviously got its name from the sport of baseball, but it didn't originally have a shade-creating bill. The bill-less kind was first worn around 1860, and the hat underwent its design change later in the early 1900s. In the 1920s, the billed-style hat became popular among the masses, as fans emulated their favorite players like superstar Babe Ruth.

Source: Fashion 101: A Crash Course in Clothing (Zest Books, 2008)

Exercise 3.7   **Sentence Writing**

Write ten short sentences (under ten words each) about the good qualities of a person you know well, perhaps a sibling or close friend. Be sure to avoid using "to ___" forms of verbs. Label the parts of speech above the words in your sentences.

4. Adjectives and Adverbs

English has two kinds of modifiers: adjectives and adverbs. "To modify" means to change or improve something, usually by adding to it. The role of these two parts of speech, adjectives and adverbs, is to *add* information. Notice that both of these words begin with *ad*. If you keep in mind that *ad*jectives and *ad*verbs *add* information to other words or phrases, you can understand the unique roles they play in sentences.

ADJECTIVES

- **Adjectives add to nouns and pronouns by answering these questions**: *Which one? What kind? How much or how many? What size, color, or shape?*

  adj   n   adj   n   adj adj adj
  She bought a *new* textbook with *multicolored* tabs. It has *one large blue*

  n   adj   adj   adj   n   adj   adj   adj   pro
  tab, *two medium yellow* tabs, and *three small red* ones.

- **Adjectives usually come *before* the nouns they modify.**

  adj   n   adj   n   adj adj   adj   n
  The *new* library stands on the *north* side of *our big, beautiful* campus.

- **Adjectives can sometimes come *after* the nouns they modify.**

  n   adj   adj   adj
  That piece of land—*flat, wide,* and *accessible*—inspired the architect of the building.

- **Adjectives may also come *after linking verbs*** (*is, am, are, was, were, feel, seem, appear, taste* . . .) to add description to the subject. For further discussion of these special verbs, see Sections 9, 15, and 20.

  n   lv   adj   adj
  The oranges were *ripe* and *juicy.*

  n   lv   adj   adj   n   lv   adj   adj
  Their juice tasted *sweet* and *delicious.* (or) Their juice was *sweet* and *delicious.*

- **Adjectives can be possessive *forms of nouns and pronouns*** whose only job is to add information to other nouns.

  adj   n   adj   n   adj   adj   n
  The *tree's* owner always picks *its* fruit during *his summer* vacation.

  adj   n   adj   n
  I love to eat *chocolate* cake on *my* birthday.

ADVERBS

- **Adverbs add to verbs, adjectives, other adverbs, and whole clauses** by answering these questions: *How? When? Where? Why? In what way?*

  adv   v   adv   v   adv adv
  I *quickly* typed my paper and *reluctantly* turned it *in late*.

  v adv v
  My teacher did *not* accept my paper at first.

  adv   adj
  I was *very* nervous about it.

  adv   adj   n
  She had an *extremely* disappointed look on her face.

  adv adj   adv   adj
  The deadline was *very* clear and *quite* reasonable.

  adv   adv adv
  Students *often* work *really hard* at the end of the term.

- **Unlike adjectives, some adverbs can move around in sentences without changing the meaning**.

  adv
  Now I have enough money for a vacation.

  adv
  I *now* have enough money for a vacation.

  adv
  I have enough money *now* for a vacation.

  adv
  I have enough money for a vacation *now*.

Many—but not all—adverbs end in *ly*. Adjectives can also end in *ly*. Remember that a word's part of speech depends on *how* the word participates with other words in a particular sentence. For instance, in the old saying "The early bird catches the worm," *early* acts as an adjective; it adds to a noun, telling which bird. However, in the sentence "The teacher arrived early," *early* acts as an adverb; it adds to the verb, telling when the teacher arrived.

Now that you've read about adjectives and adverbs, try to identify the question that each modifier (adj or adv) answers in the sample sentences below. Refer back to the questions listed under Adjectives and Adverbs.

adj   n   adj   n   adv   adv   v
My family and I went to the farmer's market yesterday. There we watched the

adj adj   n   adv   v   adv adj
decoration of a huge wedding cake. The baker skillfully squeezed out yellow

n   adj   adj   n   adv adj adj   n   adj   adj
flowers, green leaf patterns, and a light pink curly border made of smooth, creamy

n
frosting.

> **NOTE 4.A**—Although we discuss only single-word adjectives and adverbs here, phrases and clauses can also function as adjectives and adverbs following similar patterns.

CHOOSING BETWEEN ADJECTIVES AND ADVERBS

Knowing how to choose between adjectives and adverbs is important, especially in sentences that describe feelings, add emphasis, or make comparisons. See if you can make the correct choices in these three sentences:

We did (good, well) on that test.

I feel (bad, badly) about quitting my job.

Your friend speaks (really clear/really clearly).

Did you choose *well, bad,* and *really clearly?* If you missed *bad,* you're not alone. You might have reasoned that *badly* adds to the verb *feel,* but *feel* is acting in a

v
special way here—not naming the action of feeling with your fingertips (as in "I *feel*

adv   n   adj
the fabric *carefully*"), but describing the feeling of it (as in "The *fabric* feels *smooth*"). To understand this concept, try substituting "I feel (happy, happily)" instead of "I feel (bad, badly)" and note how easy it is to choose.

Another way that adjectives and adverbs work is to compare two or more things by describing them in relation to one another. The *er* ending is added to both adjectives and adverbs when comparing two items, and the *est* ending is added when comparing three or more items.

adj   n   adj   adj   n   adj   adj   n
The *first* peach was *sweet*. The *second* peach was *sweeter*. The *third* peach was

adj   pro
the *sweetest* one of all.

v   adv   v   adv   v   adv
You work *hard;* he works *harder;* I work the *hardest*.

In some cases, such comparisons require the addition of a word (*more* or *most, less* or *least*) instead of a change in the ending from *er* to *est*. Longer adjectives and adverbs usually require these extra adverbs to help with comparisons.

                adj   adv   adj   adv   adj
Gas is *expensive;* food is *more expensive;* rent is the *most expensive.*
                      adv   adv   adv   adv   adv
He dances *gracefully;* you dance *less gracefully;* I dance *least gracefully.*

EXERCISES

Remember that adjectives add to nouns and pronouns, while adverbs add to verbs, adjectives, and other adverbs. The following exercises will help you learn the difference between adjectives and adverbs and practice choosing the correct forms in particular sentences. Check your answers frequently to make the most progress.

Exercise 4.1

Identify whether each *italicized* word is used as an *adjective* or an *adverb* in the following sentences from a book written for new nurses by Kathy Quan. These sentences discuss the importance of teamwork.

1. The *team* leader keeps the team on track. (adjective, adverb)

2. Teamwork always works *best* when everyone is a team player. (adjective, adverb)

3. As team members, you work *collectively* toward a common goal. (adjective, adverb)

4. If each person is working *alone* and for his individual stardom, you won't have a team. (adjective, adverb)

5. *One* person who is not a team player can spoil the effort for everyone else. (adjective, adverb)

6. The team leader or *unit* manager sets the tone and is responsible for keeping the team intact. (adjective, adverb)

7. All team members have to be dedicated to the *common* goal as well. (adjective, adverb)

8. If someone isn't working out, the entire team needs to work toward pulling her *in.* (adjective, adverb)

9. But the team leader is *ultimately* responsible to support the team in doing this. (adjective, adverb)

10. *Sometimes* that's just not possible, and the spirit of the team is broken. (adjective, adverb)

Source: 150 Tips and Tricks for New Nurses (Adams Media, 2009)

Exercise 4.2

Identify whether the word *only* is used as an adjective or an adverb in the following sentences. In each sentence, try to link the word *only* with another word to figure out if *only* is an adjective (adding to a noun or pronoun) or an adverb (adding to a verb, adjective, or other adverb). Have fun with this exercise!

1. I reached into my wallet and pulled out my *only* coupon.

2. I had *only* one coupon.

3. *Only* I had a coupon.

4. That company *only* sells the software; it doesn't create the software.

5. That company sells *only* software, not hardware.

6. Other companies deal in hardware *only*.

7. In my Spanish class, the teacher speaks in Spanish *only*.

8. *Only* the students use English to ask questions or to clarify something.

9. My best friend is an *only* child, and so am I.

10. *Only* she understands how I feel.

Exercise 4.3

Choose the correct adjective or adverb form required to complete each sentence.

1. We have many (close, closely) relatives who live in the area.

2. We are (close, closely) related to many of the people in this area.

3. During the holidays, we feel (close, closely) to everyone in town.

4. My sister suffered (bad, badly) after she fell and broke her leg.

5. She felt (bad, badly) about tripping on a silly little rug.

6. Her leg itched really (bad, badly) under her cast.

7. The classroom hamster runs (very happy, very happily) on his exercise wheel.

8. The children are always (very happy, very happily) when he exercises.

9. My group received a (good, well) grade on our project.

10. The four of us worked (good, well) together.

Exercise 4.4

Choose the correct adjective or adverb form required to complete each sentence.

1. Of all my friends' cars, Jake's is (small, smaller, the smallest).

2. Janna has (a small, a smaller, the smallest) car, too.

3. Her car is (small, smaller, smallest) than mine.

4. Ken bought his car last week, so it's (a new, a newer, the newest) one.

5. Mine has (new, newer, newest) tires than Ken's since my tires were put on yesterday.

6. Jake's car is (new, newer, newest) than Janna's.

7. Ken looked for a car with (good, better, best) gas mileage than his old one.

8. Of course, Jake's tiny car gets (good, better, the best) gas mileage of all.

9. I do get (good, better, best) gas mileage now that I have new tires.

10. These days, gas mileage is (important, more important, most important) than it used to be.

Exercise 4.5

Label all of the adjectives (adj) and adverbs (adv) in the following sentences. Mark the ones you are sure of; then check your answers and find the ones you missed.

1. I took a helpful class online in the spring.

2. An Internet specialist taught me research skills.

3. I discovered very useful tools for Web research.

4. The instructor clearly explained various kinds of online resources.

5. She gave me several optional topics for each assignment.

6. I especially enjoyed the articles from my two projects about world music.

7. Now I fully understand the benefits of online classes.

8. They are fun and rewarding because students work at their own pace.

9. I am definitely less confused about online sources.

10. I can do research online and enjoy the process completely.

Exercise 4.6   *Proofreading Practice*

Correct the five errors in the use of adjectives and adverbs in the following paragraph. Then try to label all of the adjectives (adj) and adverbs (adv) in the paragraph for practice.

I didn't do very good during my first semester at community college. I feel badly whenever I think of it. I skipped classes and turned in sloppy work. My counselor warned me about my negative attitude, but I was real stubborn. I dropped out for a year and a half. Now that I have come back to college, I am even stubborner than before. I go to every class and always do my best. Today, a college degree is only my goal.

Exercise 4.7   *Sentence Writing*

Write a short paragraph (five to seven sentences) describing your favorite singer and song at the moment. Then go back through the paragraph and label your single-word adjectives and adverbs.

5. Contractions

When two words are shortened into one by removing letters and adding an apostrophe in their place, the result is called a *contraction*. A contraction pulls the two words together in the same way that a muscle contraction pulls your forearm and upper arm together. Use an apostrophe to show where the letter or letters have been squeezed out in most contractions.

is not ·····➤ *isn't*   you have ·····➤ *you've*

Here's a list of the most common contractions:

I am	I'm
I have	I've
I shall, I will	I'll
I would	I'd
you are	you're
you have	you've
you will	you'll
she is, she has	she's
he is, he has	he's
it is, it has	it's
we are	we're
we have	we've
we will, we shall	we'll
they are	they're
they have	they've
are not	aren't
cannot	can't
do not	don't
does not	doesn't
have not	haven't
let us	let's
who is, who has	who's

where is	where's
were not	weren't
would not	wouldn't
could not	couldn't
should not	shouldn't
would have	would've
could have	could've
should have	should've
that is	that's
there is	there's
what is	what's

Notice that one contraction does not follow this rule: *will not* becomes *won't.*

In all other contractions that you're likely to use, the apostrophe goes exactly where the letter or letters are left out. Note especially that *it's, they're, who's,* and *you're* are contractions. Use them when you mean *two* words. (See Section 6 for more about the possessive forms—*its, their, whose,* and *your*—which *don't* need apostrophes.)

EXERCISES

Add the missing apostrophes to any contractions in the following sentences. We have added more contractions than sentences usually have to allow for extensive practice in these exercises. A few of the sentences do not include any contractions. Be sure to check your answers after each exercise to make the most progress.

Exercise 5.1

1. Psychologists have identified a new kind of addiction thats affecting many people's lives.

2. Its called "infomania."

3. If someones addicted to catching every email, phone, or text message—even the latest viral video—as soon as it happens, that person suffers from infomania.

4. And that persons not alone.

5. A recent study shows that over sixty percent of people admit to having at least a mild case of infomania.

6. If theres a smartphone or computer around, theyll check it for updates, even if theyre in the middle of another, more important activity.

7. Infomaniacs continue to after hunger for the latest information after theyve gone home, are getting ready to sleep, or just trying to relax on vacation.

8. The results of the study show that people with infomania are feeling its effects.

9. Theyre losing the ability to focus on tasks or retain information by constantly interrupting themselves to check on the latest digital developments.

10. If people limit their online interests to one or two areas and value the time it takes to absorb what they really need or want to know, they can lesson the effects of infomania.

Source: Los Angeles Times, January 19, 2016 [http://www.latimes.com/business/technology/la-fi-thedownload-infomania-20160119-story.html]

Exercise 5.2

1. We modern folks arent the only ones to love movies and animation.

2. Ancient Europeans created their own animated images in caves 30,000 years ago.

3. Their moving pictures werent projected but painted on walls and twirled on strings.

4. The walls of prehistoric caves in France display scenes that appear to move due to tricks of perspective and repetition.

5. In one image, theres a bison painted in various positions with eight legs instead of four to suggest running.

6. In parts of France and Spain, scientists have also discovered ancient animated toys.

7. Theyve found flat, two-sided objects carved with pictures of the same animal on both sides.

8. On one side, the animal is lying down, and on the other, its standing on four legs.

9. When the disk is spun on string, the viewer sees a moving image of the animal standing up by itself.

10. Its fascinating to think of people creating animated images so long ago.

Source: Science News, June 1, 2012 *https://www.sciencenews.org/article/stone-age-art-gets-animated*

Exercise 5.3

1. Whats a strong natural substance that might save thousands of lives in the future?

2. Youre right if youre thinking of bamboo.

3. Engineers from around the world have recently tested its strength and flexibility.

4. Experts found that its equally impressive when its used in its natural state and when its mixed with more traditional building materials, such as concrete.

5. Structures made from bamboo-based products are clearly safer when theres an earthquake.

6. They dont crack or crumble, even when theyre shaken violently by powerful earthquake simulators.

7. Theres a long list of factors that make bamboo a promising building material of the future.

8. It doesnt cost much and wont catch on fire.

9. Its lightweight but isnt brittle.

10. And although theyll be easy and quick to build, bamboo-reinforced buildings wont need repair for decades.

Source: Discover, August 2004 *[http://discovermagazine.com/2004/aug/bamboo-cures-earthquakes/]*

Exercise 5.4

1. "Music wasnt made to make us wise, but better natured." Josh Billings

2. "Give me a laundry list, and Ill set it to music." Rossini

3. "I know only two tunes. One of them is 'Yankee Doodle'—and the other one isnt." Ulysses S. Grant

4. "Its not me. Its the songs. Im just the postman. I deliver the songs." Bob Dylan

5. "If you think youve hit a false note, sing loud. When in doubt, sing loud." Robert Merrill

6. "I dont know anything about music. In my line, you dont have to." Elvis Presley

7. "If the king loves music, theres little wrong in the land." Mencius

8. "When you got to ask what jazz is, youll never get to know." Louis Armstrong

9. "I havent understood a bar of music in my life, but I have felt it." Igor Stravinsky

10. "There are more love songs than anything else. If songs could make you do something, wed all love one another." Frank Zappa

Source: Music: A Book of Quotations (Dover, 2001)

Exercise 5.5

1. This week, Im helping my sister with her research paper, and shes chosen chocolate as her topic.

2. Weve been surprised by some of the things weve discovered.

3. First, the cocoa beans arent very appetizing in their natural form.

4. They grow inside an odd-shaped, alien-looking pod, and theyre surrounded by white mushy pulp.

5. After cocoa beans have been removed from the pods, theyre dried, blended almost like coffee beans, and processed into the many types of chocolate foods available.

6. In fact, the Aztecs enjoyed chocolate as a heavily spiced hot drink that was more like coffee than the sweet, creamy chocolate thats popular today.

7. Weve also learned that white chocolate cant be called chocolate at all since it doesnt contain any cocoa solids, only cocoa butter.

8. With an interest in organic foods, wed assumed that organic chocolate would be better than conventional chocolate.

9. But thats not true either because its got to be grown on pesticide-free trees, and theyre the strongest but not the tastiest sources of chocolate.

10. Unfortunately, the best cocoa trees are also the most vulnerable to disease, so it isnt easy to grow them organically.

Source: The Chocolate Companion (Simon & Schuster, 1995)

Exercise 5.6   Paragraph Practice

In the following paragraph, cross out the ten pairs of italicized words and rewrite them as correct contractions (ex., ~~you are~~ = *you're*).

   I have had the same group of friends since I was in junior high school. Now that *we are* all in college, my friends *do not* spend as much time on schoolwork as I do. Whenever *I am* studying for an exam or working on a project, they call and ask if *I would* like to see a movie or go to a game. *It is* the worst in the summer. *I have* been enrolling in summer school classes for the past two years so that *I will* be ready to transfer soon. However, none of my friends has taken a class during the summer. At the rate *they are* going, my friends *will not* ever transfer.

Exercise 5.7   Sentence Writing

Write ten sentences to practice using contractions. In these sentences, try to describe your dream vacation or the types of recycling you participate in at home, at work, or at school.

6. Possessives

Words that clarify ownership are called *possessives*. The trick in writing possessives is to ask the question "Who (or what) does the item belong to?" Modern usage has made *who* acceptable when it begins a question. More correctly, of course, the phrasing should be "*Whom* does the item belong to?" or even "*To whom* does the item belong?"

In any case, if the answer to this question does not end in *s* (as in *player, person, people, children, month*), simply add an *apostrophe* and *s* to show the possessive. Look at the first five examples in the chart below.

However, if the answer to the question already ends in *s* (as in *players and Brahms*), add only an apostrophe after the *s* to show the possessive. See these two examples in the chart and say them aloud to hear that their sound does not need to change when made possessive.

Finally, some *s*-ending words need another sound to make the possessive clear. If you need another *s* sound when you *say* the possessive (ex., *the office of my boss* becomes *my boss's office*), add the apostrophe and another *s* to show the added sound.

a player (uniform)	Who does the uniform belong to?	a player	Add 's	a player's uniform
a person (clothes)	Who do the clothes belong to?	a person	Add 's	a person's clothes
people (clothes)	Who do the clothes belong to?	people	Add 's	people's clothes
children (games)	Who do the games belong to?	children	Add 's	children's games
a month (pay)	What does the pay belong to?	a month	Add 's	a month's pay
players (uniforms)	Who do the uniforms belong to?	players	Add '	players' uniforms
Brahms (Lullaby)	Who does the Lullaby belong to?	Brahms	Add '	Brahms' Lullaby
my boss (office)	Who does the office belong to?	my boss	Add 's	my boss's office

The trick of asking "Who does the item belong to?" will always work, but you must ask the question every time. Remember that the key word is *belong*. If you ask the question another way, you may get an answer that won't help you. Also, notice that the trick does not depend on whether the answer is *singular* or *plural*, but on whether it ends in *s* or not.

TABLE 6.A TO MAKE A POSSESSIVE

1. Ask "Who (or what) does the item belong to?"
2. If the answer doesn't end in *s,* add an *apostrophe* and *s.*
3. If the answer already ends in *s,* add just an *apostrophe* or
an *apostrophe* and *s* if you need an extra sound to show the
possessive (as in *boss's office*).

Cover the right column and see if you can create the following possessives using the method explained above. Ask the question "Who (or what) does the item belong to?" each time. Try not to look at the answers before you try!

1. the jury (reaction)   _____   the jury's reaction

2. an umpire (decision)   _____   an umpire's decision

3. Jess (remarks)   _____   Jess's (or Jess') remarks

4. Alice (company)   _____   Alice's company

5. Dr. Porter (car)   _____   Dr. Porter's car

6. the Johnsons (cat)   _____   the Johnsons' cat

7. a parent (advice)   _____   a parent's advice

8. parents (advice)   _____   parents' advice

9. a woman (watch)   _____   a woman's watch

10. two women (watches)   _____   two women's watches

(Sometimes you may have a choice when the word ends in *s. Jess's remarks* may be written *Jess' remarks.* Whether you want your reader to say it with or without an extra *s* sound, be consistent when given such choices.)

NOTE 6.A—Don't assume that every word that ends in *s* is a possessive. The *s* may indicate more than one of something, a plural noun. Make sure the word actually possesses something before you add an apostrophe.

A few commonly used pronoun forms are already possessive and don't need apostrophes added to them. Some of these words act primarily as *adjectives* to clarify ownership of a noun (*our* house, *its* roof, *your* car, *their* dog). For now, try to memorize this list of words that do not require apostrophes for possession:

our, ours	its
your, yours	their, theirs
his, her, hers	whose

Note particularly that the **possessives** *its, their, whose,* and *your* don't take an apostrophe, but these words sound like the **contractions** *it's, they're, who's,* and *you're* that do use an apostrophe to show that they combine the words *it is, they are, who is,* and *you are.*

Here's another chance to practice with possessives. Cover the right column again, and add apostrophes to any possessives. Each correct answer includes an explanation.

1. The students went to their counselors offices.	counselors' (You didn't add an apostrophe to *students,* did you? The students don't possess anything.)
2. The teams bus broke down with all the players on board.	The team's (The bus belongs to the *team.* The players don't possess anything.)
3. I was invited to my friends graduation.	friend's (if it's the graduation of one *friend*), friends' (if it belongs to two or more *friends*)
4. That writers ideas are very clever.	writer's (The ideas belong the *writer,* the ideas themselves don't possess anything.)
5. Gus opinion is similar to mine.	Gus's (The s after the apostrophe adds the extra letter *Gus'* needs to *sound* possessive.)
6. The bus that is ours has a red arrow on its side.	No apostrophe. *Ours* and *its* are already possessive.
7. The Millers house is just outside of the city.	The Millers' (The house belongs to the *Millers.* There is no need to add an extra s sound to the *Millers'.*)
8. I'm reading many books in my childrens literature class.	children's (The literature belongs to *children,* but the books don't possess anything.)
9. The students handed the teacher their essays.	No apostrophe. *Their* is already possessive.
10. The sign on the door said, "Employees Entrance."	Employees' (The entrance is for *employees* only.)

EXERCISES

Now you're ready to add apostrophes to any possessives in the exercises that follow. But be careful. *First*, make sure the word really possesses something; not every word ending in *s* is a possessive. *Second,* remember that certain words already have possessive forms and don't use apostrophes. *Third,* even though a word ends in *s,* you can't tell where the apostrophe goes until you ask the question, "Who (or what) does the item belong to?" The apostrophe or apostrophe and *s* should follow the answer to that question. Check your answers after the first set.

Exercise 6.1

1. It is many peoples dream to live in a penthouse.

2. Researchers in Canada have found that a buildings height affects the health of the people who live there.

3. Specifically, scientists at St. Michaels Hospital in Toronto have found a link between living at the top of a tall building and dying of a heart attack.

4. The link exists regardless of a neighborhoods wealth or geographical location.

5. The study shows that a heart attack victims chance of survival above the 16th floor is "less than one percent."

6. The studys results do not blame this low survival rate on high-rise residents exposure to higher air pressure or the stress of living above others.

7. The results point to rescuers inability to reach heart attack victims on the top floors in time to help.

8. And the higher someones apartment is, the higher the risk is.

9. Scientists suggestions to reduce this risk include giving universal elevator keys to emergency personnel and placing special defibrillators on the upper floors.

10. As a result of this study, however, some peoples dreams of living in a penthouse might change.

Source: The Toronto Star, January 18, 2016 *[www.thestar.com/life/health_wellness/2016/01/18/heart-attacks-in-highrises-a-deadly-combination-toronto-study-shows.html]*

Exercise 6.2

1. Claude Monets paintings of water lilies are world famous.

2. Monet also created a series of paintings that captured the beauty of Londons bridges at the turn of the twentieth century.

3. Monet was inspired by the fogs influence on light, color, and texture.

4. He wrote about the foggy weathers positive effect on his mood and creativity.

5. Now historians and scientists know more about the unusually thick fog that hung over London at that time.

6. It was really smog—fog mixed with soot, smoke, and other pollutants.

7. Peoples health suffered so much that hundreds died each week at its worst.

8. Monet himself had lung disease.

9. The artists views of London in the fog went on tour as an exhibition in 2005.

10. The exhibit was called "Monets London."

Source: Discover, September 2005, and http://www.nytimes.com/2015/11/01/books/review/london-fog-the-biography-by-christine-l-corton.html

Exercise 6.3

1. David Mannings reputation as a movie reviewer was destroyed in the spring of 2001.

2. This critics words of praise had been printed on several of Columbia Pictures movie posters at the time and had helped to convince the public to see the films.

3. Mannings glowing quotations appeared on ads for *A Knights Tale, The Patriot,* and *Hollow Man.*

4. However, there was a problem with this particular writers opinions.

5. David Mannings praise was empty because David Manning didn't exist.

6. One of the movie studios executives had invented Manning and made up the quotations printed on the posters.

7. A news writer discovered that Mannings identity was a fake.

8. The studios reaction surprised both news people and other entertainment industry executives.

9. After the executive admitted the truth, the studio argued that these fake reviews were a form of free speech.

10. The courts took the deception very seriously, however, with fines and an order to remove any of the films posters with this imaginary critics quotes on them.

Source: BBC News, August 3, 2005, and *http://hoaxes.org/archive/permalink/david_manning*

Exercise 6.4

1. I'm not satisfied with my cars ride; it's too rough.

2. Bumps and potholes usually send my passengers heads straight into the roof.

3. My tires tread pattern also seems too deep for ordinary city driving.

4. If a roads surface has grooves in it, my wheels get pulled in every direction.

5. During my first test drive of the car, I asked about its rough suspension and heavy-duty tires.

6. The salesperson told me that the suspensions stiffness would eventually soften.

7. My fathers opinion matched the salespersons, so I bought the car.

8. I've been driving around waiting for its ride to become smoother over time.

9. That hasn't happened yet, and I know that some of my friends even avoid driving with me.

10. Next time I buy a car, I won't trust anyone elses opinion more than my own.

Exercise 6.5

1. According to Eric Sloanes book *Skies and the Artist,* it isn't easy to draw or paint clouds.

2. Most peoples perception of clouds is that they are static bumps floating in the sky.

3. But clouds shapes are difficult to capture because they're actually always moving.

4. Also, a clouds density isn't as solid as it seems.

5. Each clouds structure constantly builds up and disintegrates.

6. According to Sloane, artists must treat clouds as "wet air in action."

7. Sloanes suggestions for capturing clouds beauty make good sense.

8. Color choices affect any artists ability to recreate clouds on paper or canvas.

9. Artists who want to paint a cloudy sky should not rely on blue and white alone.

10. It's better to use gray, yellow, and pink to capture a cloudscapes full effect.

Source: Skies and the Artist (Dover, 2006)

Exercise 6.6   Paragraph Practice

Add necessary apostrophes to the five possessive nouns in the following paragraph. The name Alexis is used as a possessive noun only once.

I consider my friend Alexis to be one of the smartest people I know. Alexis is a twenty-five-year-old film student at a nearby university. She's presently in her senior year, but that is just the beginning for Alexis. She plans to take full advantage of her universitys resources to learn what she needs before starting her own filmmaking career. She has access to her fellow students talents, her different teachers experiences, and the film schools state-of-the-art equipment and industry contacts. I've always been impressed by Alexis self-confidence, and it has inspired me to make a plan of my own for the future.

Exercise 6.7   Sentence Writing

Write ten sentences using the possessive forms of the names of your family members or the names of your friends. You could write about a recent event that brought your family or friends together. Just narrate a few of the events that happened that day.

7. Consulting a Dictionary

Imagine having a professional on call every hour of every day, waiting to answer your questions about word use. That's just what a dictionary is, if you think about it, but do you take full advantage of this 24-hour resource? Many computers even come with a dictionary program preinstalled and ready to consult. A college-level dictionary—whether in print, online, or on your computer—can offer help with spelling, pronunciation, definitions, uses and sources of words, as well as foreign phrases, famous names, and geographical locations.

The opportunities for learning by consulting a dictionary are nearly endless, yet instead of consulting a real dictionary within reach of our fingertips, many of us rely on spell-checkers to "fix" words or phrasing that the program identifies as errors. Sometimes these changes don't convey our intended meaning, and they often create new errors. Let's take a "least you should know" look at the many types of information available in a good dictionary to discover what a valuable resource it can be.

Spelling

By looking up words that you aren't sure how to spell, you can become more familiar with how words work. For instance, when the dictionary lists two or more spellings for a word, the first one with the pronunciation is usually preferred. In addition, the spellings of many words differ in American English (*color*) and British English (*colour*), and this pattern repeats itself in *glamor* and *glamour,* as well as many other word pairs.

Capitalization

If a word is capitalized in the dictionary, it should always be capitalized. Other words may or may not be capitalized, depending on their use. For example, the word *American* is always capitalized, but the word *Internet* is usually capitalized but may not be if the writing is informal. For more information about the use of "Capital Letters," see Section 29.

Compound Words

Compound words and phrases are made up of two or more words that work together as one. A dictionary will clarify whether compound words or phrases should be written separately, as in *hot dog;* written with a hyphen (-) between them, as in *father-in-law;* or written as one word, as in *handmade.*

Pronunciation

A word's pronunciation is important since most people *hear* words either inwardly or aloud as they read them. Once again, a dictionary is available to help. For example, next to the word *vigilant* in a dictionary entry, you will find its pronunciation written like this: *'vijələnt* or *'vi-jə-lənt*. The upside-down *e* (ə) that dictionaries use to represent an *uh* sound like the *a* in *about* or *ago* is found in many words. Through the practice and experience of consulting a dictionary, you can quickly learn what the other sound representations mean.

Pronunciation also involves paying attention to syllables. If a word has more than one syllable, the dictionary marks the stressed syllable with an accent mark (*'*). In most dictionaries, an accent mark will point to the stressed syllable or will come right before it. The stressed syllable in *vigilant* is *'vij*, so you should let the full force of your voice fall on the first syllable. Here is a pair of examples to illustrate how stressing a different syllable changes the meaning of a word: "I drove through the *desert*" and "Please don't *desert* me at the party." The first example stresses the first syllable (*'desert*), and the second stresses the second syllable (*de'sert*).

Luckily, next to a word's written pronunciation, most online dictionaries include a speaker icon that links to an audio clip of a person's voice pronouncing the word to demonstrate how it sounds.

Parts of Speech

As explained in Section 3, English has eight parts of speech: *noun, pronoun, verb, adjective, adverb, preposition, conjunction,* and *interjection.* Think of these as the eight jobs that words can do. Luckily, dictionaries list the jobs that each particular word can do. Some words have just one job, such as *during,* a *preposition* that tells *when* something takes place (*during* the summer). Other words have more than one job and play multiple parts of speech. The word *back* performs four different jobs in the following sentence: The *back* of their car *backed* into our *back* fence, so they must go *back* to the body shop. *Back* is a *noun* that names a part of their car, then a *verb* that shows an action, next an *adjective* that identifies which fence, and finally an *adverb* that tells how they must go to the body shop. For each definition of a word, a dictionary lists the abbreviation *n., pron., v., adj., adv., prep., conj.,* or *interj.*

Definitions

A dictionary also shows whether a word or term has one definition or multiple definitions. Even a simple word like *set* has dozens of meanings in English, depending on its use in a particular phrase or sentence. From people who "*set* the table" or "play a *set*" of tennis to yesterday's sun that "*set* slowly in the west" or last night's movie that was "*set* in Paris," each use has a different meaning. Fortunately, most dictionaries provide sample phrases or sentences like these to demonstrate each of a word's uses when it has multiple definitions.

Abbreviations

Abbreviations such as *RSVP* are commonly used as words in English. By consulting a dictionary, you can discover what the letters in these and other abbreviations stand for, how to capitalize them, and whether to punctuate them with periods or not. For example, *RSVP* stands for *"Répondez s'il vous plaît,"* a French expression that asks people who have been invited somewhere to "Please reply."

Usage Labels

Just because a word appears in a dictionary doesn't mean that it is appropriate for all uses. A dictionary will label some words in the following way to indicate their limited uses.

archaic, dated	not in current use but still found in some biblical, literary, and legal expressions (ex. *yesternight*)
informal	used in conversation but not in formal or academic writing (ex. *bro*)
dialect, regional	used in particular locations but not everywhere (ex. *y'all*)
slang, colloquial	popular but not used in standard written expression (ex. *gonna*)

Word Origins

Knowing the origin of—or the story behind—a word often helps us remember its meaning. For example, if we read that someone is *narcissistic* and consult a dictionary, we find that *narcissism* is a condition named after *Narcissus,* a handsome young man in Greek mythology. One day Narcissus fell in love with his own reflection in a pool, but when he tried to get closer to it, he fell in the water and drowned. A flower that grew nearby is now named for Narcissus. And *narcissistic* has come to mean "in love with oneself."

Names of People

Knowing who famous people are and how to pronounce their names can give anyone a boost in confidence. College-level print dictionaries include the names of famous people either in the main part or in a separate biographical names section at the back. Online searches will produce a variety of results about people, so remember to add the word *definition* after people's names to get to a list of brief but detailed dictionary entries about them, including how to pronounce them. By searching *"Disney definition,"* for example, we can find that *Disney* was an American creator, animator, and film producer; that his last name is pronounced *'diz-nee;* that his full name was Walter E. Disney; and that he lived from 1901 to 1966.

Names of Places

Like the names of people, the names of places appear either in the main part of a college-level print dictionary or in a separate geographical names section at the back. Online searches will produce a variety of results about places, so remember to add the word *definition* after a place's name to find a list of dictionary entries about it, including how to pronounce them. By searching "*Okracoke Island definition*," for example, we can find that *Okracoke* is an island off North Carolina; that it is pronounced ōkrəkōk īlənd; that it covers about 10 square miles of land; and that Blackbeard the Pirate died there in 1718.

EXERCISES

Complete the following brief exercises by consulting a recently published, college-level dictionary. You may search a print dictionary, the dictionary program on your computer (if available), or an online dictionary by typing the word, phrase, person, or place plus the word *definition* after it. For example, to find out if the word *internet* should be capitalized, type "*internet definition*" into the search space. From your search results, consult one or more of the dictionary sites to help you find the answers.

Exercise 7.1

Search the following words and phrases to find and write the correct or preferred *spelling* (including *capitalization* and *spacing* or *hyphenation* if they are *compound words*). After each corrected form, carefully copy the dictionary's *pronunciation* of the term. When using an online search engine, be sure to include the term followed by the word *definition* (ex. *web site definition*) in the search box to bring up brief, detailed dictionary entries.

1. web site
2. judgement
3. half moon
4. greenwich mean time
5. velocipede
6. occured
7. dialog
8. teritory
9. bollywood
10. take home pay

Exercise 7.2

Search the following words to locate and write all of the parts of speech that they can play. The parts of speech are listed before the definitions as *noun* (*n.*), *pronoun* (*pro.*), *verb* (*v.*), *adjective* (*adj.*), *adverb* (*adv.*), *preposition* (*prep.*), *conjunction* (*conj.*), and *interjection* (*int.* or *exclam.*). When using an online search engine, be sure to include the term followed by the word *definition* (ex. *debate definition*) in the search box to bring up brief, detailed dictionary entries.

1. debate
2. before
3. help
4. that
5. early
6. someone
7. swell
8. about
9. front
10. while

Exercise 7.3

Search the following words to locate their dictionary *definitions*. Write *one* of the definitions here, and include the part of speech that the word plays for that definition. When using an online search engine, be sure to include the term followed by the word *definition* (ex. *segue definition*) in the search box to bring up brief, detailed dictionary entries.

1. segue
2. twiddle
3. dunce
4. assuage
5. vapid
6. fend
7. collude

8. utopian

9. Dada (with a capital D)

10. cogitate

Exercise 7.4

Search recent print or online dictionaries to find what the letters in the following common *abbreviations* stand for and how they are capitalized and punctuated. When searching for online dictionary entries, be sure to type the *abbreviation* followed by the word *definition* (ex. *bce definition*) in the search box. Correct the capitalization and punctuation (if any) of the *abbreviations* and write their full meaning after each sentence.

1. That film takes place in the year 304 *bce*.

2. My sister plans to graduate with a *phd* before she is 30.

3. One organization called *madd* has been very effective.

4. The use of the *potus* abbreviation began as a telegraph code.

5. I saw the abbreviation *ie* next to an example.

6. The library closes at 10:30 *pm* on weekdays.

7. Their flight's *eta* has been adjusted.

8. The envelope had the abbreviation *attn* on it.

9. We saw company names that end in *ltd* on our trip.

10. Before I apply, I need to increase my *wpm* score.

Exercise 7.5

Correct the *capitalization,* and write the *origins* after each word in 1–5 and the *details* after each of the *people* or *places* in 6–10. When using an online search engine, be sure to include the term followed by the word *definition* (ex. *procrustean definition* or *mumbai definition*) in the search box to bring up brief, detailed dictionary entries.

1. procrustean (procrustes)

2. frankenfish

3. boycott

4. sabotage

5. plagiarism

6. mumbai

7. thorstein veblen

8. sarah breedlove walker

9. antonia novello

10. katherine sui fun cheung

Exercise 7.6 Paragraph Exercise

Consult a dictionary to find the meaning of and details about the ten italicized *words, phrases, abbreviations, names,* and *places* in the following excerpt from Todd Aaron Jensen's book *On Gratitude*. In his book, Jensen introduces an interview with the late Ray Bradbury by describing Bradbury's unique persona and contribution to the world of writing. Be sure to find the meaning of each word as Jensen uses it in his paragraph.

Bradbury, crowned with a *shock* of snow-white hair cropped to *Dutch*-boy length, his facial features slightly larger than life, in a way that makes him look wizardly, is our *Father Time*. He's here to say, as he always has, that everything is going to be all right. Listen to him today, wedged into an easy chair in the study of his home in Los Angeles, surrounded by decades of vintage film *memorabilia*, highly collectible comic books, half-done paintings, *VHS* tapes, and a battlefield of used pens. In person, Bradbury is grand, the author as mythological beast, a *winsome* character who may have sprung to life from a *Maurice Sendak* story . . . . And what does Bradbury, the Willy Wonka of words, announce on this visit? "Love is the answer to everything. It's the only reason to do anything." That's what Ray Bradbury says, an *evergreen* message from the *Oracle* of *Optimism*.

Source: On Gratitude (Adams Media, 2010)

Exercise 7.7   Sentence Writing

Choose ten words and abbreviations from Exercises 7.1, 7.3, and 7.4, and write ten *new* sentences that demonstrate knowledge of their spelling, pronunciation, capitalization, punctuation, and meaning. The sentences can be on different subjects and can be written separately as a list.

Word Use Progress Test

This test will help you gauge your progress and identify areas of Word Use that you could still know better. Be confident, and check your answers only after trying your best. Read each of the following sentences carefully, and choose the word or term that successfully completes its meaning:

1. Fans often have (a, an) unique perspective that others don't understand.

2. Counselors (advice, advise) many students to earn certificates along with their degrees.

3. Some people could (have, of) dressed better for the graduation ceremony.

4. Honesty is a guiding (principal, principle) in my life.

5. In the sentence "The midterm *took* an hour to complete," *took* is (an adverb, a verb).

6. In the sentence "*Someone* returned the money," *someone* is a (noun, pronoun).

7. In the sentence "We moved *inside* because of the rain," inside is an (*adjective, adverb*).

8. In the sentence "Early students received extra credit," *early* is an (adjective, adverb).

9. I did (well, better) than most of my classmates on the surprise quiz.

10. Sandbags should be ready before (there, they're) needed.

11. We compared our phones to see (who's, whose) phone was the oldest.

12. Our neighbors want to put a gate between (their, they're) property and ours.

13. These days, (children's, childrens') clothes look just like adults' clothes.

14. College classes have taught me to trust my own (judgement, judgment).

15. A (self-made, self made) success story is always the most motivating.

Word Use Practice

Find and correct the ten errors in this paragraph. The errors cover all areas of word use.

On a recent expedition in Siberia, scientists made an un-expected discovery. They found a pair of baby lion cubs that have been frozen for over 10,000 years. Whats amazing about they're discovery is the condition of the two cub's. The little lions look as if they were frozen yesterday. Thousands of years in ice have had almost no affect on the cub's fur and physical features. Its clear that the cubs were about two weeks old when they died, since they did not have their baby teeth even yet. The cubs belonged to a species that is now extinct—the cave lions of Siberia. By studying these perfect preserved lion cubs, scientists can learn more about how the cave lion species lived and how these two tiniest cubs died.

Source: http://news.nationalgeographic.com/2015/10/151028-cave-lion-frozen-permafrost-science/,
November 19, 2015

PART TWO

Sentence Structure

WHAT IS THE LEAST YOU SHOULD KNOW ABOUT SENTENCE STRUCTURE?

Sentence structure refers to the way sentences are built using words, phrases, and clauses. Words are single units, and words combine to form clauses and phrases. **Clauses** are word groups *with* subjects and verbs, and **phrases** are word groups *without* subjects and verbs. Clauses are the most important structures because they make statements—they tell *who did what* or *what something is* in a sentence. Look at the following sentence as an example:

During the summer, we visited the Grand Canyon.

It contains eight words, each playing its own part in the meaning of the sentence. But which of the words join together to tell who did what? *We visited the Grand Canyon* is correct. That word group is a *clause*. Notice that the three words *during the summer* also form a word group, but it doesn't include somebody—a subject— doing something—a verb. Instead, *during the summer* is just a *phrase* to clarify *when* we visited the Grand Canyon.

Importantly, you could delete the opening phrase and still have a sentence: *We visited the Grand Canyon.* However, if you leave the clause out, you just have *During the summer,* not a sentence. Remember, every sentence must include a *clause* that can stand by itself.

Learning about the structure of sentences helps you control your own. Once you know more about sentence structure, you can understand writing errors and learn to avoid and correct them.

Among the most common errors in writing are fragments, run-ons, and awkward phrasing.

Here are a few examples of fragments:

Wandering around the museum all afternoon.

Because I tried to handle too many responsibilities at once.

By tutoring the students in groups.

These groups of words don't make complete statements—not one has a clause that can stand by itself. Who was "wandering around the museum"? What happened "because I tried to handle too many responsibilities at once"? What did someone gain "by tutoring the students in groups"? These incomplete sentence structures fail to communicate a complete thought.

In contrast, look at these examples of run-on sentences:

The yearly forecast calls for heavy rain the drought might be at an end.

Taking the train cuts my travel time in half carpooling is also an option.

My boss offers incentives and they motivate us to work harder.

Unlike fragments, run-on sentences do make complete statements, but the trouble is they make *two* complete statements; the first *runs on* into the second. Without the help of punctuation, the reader has to go back and find the break between the two ideas.

Fragments don't make any complete statements, and run-ons make too many complete statements without punctuating between them. Another problem occurs when the phrasing in a sentence just doesn't make sense.

Read these sentences with examples of awkward phrasing:

The problem from my grades started to end.

It was a great time at my sister's graduation.

She won me at chess every time we played.

Try to find the word groups that show who did what—that is, the clauses (*The problem started, It was,* and *She won*). Now try to put the clauses and phrases together to form a precise meaning. It's difficult, isn't it? You'll see that many of the words don't work together, such as "problem from my grades," "started to end," "it was a great time at," and "won me at chess." These sentences don't communicate clearly due to awkward phrasing.

Fragments, run-ons, and awkward phrasing confuse the reader. When you learn to avoid these and other sentence structure errors, your writing will be stronger and easier to understand. Unfortunately, there is no quick, effortless way to strengthen sentence structure. First, you need to understand how clear sentences are built. Then you can eliminate common errors in your own writing.

Part Two will describe areas of sentence structure one at a time and then explain how to avoid errors associated with the different areas. For instance, we start by helping you find subjects and verbs and understand dependent clauses; then we show you how to correct fragments. You can go through the whole part yourself to learn and practice all of the concepts and structures. Or your teacher may assign only certain sections based on the structures the class needs to review. Before you begin, take this Sentence Structure Preview Test.

Sentence Structure Preview Test

Think of this preview test as an opportunity to discover how much you already know about sentence structure, rather than as a test to be graded. A full explanation follows each of the answers, but first try your best. One sentence in each pair contains an error in sentence structure or phrasing. Read both sentences carefully to find a clear fault in one of them. Then write the letter of the *correct* sentence in the blank:

1. _____ **A.** Taking a family cruise is a popular form of vacation.

   B. Taking a family cruise to Alaska, our ship was magnificent.

2. _____ **A.** My speech teacher is much luckier than me.

   B. She has already won two big prizes in the lottery.

3. _____ **A.** Community colleges offer day, night, and weekend classes.

   B. I have taken day and night classes but never weekends.

4. _____ **A.** As the teacher entered the classroom and took off his headphones and his backpack.

   B. He put them on the podium and immediately started lecturing.

5. _____ **A.** The tutors always lock the door to the language lab.

   B. Too many students wandered in if they don't.

6. _____ **A.** In today's society, people usually mind their own business.

   B. If I see someone who really needs help, I get involved.

7. _____ **A.** The librarian gave my friend and I a two-week extension.

   B. The librarian gave my friend and me a two-week extension.

8. _____ **A.** The store was offering the free gift of a coffee maker.

   B. My uncle gave me a new coffee maker as a gift.

9. _____ **A.** My essay is full of details and it has a strong thesis.

   B. I'll type the final copy tonight and submit it on Monday.

10. _____ **A.** The band members arrived in a limousine and took their guitars out of the trunk.

    B. Everyone stood there with a shocked look on their faces.

11. _____ **A.** Some of the new furniture has scratches on them already.

    B. The delivery company should have been more careful.

12. _____ **A.** Water bottles are available in many sizes.

B. From the size of a baby bottle to a magnum of champagne.

13. _____ **A.** Walking around the park before dinner last night.

B. We watched a beautiful metallic kite soaring in the sky.

14. _____ **A.** Shawn and Sharon, my twin cousins who are both talented musicians.

B. Shawn, however, is not as ambitious as Sharon is.

15. _____ **A.** Whenever I plan a whole meal around a single specific ingredient, the different dishes themselves don't always taste very good.

B. I like the flavor of curry with chicken but not with vegetables.

8. Locating Prepositional Phrases

Prepositional phrases are among the easiest sentence structures in English to learn, so we will begin with them. Remember that a **phrase** is just a group of related words *without* a subject and a verb. And don't let a term like ***prepositional*** scare you. If you look in the middle of that long word, you'll find a familiar one—*position*. In English, we tell the *positions* of people and things in sentences using prepositional phrases. Think of prepositional phrases as a type of GPS—a *grammatical* positioning system—in the sentences that you write and read.

Look at the following sentence with its prepositional phrases in parentheses:

Our trip (to the desert) begins (at 6:00) (in the morning) (on Friday).

One phrase tells *where* the trip will take us (*to the desert*), and three phrases tell *when* the trip will begin (*at 6:00, in the morning,* and *on Friday*). Most prepositional phrases show the position of someone or something in *space* or in *time*.

Here is a list of prepositions that can show *positions in space:*

to	across	over	against	with
at	through	inside	under	within
in	beyond	between	beneath	without
on	among	above	around	below
by	near	behind	past	from

Other prepositions can show *positions in time.* Note that some prepositions appear in both lists:

at	for	past	within	from
by	after	until	since	between
in	before	during	throughout	around

These lists include only individual words, *not phrases.* To form *a prepositional phrase*, a noun or pronoun object—a person, place, thing, or idea—must follow the preposition. For example, imagine a plane flying across a sky full of clouds. Notice that we can change the plane's *position in space* by using prepositions from the first list plus the object of the clouds in the examples below:

The plane flew *above* the clouds.
           below the clouds.
           within the clouds.
           between the clouds.
           past the clouds.
           behind the clouds.

Now notice how we can specify a *position in time* by using prepositions from the second list plus the object of a particular hour or event:

The plane landed *at* 3:30.
                 by 3:30.
                 after 3:30.
                 before the thunderstorm.
                 during the thunderstorm.
                 between two thunderstorms.

NOTE 8.A—Don't mistake *to* plus a verb for a prepositional phrase. Special forms of verbals always start with *to,* but they are not prepositional phrases (see Section 18). For example, in the sentence "I like to take the train to school," *to take* is a verbal, not a prepositional phrase. However, *to school* is a prepositional phrase because it begins with a preposition (to), ends with a noun (school), and shows position in space.

Locating prepositional phrases will help you find subjects and verbs more easily. For example, it might be difficult to find the subject and verb in a long sentence like this:

In the rainy season, one of our windows leaked at all four corners.

But notice how easy it is to see them after we put parentheses around the prepositional phrases:

(In the rainy season), one (of our windows) leaked (at all four corners).

Only two words remain—the pronoun *one* is the subject, and the action word *leaked* is the verb. Even in short sentences like the following, you might think that the words *books* and *campus* are the subjects if you don't put parentheses around the prepositional phrases first:

A box (of books) arrived (with a return address) (from Italy).

The mood (around campus) is cheerful today.

As you can see from the parentheses, *books* and *campus* are actually the noun objects that follow *of* and *around* to form prepositional phrases.

NOTE 8.B—A few words—*of, as,* and *like*—are prepositions that do not fit neatly into either the space or time category, yet they are very common prepositions (book of *essays,* note *of apology,* type *of bicycle;* act *as a substitute,* use *as an example,* testified *as an expert;* sounds *like a computer,* works *like magic,* moves *like an athlete*).

EXERCISES

Put parentheses around all of the prepositional phrases in the following sentences. Be sure to start with the prepositions themselves (*to, in, with, of . . .*) and include the noun or pronoun objects that complete them (*to Hawaii, in a democracy, with her, of our psychology book . . .*). Check your answers often to make the most progress as you continue to practice. Try to think of it as a game, and motivate yourself to find them all on your own.

Exercise 8.1

1. Viganella is a tiny village at the bottom of the Alps in Italy.
2. Due to its physical position between the mountains, the town of Viganella suffered from an unusual problem.
3. The sun's rays never reached the village from the middle of November to the first week in February.
4. The mountains kept the little town in shadow without any direct sunlight for several months each year.
5. Then Giacomo Bonzani found a high-tech solution to Viganella's dreary situation.
6. In 2006, engineers installed a huge mirror thousands of feet above Viganella on the side of one of the mountains around it.
7. A computer at the mirror's location keeps track of the sun's movements.
8. The computer's software rotates the mirror into the perfect position to reflect sunlight into the village square.
9. The mirror began its work in December of 2006.
10. Now the sun "shines" on the town of Viganella during all months of the year.

Source: International Herald Tribune, February 5, 2007

Exercise 8.2

1. One fact about William Shakespeare and his work always surprises people.
2. There are no copies of his original manuscripts.

3. No museum or library has even one page from a Shakespeare play in Shakespeare's own handwriting.

4. Museums and libraries have copies of the First Folio instead.

5. After Shakespeare's death in 1616, actors from his company gathered the texts of his plays and published them as one book, the First Folio, in 1623.

6. They printed approximately 750 copies at the time.

7. Currently, there are 230 known copies of the First Folio in the world.

8. Many owners of the Folio remain anonymous by choice.

9. One woman inherited her copy of the Folio from a distant relative.

10. Another copy of the First Folio recently sold for five million dollars.

Source: Smithsonian, September 2006

Exercise 8.3

1. Most of us remember playing with Frisbees in our front yards in the early evenings and at parks or beaches on weekend afternoons.

2. Fred Morrison invented the original flat Frisbee for the Wham-O toy company in the 1950s.

3. Ed Headrick, designer of the professional Frisbee, passed away at his home in California in August of 2002.

4. Working at Wham-O in the 1960s, Headrick improved the performance of the existing Frisbee with the addition of ridges in the surface of the disc.

5. Headrick's improvements led to increased sales of his "professional model" Frisbee and to the popularity of Frisbee tournaments.

6. After Headrick's redesign, Wham-O sold 100 million of the flying discs.

7. Headrick also invented the game of disc golf.

8. Like regular golf but with discs, the game takes place on special disc golf courses like the first one at Oak Grove Park in California.

9. Before his death, Headrick asked for his ashes to be formed into memorial flying discs for select family and friends.

10. Donations from sales of the remaining memorial discs went toward the establishment of a museum on the history of the Frisbee and disc golf.

Source: Los Angeles Times, August 14, 2002

Exercise 8.4

1. Roald Dahl is the author of *Charlie and the Chocolate Factory.*
2. In his youth, Dahl had two memorable experiences with sweets.
3. One of them involved the owner of a candy store.
4. Dahl and his young friends had a bad relationship with this particular woman.
5. On one visit to her store, Dahl put a dead mouse into one of the candy jars behind her back.
6. The woman later went to his school and demanded his punishment.
7. He and his friends received several lashes from a cane in her presence.
8. During his later childhood years, Dahl became a taste-tester for the Cadbury chocolate company.
9. Cadbury sent him and other schoolchildren boxes of sweets to evaluate.
10. Dahl tried each candy and made a list of his reactions and recommendations.

Source: Sweets: A History of Candy (Bloomsbury, 2002)

Exercise 8.5

1. At 2 a.m. on the second Sunday in March, something happens to nearly everyone in America: Daylight Saving Time.
2. But few people are awake at two in the morning.
3. So we set the hands or digits of our clocks ahead one hour on Saturday night in preparation for it.
4. And before bed on the first Saturday in November, we turn them back again.

5. For days after both events, I have trouble with my sleep patterns and my mood.

6. In spring, the feeling is one of loss.

7. That Saturday-night sleep into Sunday is one hour shorter than usual.

8. But in fall, I gain a false sense of security about time.

9. That endless Sunday morning quickly melts into the start of a hectic week like the other fifty-one in the year.

10. All of this upheaval is due to the Uniform Time Act of 1966.

Exercise 8.6   Paragraph Practice

Put parentheses around the prepositional phrases in the following paragraph from the book *One Red Paperclip* by Kyle MacDonald. MacDonald is the young man who turned one red paperclip into a house of his own by trading it each time for something "bigger and better." In the following paragraph, MacDonald describes the first moments of his world-famous adventure when he decided, "All I had to do was go outside and trade with somebody. Surely *somebody* would have something bigger and better than one red paperclip." Remember that a prepositional phrase must include a preposition followed by a noun or pronoun.

I put the red paperclip on the desk and took a picture of it. I walked to the door and pulled the handle. The door swung open. I lifted my right foot into the air. As my right foot came forward to the threshold of the doorframe, the phone rang. My foot hung in the air, just short of the outside hallway. The phone rang again. I spun around slowly, almost in slow motion. I slowly slunk away from the door and lifted the phone from the receiver.

Exercise 8.7   Sentence Writing

Write ten sentences describing memorable moments in your own life that may be similar to Kyle MacDonald's paper clip moment in Exercise 8.6. When you finish your sentences, put parentheses around any prepositional phrases. For example, if you had been a contestant on a game show, you might write, "I stood (in front) (of the enormous wheel) and reached (for one) (of the pegs) (with my hand)."

9. Finding Subjects and Verbs

The most important words in sentences are those that make up its independent clause—the **subject** and the **verb**. When you write a sentence, you write about a noun or pronoun (a person, place, thing, or idea). That's the *subject*. Then you write the action that the subject *does* or *is*. That's the *verb*.

Lightning strikes.

Lightning is the thing you are writing about; it's the subject, and we'll underline all subjects once. *Strikes* tells what the subject does, showing the action in the sentence. It's the verb, and we'll underline all verbs twice. Of course, few sentences contain just two words, the subject and the verb. Nevertheless, they still make up the core of any clause or sentence, even if many other words and phrases are included with them.

As we learned in Section 8 on "Locating Prepositional Phrases," when many words appear in a sentence, the subject and verb can be harder to find.

At certain times of year, lightning strikes in predictable places.

In summer, it strikes in parks, near lakes, and at golf courses.

But once we put the prepositional phrases in parentheses, the subject and verb in these sentences are left over—"lightning strikes" and "it strikes"—just waiting to be underlined:

(At certain times) (of year), lightning strikes (in predictable places).

(In summer), it strikes (in parks), (near lakes), and (at golf courses).

For the remaining examples in this section, we will put parentheses around prepositional phrases. After identifying any prepositional phrases in sentences, always look for their verbs *next*. Because verbs usually show some kind of action, they're easier to locate than subjects. For example, read this sentence that has no prepositional phrases to see if you can find the verb:

My neighbor's cat gracefully cleans its paws and face all day.

Just ask, "Which word shows the *action*?" The action word is cleans. It's the verb, so we'll underline it twice. Now ask, "*Who* or *what* cleans?" The answer is cat. That's the subject, so we'll underline it once. The following sentences further demonstrate how to find subjects and verbs:

The college celebrates its fiftieth anniversary tomorrow.

Which word shows the *action*? The action word is celebrates. It's the verb, so we'll underline it twice. *Who* or *what* celebrates? The college does. It's the subject. We'll underline it once.

The team members shared several boxes (of chocolates).

Which word shows the *action*? Shared shows the action. *Who* or *what* shared? Members shared.

Internet users often crowd (into the computer labs) (on campus).

Which word shows the *action*? The verb is crowd. *Who* or *what* crowd? Users crowd.

In some sentences, the verb doesn't show an action but *links* the subject with a description. Learn to recognize such linking verbs—*is, am, are, was, were, has been, seem, feel, appear, become, look* . . . (for more, see Section 20). Here are two examples:

Marshall is a popular neon artist (with his own studio).

First spot the *verb* is. Then ask *who* or *what* is? Marshall is.

The sandwiches (in the cafeteria) look really fresh today.

First spot the *verb* look. Then ask *who* or *what* look? Sandwiches look.

Occasionally, the subject comes *after* the verb, especially when a word like *there* or *here* begins the sentence without being a real subject.

(In the audience) were two famous bloggers.

Who or *what* were in the audience? Two famous bloggers were.

There was a fortune-teller (at the carnival).

Who or *what* was there? A fortune-teller was.

(At the top) (of the box), there is an ID tag (with your name) (on it).

Who or *what* is there? A tag is.

Here are two suggestions (for scholarship applicants).

Who or *what* are here? The suggestions are.

NOTE 9.A—Remember that *there* and *here* (as used in the last three examples) are not subjects. They simply point to something.

When a sentence is a command, it may appear to be missing a subject. However, an unwritten *you* is understood by the reader.

Fill in all spaces (on the form). → You <u>fill</u> in all spaces (on the form).

Attach two reference letters. → You <u>attach</u> two reference letters.

Mail it back (by Friday). → You <u>mail</u> it back (by Friday).

Finally, a sentence may have more than one subject.

<u>Toys</u> and <u>memorabilia</u> (from the 1950s) (to the 1990s) <u>are</u> valuable these days.

Collectible <u>dolls</u>, board <u>games</u>, and even cereal <u>boxes</u> (from those decades) <u>sell</u> (for high prices) online.

A sentence may also have more than one verb.

Water <u>boils</u> (at a certain temperature) and <u>freezes</u> (at another).

The ice <u>tray</u> <u>fell</u> (from my hand), <u>skidded</u> (across the floor), and <u>landed</u> (under the table).

EXERCISES

Identify the subjects and verbs in the following sentences. Start by putting parentheses around prepositional phrases. Remember that a sentence's subject and verb will *not* be inside prepositional phrases, so marking them first will help you shorten the sentence to just a few words. Then you can double underline the verbs and single underline their subjects. As you finish each exercise, compare your markings carefully with the answers. Revisit the explanations and examples in this section whenever necessary.

Exercise 9.1

1. Many people know the name of Uggie, the dog actor.
2. Uggie became famous in the Oscar-winning silent movie *The Artist*.
3. His big break came after ten years of work in other films and projects.
4. With his role in *The Artist,* Uggie showcased the skills and expressions of Jack Russell terriers and made them very popular.
5. Originally, Uggie's trainer rescued him from an animal shelter.
6. In June 2012, Uggie retired from his long acting career due to a physical setback.

7. Before his retirement, this famous little dog left his mark on Hollywood—literally.

8. On June 25, 2012, Uggie put his paw prints in cement at Grauman's Chinese Theater.

9. Crowds of fans gathered on Hollywood Blvd. in honor of Uggie's work in films.

10. They were the first canine footprints in the history of this famous landmark.

Source: San Francisco Chronicle, June 28, 2012

Exercise 9.2

1. In 1940, four teenagers took a walk and discovered something marvelous.

2. They entered an underground cavern in Lascaux, France, and found vivid images of animals on its walls.

3. There were horses, deer, bulls, cats, and oxen.

4. The prehistoric artists also left tracings of their handprints on the walls.

5. Scientists dated the paintings and engravings at approximately 17,000 years old.

6. After its discovery, the Lascaux cave became a popular tourist attraction.

7. Twelve hundred people visited the site daily.

8. These visitors had a negative impact on the cave's prehistoric artwork.

9. They breathed carbon dioxide into the cave and increased its humidity.

10. French officials closed the Lascaux cave to the public in 1963.

Source: The Cave of Lascaux official web site (http://www.culture.gouv.fr:80/culture/arcnat/lascaux/en/)

Exercise 9.3

1. Harold Lloyd became a star of comic films during the silent era of Hollywood.

2. Lloyd worked in Hollywood at the same time as Charlie Chaplin and Buster Keaton.

3. The name of Harold Lloyd's character in many of his films was also Harold.

4. One accessory distinguished Harold from other silent-film characters—a pair of perfectly round eyeglasses.

5. The glasses had no lenses but fit his face and gave him a distinct personality.

6. A suit and a straw hat completed Harold's simple yet memorable costume.

7. Unlike Chaplin and Keaton's clownish characters, Harold looked like a normal young man out for adventure—anything from good fun to a great fight.

8. As Harold, Lloyd performed incredible stunts in spite of an injury from an accident with a prop bomb early in his career.

9. He lost part of his hand and covered it in his films with a special glove.

10. In his most famous film, *Safety Last!,* Harold climbed outside a tall building and dangled dangerously from the hands of its clock.

Source: Harold Lloyd: Magic in a Pair of Horn-Rimmed Glasses (Bear Manor Media, 2009)

Exercise 9.4

1. There are many world-famous trees in California.

2. Among them are the oldest trees on the planet.

3. These trees live somewhere in Inyo National Forest.

4. One of these ancient trees is a bristlecone pine.

5. Scientists call it the Methuselah Tree.

6. They place its age at five thousand years.

7. The soil and temperatures around it seem too poor for a tree's health.

8. But the Methuselah Tree and its neighbors obviously thrive in such conditions.

9. Due to its importance, the Methuselah Tree's exact location is a secret.

10. Such important natural specimens need protection.

Source: Current Science, May 3, 2002

Exercise 9.5

1. Ancient Egyptians worshipped cats of all sizes.

2. Archaeologists find many mummies of cats in Egyptian tombs.

3. Carvings in the tombs reveal a strong belief in the god-like powers of large cats.

4. Scientists always look for new evidence of ancient beliefs.

5. Archaeologists recently discovered the mummy of a lion in a tomb in Saqqara, Egypt.

6. It is the first discovery of a lion skeleton in an Egyptian tomb.

7. There were no bandages around the lion.

8. But there were other signs of mummification.

9. The lion rested in the tomb of King Tutankhamen's nurse.

10. Archaeologists now have real evidence of lion worship in Egypt.

Source: Science News, January 31, 2004

Exercise 9.6   Paragraph Practice

Identify the subjects and verbs in the following excerpt from *The Writer's Almanac* about the history of the modern pencil. We have shortened the excerpt and simplified some of its phrasing for this exercise. Remember to double underline the verbs first; then single underline their subjects. Check your answers often, and refer to the explanations and examples whenever necessary.

On March 30, 1858, Hymen Lipman of Philadelphia patented the first pencil with an attached eraser. The eraser-tipped pencil is something of an American phenomenon. Most European pencils are still eraserless. The humble pencil has a long history. It goes back to the Roman stylus, a pointed piece of lead. We still call the business end of the pencil the "lead." However, it is really nontoxic graphite.

Mass-production of the pencil began in Nuremburg, Germany, in 1662 and later flourished as a result of the Industrial Revolution of the 19th century. Henry David Thoreau and his father made the hardest, blackest pencils in the United

States. Thomas Edison was fond of short pencils and kept them in his vest pocket, ready for ideas. John Steinbeck loved the pencil and started every day with 24 fresh, sharp ones. He used 300 pencils to write *East of Eden* and needed 60 a day for *The Grapes of Wrath.*

There are many more interesting facts about pencils. A single pencil can draw a line 35 miles long or write around 45,000 words. And if you make a mistake, thanks to Hymen Lipman, you have an eraser handy.

Source: http://writersalmanac.org/episodes/20150330/

Exercise 9.7   Sentence Writing

Write ten sentences about any subject—your friends' or family's favorite movie snacks, for instance. To make it easy to find your subjects and verbs, keep these sentences as simple as possible. After you have written your sentences, put parentheses around any prepositional phrases and underline the verbs twice and their subjects once. For example, "My <u>brother</u> and <u>I</u> always <u>eat</u> popcorn (at the movies)."

10. Understanding Dependent Clauses

All clauses are groups of related words that contain a subject and a verb. However, there are two kinds of clauses: *independent* and *dependent*. **Independent clauses** include a subject and a verb and make complete statements by themselves. **Dependent clauses** also include a subject and a verb, but these clauses don't make complete statements because of the words that *begin* them. Here are some of the words (conjunctions and pronouns) that can begin dependent clauses:

after	since	where
although	so that	whereas
as	than	wherever
because	that	whether
before	though	which
even if	unless	whichever
even though	until	while
ever since	what	who
how	whatever	whom
if	when	whose
once	whenever	why

When a clause begins with one of these dependent words, it is usually a dependent clause. To see the difference between an independent and a dependent clause, look at this example of an independent clause:

We studied history together.

It includes a subject (We) and a verb (studied), and it makes a complete statement. But as soon as we put one of the dependent words in *front* of it, the clause becomes *dependent* because it no longer makes a complete statement:

After we studied history together . . .

Although we studied history together . . .

As we studied history together . . .

Before we studied history together . . .

Since we studied history together . . .

That we studied history together . . .

When we studied history together . . .

While we studied history together . . .

Each of these dependent clauses leaves the reader expecting something more. Each would *depend* on another clause—an independent clause—to make it a sentence. For the rest of this discussion, we'll place a dotted line beneath dependent clauses.

After we studied history together, we went to the evening seminar.

We went to the evening seminar *after* we studied history together.

The speaker didn't know *that* we studied history together.

While we studied history together, we often quizzed each other.

As you can see in the examples, *when a dependent clause comes before an independent clause, a comma should separate it from the rest of the sentence.* Often the comma prevents misreading, as in the following sentence:

When we returned, our library books were on the floor.

Without a comma after *returned,* the reader would get as far as "When we returned our library books" before realizing that this was not what the writer meant. The comma after "returned" prevents such a misreading. Sometimes, if the dependent clause is short and there is no danger of misreading, the comma can be left off, but it's safer simply to make a habit of adding a comma after a dependent clause that introduces an independent clause. You can learn more about the punctuation of clauses in Table 10.A and Table 10.B at the end of this section.

Note that a few of the dependent words (*that, who, which, what*) can do "double duty" as both the dependent word and the subject of the dependent clause:

Thelma wrote a poetry book *that* sold a thousand copies.

The manager saw *what* happened.

Sometimes the dependent clause is in the middle of the independent clause:

The book *that* sold a thousand copies was Thelma's.

The events *that* followed the parade delighted everyone.

The dependent clause can even be the subject of the entire sentence:

What you do also affects me.

How your project looks counts for ten percent of the grade.

Also note that sometimes the *that* of a dependent clause is omitted:

I know *that* you feel strongly about this issue.

I know you feel strongly about this issue.

Everyone received the classes *that* they wanted.

Everyone received the classes they wanted.

Of course, the word *that* doesn't always introduce a dependent clause. It may be a regular pronoun that serves as the subject or object of a sentence or the object of a prepositional phrase:

That was a really long movie.

The answer is 185. We know *that* already.

I found an inspirational quotation; I will begin my speech (with *that*).

That can also be an adjective, a descriptive word telling *which one:*

That comic always makes me laugh.

We took them to *that* park last week.

EXERCISES

Exercise 10.1

Each of the following sentences contains one independent and one dependent clause. Draw a dotted line beneath the dependent clause in each sentence. Start at the dependent word and include all of the words that go with it, including any prepositional phrases that they contain. You do not need to mark prepositional phrases here. Just focus on finding dependent clauses, and remember that they can appear at the beginning, in the middle, or at the end of a sentence.

Example: We study together whenever we meet in the library.

1. Edgar and Nina Otto, who live in Florida, were the winning bidders in an unusual auction in 2008.

2. Whoever placed the highest bid won the opportunity of a lifetime: a chance to clone their dog.

3. The company that held the auction and provided the service was BioArts International.

4. The Ottos wanted to clone Sir Lancelot, a yellow Labrador that died in 2008.

5. The price that they paid exceeded $150,000.

6. Once the auction ended, the scientists at BioArts went to work.

7. They used the DNA that the Ottos saved from Sir Lancelot to produce a genetic match.

8. The complex process, which took place in South Korea, yielded an adorable puppy.

9. The puppy looked so much like Sir Lancelot that the company named him Encore Lancelot, Lancey for short.

10. At the first meeting with their new dog in January of 2009, the Ottos were overjoyed that Lancey walked with crossed feet, just like Sir Lancelot.

Source: www.Today.com, January 28, 2009

Exercises 10.2–5

Follow the same directions as in Exercise 10.1; however, this time draw your dotted lines far below the dependent clauses. Then go back to both the independent and dependent clauses to double underline their verbs and single underline their subjects.

Example: We study together whenever we meet in the library.

Exercise 10.2

1. When I was on vacation in New York City, I loved the look of the Empire State Building at night.

2. I thought that the colored lights at the top of this landmark were just decorative.

3. I did not know that their patterns also have meaning.

4. While I waited at the airport, I visited the building's web site and read about the patterns.

5. Some of the light combinations reveal connections that are obvious.

6. For instance, if the occasion is St. Patrick's Day, the top of the building glows with green lights.

7. When the holiday involves a celebration of America, the three levels of lights shine red, white, and blue.

8. There are other combinations that are less well known.

9. Red–black–green is a pattern that signals Martin Luther King Jr. Day.

10. Whenever I visit the city again, I'll know that the lights on the Empire State Building have meaning.

Source: http://www.esbnyc.com/esb_led_lights.asp

Exercise 10.3

1. When people visit Google's homepage on one evening in March each year, they are often surprised.

2. They notice immediately that the whole page is black instead of white.

3. After they look into it further, they discover the reason for the temporary color change.

4. The black page signifies that Google is a participant in Earth Hour.

5. In 2008, Google joined countless cities, companies, and individuals who turn their lights off for one hour in an international effort to encourage energy conservation.

6. People around the globe cut their electricity and live in the dark as soon as the clocks strike the appointed hour in their locations.

7. When the hour is up, they turn the electricity back on.

8. Earth Hour is an idea that began in Australia.

9. In 2007, the first Earth Hour that the Australians celebrated occurred between 7:30 and 8:30 p.m. on March 31.

10. Even though some people dismiss Earth Hour as a minor event, others believe in its power as a symbol of environmental awareness.

Source: http://www.earthhour.org

Exercise 10.4

1. On June 8, 1924, George Mallory and Andrew Irvine disappeared as they climbed to the top of Mount Everest.

2. Earlier, when a reporter asked Mallory why he climbed Everest, his response became legendary.

3. "Because it is there," Mallory replied.

4. No living person knows whether the two British men reached the summit of Everest before they died.

5. Nine years after Mallory and Irvine disappeared, English climbers found Irvine's ice ax.

6. In 1975, a Chinese climber spotted a body that was frozen in deep snow on the side of the mountain.

7. He kept the news secret for several years but finally told a fellow climber on the day before he died himself in an avalanche on Everest.

8. In May 1999, a team of mountaineers searched the area that the Chinese man described and found George Mallory's frozen body, still intact after seventy-five years.

9. After they took DNA samples for identification, the mountaineers buried the famous climber on the mountainside where he fell.

10. The question remains whether Mallory was on his way up or down when he met his fate.

Source: Newsweek, May 17, 1999

Exercise 10.5

1. I just read an article with a list of "What Doctors Wish You Knew."

2. One fact is that red and blue fruits are the healthiest.

3. Patients who have doctor's appointments after lunchtime spend less time in the waiting room.

4. Drivers who apply more sunscreen to their left sides get less skin cancer.

5. People who take ten deep breaths in the morning and evening feel less stress.

6. A clock that is visible from the bed makes insomnia worse.

7. People often suffer from weekend headaches because they get up too late.

8. They withdraw from caffeine by skipping the coffee that they usually drink on workdays.

9. Doctors suggest that people maintain weekday hours on weekends.

10. I am glad that I found this list.

Source: Good Housekeeping, November 2005

Exercise 10.6 Paragraph Practice

Draw a dotted line beneath the dependent clauses in the following paragraphs about how gender stereotypes affect parents and babies from the book *Parenting beyond Pink and Blue* by Christia Spears Brown, Ph.D. See if you can find all eleven dependent clauses in this excerpt.

PARENTING BABIES

We are most prone to rely on stereotypes when our children are babies. It is difficult to pay attention to their unique qualities when they just lie there, cry, and drool. They don't show much interest in toys yet. They are primarily interested in milk and our dangling car keys. So we fill in the missing information about their personality and interests with stereotypes about what they should like. We don't know much about them as individuals, but we do know their gender. So we let gender drive a lot of our own behavior.

Not surprisingly, when researchers examined the rooms of infant boys and girls, they found differences in what babies are exposed to right from the start. Boys had more "toys of the world," like cars, trains, and machines; girls had more "toys of the home," like dolls and housekeeping toys. Right from the start, parents are shaping whether their children will gravitate toward trucks or dolls once they become mobile.

Parents also differ in how they interact with their babies. Mothers talk more, interact more, and are more sensitive to the smiles of girl babies than boy babies. Baby boys are handled more roughly than baby girls. This is even true when the baby is a stranger in a research study and the researchers alternate whether they call the baby a boy or a girl. The "boy" gets handled like a boy, even when she is secretly a girl.

Exercise 10.7 Sentence Writing

Write ten sentences of your *own* in response to the excerpt "Parenting Babies" in Exercise 10.6. Try to write sentences that contain both independent and dependent clauses. Then underline your verbs twice, their subjects once, and draw a broken line beneath any dependent clauses. Take care not to use Brown's exact phrasing, unless you punctuate it correctly as a quotation. For more about quoting from and responding to readings, see Section 36 on "Choosing and Using Quotations" and Section 37 on "Writing in Response to a Reading."

To see how independent and dependent clauses affect sentence types and punctuation, review the following tables:

TABLE 10.A SENTENCE TYPES AND PUNCTUATION (WITHOUT DEPENDENT CLAUSES)

Sentences *without dependent clauses* are called **simple** or **compound** based on the number of *independent clauses* they contain.

- **A simple sentence** includes **a single independent clause** and ends with a period (or ? or !). Simple sentences can have multiple subjects and verbs, but only *one* **S + V** meet to form the main clause.

> **1)** $\underline{S} + \underline{\underline{V}}$.

> **2)** $S + \underline{S} + \underline{\underline{V}} + V$.

> **1)** $\underline{I}$ often **receive** packages on Sundays.

> **2)** My $\underline{neighbor}$ and **$\underline{I}$ work** full time and $\underline{help}$ each other with deliveries.

- **A compound sentence** contains **two or more independent clauses,** using one of three punctuation options to join them. *"Fanboys"* refers to the words *for, and, nor, but, or, yet,* and *so;* and *transitions* are words like *however, consequently,* and *therefore.*

> **3)** $\underline{S} + \underline{\underline{V}}$, *FANBOYS* $\underline{S} + \underline{\underline{V}}$.

> **4)** $\underline{S} + \underline{\underline{V}}$; $\underline{S} + \underline{\underline{V}}$.

> **5)** $\underline{S} + \underline{\underline{V}}$; *transition,* $\underline{S} + \underline{\underline{V}}$.

> **3)** $\underline{I}$ often **receive** packages on Sundays, *but* **$\underline{I}$ am** usually at work.

> **4)** $\underline{I}$ often **receive** packages on Sundays; **$\underline{I}$ am** usually at work.

> **5)** $\underline{I}$ often **receive** packages on Sundays; *however,* **$\underline{I}$ am** usually at work.

TABLE 10.B SENTENCE TYPES AND PUNCTUATION (WITH DEPENDENT CLAUSES)

Sentences *with dependent clauses* are called **complex** or **compound-complex** based on the number of *dependent* and *independent clauses* they contain.

- **A complex sentence** contains **one independent clause** and **one or more dependent clauses.** A comma separates a dependent clause from the rest of the sentence when it introduces an independent clause, but not usually if it follows one. Commas enclose dependent clauses when they are "scoopable" (see Section 27 for more about commas).

> **6) Dependent word + S + V,** S + V.

> **7)** S + V **dependent word + S + V.**

> **8)** S, **dependent word + S + V,** + V.

> **6) When I receive packages on Sundays**, I am usually at work.

> **7)** I am usually at work **when I receive packages on Sundays.**

> **8)** My new neighbor, **who has weekends off,** accepts my packages for me.

- **A compound-complex sentence** contains **two or more independent clauses** *plus* **one or more dependent clause** in any order, using the same punctuation patterns outlined in 1 to 8 above:

> **9)** I am usually at work **when I receive packages**, but my new neighbor
>
> accepts them for me.

> **10) Although my new neighbor and I work full time**, we have different
>
> schedules, so we help each other **whenever we can.**

11. Correcting Fragments

To be a **sentence,** a group of words must include at least one independent clause: a subject + verb combination that forms *a complete thought.* A sentence **fragment** is a word group that is punctuated as a sentence—with a capital letter at the beginning and a period at the end—but some part of its phrasing or meaning is missing. In short, **fragments are incomplete word groups posing as sentences.** Here are a few examples:

Always reads a magazine at the break. *(no subject—Who* reads a magazine?)

The exhibit of graphic novels in the library. *(no verb—*What did the exhibit *do?)*

Once the plane finally landed. *(no complete thought—What happened* then?)

To correct these fragments, simply add the missing information:

My philosophy teacher always reads a magazine at the break. (subject added)

The exhibit of graphic novels in the library opened on Sunday. (verb added)

Once the plane finally landed, I felt so relieved. (complete thought added)

Other fragments need to be combined with the sentences around them:

Actors gathered near the director's office. Waiting for an audition. (fragment)

Waiting for an audition, actors gathered near the director's office. (fixed)

Actors gathered near the director's office and waited for an audition. (fixed)

Finally, *dependent clauses* are fragments whenever they are punctuated as sentences because their meaning is incomplete. To correct a dependent clause fragment, combine it with an independent clause or remove the word that makes it dependent. See Section 10 for more about dependent clauses:

Our presentations went well. *Because* we practiced every day. (fragment)

Our presentations went well *because* we practiced every day. (fixed)

Our presentations went well. We practiced every day. (fixed)

NOTE 11.A—If you have trouble finding fragments, try making the word group into a question by adding *"Did you know that . . . "* in front of it and adding a question mark at the end. For example, to check whether "Water is a liquid" is a sentence, ask *"Did you know that* Water is a liquid?" Clearly, the question makes sense. "Water is a liquid" also includes a subject (water) and verb (is); therefore, this word group is a sentence.

Now try using *"Did you know that . . . "* in front of "Unless it freezes or vaporizes." The result does not make sense—*"Did you know that* Unless it freezes or vaporizes?" This word group is a fragment. It does have a subject and two verbs (it freezes and vaporizes), but they are part of a dependent clause that does not form a complete thought.

The *Did you know that . . .* method will help you identify fragments in the exercises and in your own writing. This method works with most standard sentences, but not with sentences that are already questions or commands.

To check sentences that are commands (see Section 9), use *"Did you know that you should . . . "* in front of the word group. For example, to confirm that "Insert flap A into slot B" is a sentence, ask *"Did you know that you should* Insert flap A into slot B"?

You might ask, "Are fragments ever permissible?" Professional writers sometimes use fragments in ads, articles, books, and other published writing. When professional writers use fragments, however, they do it intentionally, not in error. They understand how an occasional fragment might fulfill a stylistic purpose. Until you master writing complete sentences for academic or business purposes, you should avoid writing fragments.

EXERCISES

Some of the following word groups are sentences, and some are fragments. The sentences include subjects and verbs and make complete statements, but the fragments do not. Use the *"Did you know that . . . "* method to help you identify the fragments, as explained in Note 11.A. Write "sentence" next to the word groups that qualify, and change the fragments into sentences by adding missing information or by combining them with a sentence before or after them. Check your answers frequently, and refer back to the examples whenever necessary.

Exercise 11.1

1. Soon we will wear clothes that clean themselves.
2. Improvements in fabric coatings making it possible.
3. Clothes treated with certain chemicals.
4. These chemicals kill bacteria and keep dirt from soaking into fabrics.
5. Already tested by the military for soldiers' uniforms.
6. U.S. soldiers wore self-cleaning T-shirts and underwear in one study.
7. The chemicals worked but eventually wore off.
8. Helped cure soldiers' skin problems, too.
9. Fabric that stays clean and dry is a great idea.
10. Also could be used for hospital bedding, kitchen linens, and sport-related clothing.

Source: Sunday Telegraph, December 30, 2006

Exercise 11.2

1. Duct tape has many uses.
2. Good at holding objects together firmly.
3. Campers using it to patch holes in backpacks and tents.
4. People are very creative with duct tape.
5. Books written about the unique uses for it.
6. A yearly contest by the makers of Duck Brand duct tape.
7. For the contest, high school couples make prom clothes entirely out of duct tape.
8. Strips of duct tape to form tuxedos, cummerbunds, gowns, hats, and corsages.
9. A $5,000 prize to the couple with the best use of duct tape and another $5,000 to their high school.
10. Hundreds of couples from across the country participate in this contest every year.

Source: http://www.ducktapeclub.com

Exercise 11.3

In this exercise, each pair contains one sentence and one fragment. Correct the fragment by combining it with the complete sentence before or after it.

1. A worker at the Smithsonian discovered an important historical object. On a shelf in one of the museum's storage rooms.

2. Made of cardboard and covered with short, smooth fur. It was a tall black top hat.

3. The hat didn't look like anything special. More like an old costume or prop.

4. It was special, however. Having been worn by Abraham Lincoln on the night of his assassination.

5. Once found and identified, Lincoln's hat traveled with the 150th anniversary exhibition. Called "America's Smithsonian."

6. For such a priceless object to be able to travel around the country safely. Experts needed to build a unique display case for Lincoln's top hat.

7. The design allowed visitors to view the famous stovepipe hat. Without damaging it with their breath or hands.

8. The hat traveled in a sealed box. Designed against even earthquakes.

9. Keeping the hat earthquake-proof was an important concern. Being on display in California for part of the time.

10. President Lincoln's hat is one of the most impressive. Among the millions of objects in the archives of the Smithsonian.

Source: Saving Stuff (Fireside, 2005)

Exercise 11.4

Each pair contains one sentence and one dependent clause fragment. Correct each dependent clause fragment by combining it with the complete sentence before or after it or by eliminating its dependent word.

1. When Nathan King turned twelve. He had a heart-stopping experience.

2. Nathan was tossing a football against his bedroom wall. Which made the ball ricochet and land on his bed.

3. In a diving motion, Nathan fell on his bed to catch the ball. As it landed.

4. After he caught the ball. Nathan felt a strange sensation in his chest.

5. To his surprise, he looked down and saw the eraser end of a no. 2 pencil. That had pierced his chest and entered his heart.

6. Nathan immediately shouted for his mother. Who luckily was in the house at the time.

7. Because Nathan's mom is a nurse. She knew not to remove the pencil.

8. If she had pulled the pencil out of her son's chest. He would have died.

9. After Nathan was taken to a hospital equipped for open-heart surgery. He had the pencil carefully removed.

10. Fate may be partly responsible for Nathan's happy birthday story. Since it turned out to be his heart surgeon's birthday too.

Source: Time, March 20, 2000

Exercise 11.5

All of the following word groups are fragments, incomplete word groups punctuated as sentences. Make the necessary changes to turn each fragment into a sentence that makes sense to you. Your corrections may differ from the sample answers. By comparing your answers to ours, you'll see that there are many ways to correct a fragment.

1. One of the people sitting next to me on the train.

2. Taking good pictures with my cell phone camera.

3. Before the paint was dry in the classrooms.

4. The judge's question and the answer it received.

5. Because there were fewer students in the program this year.

6. Since his speech lasted for over an hour.

7. Whenever the teacher reminds us about the midterm exam.

8. If we move to Kentucky and stay for two years.

9. As soon as the order form reaches the warehouse.

10. Buildings with odd shapes always of interest to me.

Exercise 11.6 Proofreading Practice

Find and correct the seven fragments in the following paragraphs:

On June 15, 2012, Nik Wallenda made history. By being the first person to walk on a tightrope from the U.S. to Canada directly above the raging falls of Niagara Gorge. His trip on the high wire that misty evening took 30 minutes. A nail-biting half hour that one major network, ABC, televised live. To be on the safe side, the network made sure that Wallenda attached himself to a safety cable in case he fell off the wire on live TV. Nik Wallenda comes from a long line of daredevil performers. From the famous family known as the Flying Wallendas. Nik represents the seventh generation of people willing to risk their lives in the name of entertainment. Before attempting his spectacular walk across Niagara Falls, Wallenda fought hard to get permission from both U.S. and Canadian officials. So that he was not arrested—as previous stunt performers have been—when he reached the other side. Instead of handcuffs waiting for him on the Canadian bank of the falls. Nik Wallenda heard the cheers of 100,000 supporters welcoming him back to earth.

A year later, Wallenda also succeeded in crossing a gorge near the Grand Canyon. This time without a safety cable. His tightrope being 1,500 feet above the canyon floor. Winds were so strong that he had to stop twice in the middle of the crossing and crouch down to maintain his position on the wire.

Sources: New York Times, June 15, 2012, and CBSnews.com, June 23, 2013

Exercise 11.7 Sentence Writing

Write ten fragments like the ones in Exercise 11.5 and revise them so that they are complete sentences. For even more good practice, exchange papers with another student and turn your classmate's ten fragments into sentences.

12. Correcting Run-on Sentences

A word group with a subject and a verb is a clause. As we have seen, the clause may be independent, making a complete statement and able to stand alone as a sentence. Or it may be dependent, beginning with a dependent word and unable to stand alone as a sentence. When two *independent* clauses are written together without proper punctuation between them, the result is called a **run-on sentence.** Here are some examples.

> World music offers a lot of variety I listen to it in my car.

> I love the sound of drums therefore, bhangra is one of my favorite styles.

Run-on sentences can be corrected in one of six ways:

1) Separate the independent clauses into two sentences with a period.

> World music offers a lot of variety. I listen to it in my car.

> I love the sound of drums. Therefore, bhangra is one of my favorite styles.

2) Connect the two independent clauses with a semicolon alone.

> World music offers a lot of variety; I listen to it in my car.

> I love the sound of drums; therefore, bhangra is one of my favorite styles.

3) Connect the two independent clauses with a semicolon and a transition.

Look over the following list of connecting words (transitions):

also	however	otherwise
consequently	likewise	then
finally	moreover	therefore
furthermore	nevertheless	thus

When one of these words joins two independent clauses, a semicolon comes before the connecting word, and a comma usually comes after it, unless it is only one syllable, like *then* or *thus.*

> Mobile devices are essential in our society; however, they are very expensive.

> Earthquakes scare me; nevertheless, I live in Los Angeles.

> Yasmin traveled to London; then she took the "Chunnel" to Paris.

> The college recently built a large new library; thus we have more study areas.

NOTE 12.A—The use of the comma after the connecting word depends on how long the connecting word is. If it is only a short word, like *then* or *thus,* the comma is not necessary.

4) **Connect the two independent clauses with a comma and one of the following seven *conjunctions* called *fanboys* (an easy way to remember them): *for, and, nor, but, or, yet,* and *so.***

Swans are beautiful birds, *and* they mate for life.

New students can sign up for classes in person, *or* they can register online.

Each of the *fanboys* has its own meaning when used as a connecting word. For example, *so* means "as a result," and *for* means "because":

World music offers a lot of variety, *so* I never get bored with it.

Bhangra is one of my favorite styles, *for* I love the sound of drums.

I applied for financial aid, *but* (or *yet*) I make too much money to receive it.

My brother doesn't know how to drive, *nor* does he plan to learn.

Before you put a comma before a *fanboys,* be sure there are two independent clauses. Note that the first sentence that follows has two independent clauses. However, the second sentence contains just one clause with two verbs and therefore needs no comma.

Registration begins next week, and it continues throughout the summer.

Registration begins next week and continues throughout the summer.

5) **Add another kind of *conjunction*, a *dependent word*—such as *when, since, after, while,* or *because*—to the clause at the beginning of the sentence, and follow the dependent clause with a comma.**

Because I enjoy the mellow sounds of acoustic guitar music, I listen to it in my car.

6) **Add a *conjunction*—a *dependent word* such as *when, since, after, while,* or *because*—to the clause at the end of the sentence (no comma necessary).**

I listen to acoustic guitar music in my car *because* I enjoy its mellow sounds.

Learning these ways to join two clauses will help you avoid writing run-on sentences.

TABLE 12.A–SIX WAYS TO CORRECT RUN-ON SENTENCES

Run-on: The movie needed a better story many people left early.

1. The movie needed a better story. Many people left early. (period)
2. The movie needed a better story; many people left early. (semicolon)
3. The movie needed a better story; therefore, many people left early. (semicolon + transition)
4. The movie needed a better story, so many people left early. (comma + *fanboys*)
5. Because the movie needed a better story, many people left early. (dependent clause at the beginning + comma)
6. Many people left early because the movie needed a better story. (dependent clause at end—no comma)

EXERCISES

Exercises 12.1 and 12.2

CORRECTING RUN-ONS WITH PUNCTUATION

Some of the following sentences are run-ons. If the sentence contains two independent clauses without proper punctuation, **use one of the first four ways to correct the run-on** (using punctuation only). All existing punctuation in the sentences is correct. When correcting run-ons with punctuation, remember to capitalize after a period but not after a semicolon. Also remember to insert a comma only when one of the *fanboys* **(for, and, nor, but, or, yet,** or **so)** has already been used to join the two independent clauses.

Exercise 12.1

1. Mary Mallon is a famous name in American history but she is not famous for something good.

2. Most people know Mary Mallon by another name and that is "Typhoid Mary."

3. Mallon lived during the late nineteenth and early twentieth centuries.

4. At that time, there was little knowledge about disease carriers.

5. Mary Mallon was the first famous case of a healthy carrier of disease but she never believed the accusations against her.

6. Mallon, an Irish immigrant, was a cook she was also an infectious carrier of typhoid.

7. By the time the authorities discovered Mallon's problem, she had made many people ill a few of her "victims" actually died from the disease.

8. A health specialist approached Mallon and asked her for a blood sample she was outraged and attacked him with a long cooking fork.

9. Eventually, the authorities dragged Mallon into a hospital for testing but she fought them hysterically the entire time.

10. The lab tests proved Mallon's infectious status and health officials forced Mary Mallon to live on an island by herself for twenty-six years.

Source: Los Angeles Times, September 2, 2002

Exercise 12.2

1. I just read an article about prehistoric rodents and I was surprised by their size.

2. Scientists recently discovered the remains of a rat-like creature called *Phoberomys* it was as big as a buffalo.

3. *Phoberomys* sat back on its large rear feet and fed itself with its smaller front feet in just the way rats and mice do now.

4. This supersized rodent lived in South America but luckily that was nearly ten million years ago.

5. At that time, South America was a separate continent it had no cows or horses to graze on its open land.

6. South America and North America were separated by the sea so there were also no large cats around to hunt and kill other large animals.

7. Scientists believe that *Phoberomys* thrived and grew large because of the lack of predators and competitors for food.

8. The *Phoberomys'* carefree lifestyle eventually disappeared for the watery separation between North and South America slowly became a land route.

9. The big carnivores of North America could travel down the new land route and the big rodents were defenseless against them.

10. The rodents who survived were the smaller ones who could escape underground and that is the reason we have no buffalo-sized rats today.

Source: Science News, September 20, 2003

Exercises 12.3 and 12.4

CORRECTING RUN-ONS WITH DEPENDENT CLAUSES

Most of the following sentences are run-ons. Correct any run-on sentences by making one or more of the clauses *dependent.* You may rephrase the sentences, but be sure to use dependent words (such as *since, when, as, after, while, because,* or the other words listed in Section 10) to begin dependent clauses. Since various words can be used to form dependent clauses, your answers might differ from those suggested in the answers.

Exercise 12.3

1. In September of 2006, Pablo Wendel was a German student of art he felt a special connection with a particular group of ancient sculptures.

2. Pablo acted on this feeling it won him his "fifteen minutes of fame."

3. He had always admired the terra cotta warriors that were discovered in the 2,200-year-old tomb of a Chinese emperor.

4. Pablo decided to see the famous army of clay soldiers first-hand and to document his trip with photographs.

5. He made a special clay-covered costume it was complete with armor and a helmet.

6. Pablo took this outfit and a pedestal with him to the museum it is located in Xian, China.

7. He planned to take a picture of himself in costume outside the museum, but his dream to stand among the soldiers was too strong.

8. He entered the excavation site, jumped into the excavation pit, and joined the terra cotta army.

9. Pablo, in disguise, stood among his fellow "soldiers" and didn't move eventually someone saw him.

10. The museum guards took Pablo's clay costume they let him go with just a warning.

Source: http://news.bbc.co.uk/2/hi/asia-pacific/5355546.stm

Exercise 12.4

1. I've been reading about sleep in my psychology class I now know a lot more about it.

2. Sleep has four stages we usually go through all these stages many times during the night.

3. The first stage of sleep begins our muscles relax and mental activity slows down.

4. During stage one, we are still slightly awake.

5. Stage two takes us deeper than stage one we are no longer aware of our surroundings.

6. We spend about half our sleeping time in the second stage.

7. Next is stage three in it we become more and more relaxed and are very hard to awaken.

8. Stage four is the deepest in this stage we don't even hear loud noises.

9. The most active type of sleep is called REM (rapid eye movement) sleep our eyes move back and forth quickly behind our eyelids.

10. REM sleep is only about as deep as stage one we do all our dreaming during the REM stage.

Source: Psychology: A Journey (Cengage, 2010)

Exercise 12.5

Correct the following run-on sentences using any of the methods studied in this section: adding punctuation or using dependent words to create dependent clauses. See Table 12.A if you need to review the methods.

1. White buffalos are very rare and they are extremely important in Native American folklore.

2. Many American Indian tribes feel a strong attachment to white buffalos they are viewed as omens of peace and prosperity.

3. One farm in Wisconsin is famous as a source of white buffalos three of them have been born on this farm since 1994.

4. The owners of the farm are Valerie and Dave Heider and they are as surprised as anyone about the unusual births.

5. The Heiders' first white buffalo was a female calf she was named Miracle.

6. Miracle became a local attraction visitors to the Heider farm raised tourism in the area by twenty-two percent in 1995.

7. A second white calf was born on the farm in 1996 however, it died after a few days.

8. Miracle survived until 2004 she lived for ten years.

9. In September of 2006, the Heider farm yielded a third white buffalo calf but it was a boy.

10. The odds against one white buffalo being born are high the odds against three being born in the same place are astronomical.

Source: http://whitebuffalomiracle2.homestead.com/Miracle2_BirthStory.html

REVIEW OF FRAGMENTS AND RUN-ON SENTENCES

If you remember that all clauses include a subject and a verb, but only independent clauses can be punctuated as sentences, since only they can stand alone, then you will avoid fragments in your writing. And if you memorize these six ways to punctuate clauses, you will be able to avoid most punctuation errors. For a list of other helpful charts related to clauses and punctuation, refer to the inside back cover.

TABLE 12.B PUNCTUATING CLAUSES TO AVOID FRAGMENTS AND RUN-ONS

I am a student. I am still learning.	(two sentences)
I am a student; I am still learning.	(two independent clauses)
I am a student; *therefore,* I am still learning.	(two independent clauses connected by a transition such as *also, consequently, finally, furthermore, however, likewise, moreover, nevertheless, otherwise, then, therefore, thus*)
I am a student, *so* I am still learning.	(two independent clauses connected by a *fanboys: for, and, nor, but, or, yet, so*)
Because I am a student, I am still learning.	(dependent clause at beginning of sentence) Dependent words include *after, although, as, as if, because, before, even if, even though, ever since, how, if, since, so that, than, that, though, unless, until, what, whatever, when, whenever, where, whereas, wherever, whether, which, whichever, while, who, whom, whose,* and *why.*
I am still learning *because I am a student.*	(dependent clause at end of sentence)

It is essential that you study the previous chart to learn which of the italicized words transition between independent clauses and which of them create dependent clauses.

Exercise 12.6 Proofreading Practice

Rewrite the following student paragraph, making the necessary changes to eliminate fragments and run-on sentences.

With the focus on cleanliness lately in advertising for soaps and household cleaning products. People are surprised to hear that we may be too clean for our own good. This phenomenon is called the "hygiene hypothesis" and recent studies support its validity. For instance, one study showing the benefits of living with two or more pets. Babies may grow up with healthier immune systems and be less allergic if they live with a dog and a cat or two dogs or two cats. The old thinking was that young children would become more allergic living with many pets but they don't. Somehow the exposure to pets and all their "dirty" habits gives youngsters much-needed defenses. Maybe as much as a seventy-five percent lower allergy risk, according to this study.

Source: http://www.uofmhealth.org/news/196cleaner-lifestyles-causes-allergies

Exercise 12.7 Sentence Writing

Write a sample sentence of your own to demonstrate each of the six ways to punctuate two clauses. You may model your sentences on the examples used in Table 12.a or Table 12.b.

13. Identifying Verb Phrases

Sometimes a verb is one word, but often the verb includes two or more words. Verbs made of more than one word are called **verb phrases.** Look at that following list of forms of the verb *speak*, for example. All but the first three of them are verb phrases, made up of the main verb *speak* and one or more *helping verbs—will, have, has, had, is, am, are, was, were, been, can, must, could, should, would.*

speak	is speaking	had been speaking
speaks	am speaking	will have been speaking
spoke	are speaking	is spoken
will speak	was speaking	was spoken
has spoken	were speaking	will be spoken
have spoken	will be speaking	can speak
had spoken	has been speaking	must speak
will have spoken	have been speaking	should have spoken

Note that certain adverbs may appear in the middle of a verb phrase, but they are not part of the verb itself. For more about adverbs, see Section 4.

We <u>have</u> *already* <u>spoken</u> to the landlord and <u>will</u> *also* <u>speak</u> with other tenants.

Here are the most common adverbs used to modify verbs and verb phrases:

already	ever	not	really
also	finally	now	sometimes
always	just	often	usually
probably	never	only	possibly

Two forms of *speak—speaking* and *to speak—*look like verbs, but neither form can ever be the only verb in a sentence. No *ing* word by itself or *to* _____ form of a verb can act as the main verb of a sentence. These forms are called "verbals," see Section 18.

Jeanine speaking French. (This *ing* form needs a helping verb.)

And no verb with *to* in front of it can ever be the real verb in a sentence.

We to speak in front of groups. (This fragment needs a real verb.)

However, these two forms, *speaking* without a helping verb and *to speak*, may be used as subjects, objects, or other parts of a sentence that already has a real verb.

Public *speaking* is an art. --> *Speaking* is the subject; *is* is the real verb.

I like *to speak* in public. --> *To speak* is the object of the real verb *like*.

Ted has a *speaking* part in a film. --> *Speaking* is an adjective; *has* is the verb.

Real verb phrases contain helping verbs and main verbs that work together with subjects to form clauses. Here are several sample sentences that you can use as guides when looking for verbs and verb phrases in the exercises:

Ted has never spoken any lines in a movie before.

Tomorrow, he will speak them for the first time on the set.

Now Ted can perfectly speak even the lines that had been giving him trouble.

Have you ever listened to Jeanine when she speaks French?

By the time Jeanine moves to Paris, she will have been speaking French for a year.

EXERCISES

Following the sample sentences in this section, double underline the verbs and verb phrases in the following exercises; then single underline their subjects. You do not need to mark prepositional phrases, unless you want to for extra practice. The sentences may contain independent *and* dependent clauses, so there may be several verbs and verb phrases. Remember that *ing* verbs without helping verbs and the *to* _____ forms of verbs are never real verbs in sentences.

Exercise 13.1

1. Scientists of all kinds have been learning a lot lately.

2. Those who study traffic safety have recently discovered a puzzling truth.

3. People drive more safely when they encounter fewer traffic signs and traffic lights.

4. The reason behind the "Shared Space" theory is easy to explain.

5. Drivers will regulate their speed and pay closer attention to other drivers when they are not told to do so by signs and lights.

6. Traffic signs and signals give drivers a false sense of security that often leads to recklessness.

7. When no signs or signals exist, drivers think about their own safety and drive more cautiously.

8. Many towns in Europe and America have already taken steps to test the truth of this theory.

9. In some cases, all lights, signs, and barriers have been removed so that all drivers and pedestrians must negotiate with each other to proceed through the town.

10. These changes have usually resulted in lower speeds, fewer accidents, and shorter travel times.

Sources: Discover, May 2007, and *International Herald Tribune,* January 22, 2005

Exercise 13.2

1. Have you ever felt a craving for art?

2. Have you said to yourself, "I need a new painting, or I will lose my mind"?

3. If you do find yourself in this situation, you can get instant satisfaction.

4. I am referring to Art-o-Mat machines, of course.

5. These vending machines dispense small pieces of modern art.

6. You insert five dollars, pull a knob on a refurbished cigarette dispenser, and out comes an original art piece.

7. The artists themselves get fifty percent of the selling price.

8. Art-o-Mat machines can be found at locations across the country.

9. Art-o-Mats are currently dispensing tiny paintings, photographs, and sculptures in twenty-eight states and in Canada and Austria.

10. The machines have sold the works of hundreds of contemporary artists.

Source: www.artomat.org

Exercise 13.3

1. During my last semester of high school, our English teacher assigned a special paper.

2. He said that he was becoming depressed by all the bad news out there, so each of us was asked to find a piece of good news and write a short research paper about it.

3. I must admit that I had no idea how hard that assignment would be.

4. Finally, I found an article while I was reading my favorite magazine.

5. The title of the article was a pun; it was called "Grin Reaper."

6. I knew instantly that it must be just the kind of news my teacher wanted.

7. The article explained that one woman, Pam Johnson, had started a club that she named The Secret Society of Happy People.

8. She had even chosen August 8 as "Admit You're Happy Day" and had already convinced more than fifteen state governors to recognize the holiday.

9. The club and the holiday were created to support people who are happy so that the unhappy, negative people around will not bring the happy people down.

10. As I was writing my essay, I visited the Society of Happy People Web site, *www.sohp.com*, and signed my teacher up for their newsletter.

Source: Lawrence Journal World, July 27, 1999

Exercise 13.4

1. I have always wondered how an Etch A Sketch works.

2. This flat TV-shaped toy has been popular since it first arrived in the 1960s.

3. Now I have learned the secrets inside this popular toy.

4. An Etch A Sketch is filled with a combination of metal powder and tiny plastic particles.

5. This mixture clings to the inside of the Etch A Sketch screen.

6. When the pointer that is connected to the two knobs moves, the tip of it "draws" lines in the powder on the back of the screen.

7. The powder at the bottom of the Etch A Sketch does not fill in these lines because it is too far away.

8. But if the Etch A Sketch is turned upside down, the powder clings to the whole underside surface of the screen and "erases" the image again.

9. Although the basic Etch A Sketch has not changed since I was a kid, it now comes in several different sizes.

10. Best of all, these great drawing devices have never needed batteries, and I hope that they never will.

Source: http://www.forbes.com/sites/alexknapp/2012/03/22/how-does-an-etch-a-sketch-work-anyway/

Exercise 13.5

1. Scientists successfully cloned a dog for the first time in 2005.

2. Cloning experts had been attempting to clone a dog for many years.

3. They had had success with horses, cats, and even rats before they could clone a dog.

4. The scientists who eventually succeeded were from Seoul National University in South Korea.

5. They named the cloned dog Snuppy as a tribute to the university where the accomplishment was made, and they pronounced the name "Snoopy."

6. Of course, Snuppy could thank his "parent" dog, a three-year-old Afghan hound, for all of his great physical features.

7. Both dogs had long glossy black fur that was accentuated by identical brown markings on their paws, tails, chests, and eyebrows.

8. Unfortunately, the cloning procedure does not guarantee that the clone of a dog will share the unique features of the original dog's personality.

9. Nevertheless, now that dog cloning has been achieved, many people have shown an interest in cloning their own dogs.

10. Although some people may not be happy with just a physical copy of a beloved pet, for others, a copy is better than nothing.

Source: Science News, August 6, 2005

Exercise 13.6 Paragraph Practice

To practice finding the sentence structures we have studied so far, mark the following paragraphs in an excerpt from the book *The Birth of Korean Cool,* by Euny Hong, about how recent social changes in South Korea are affecting the world. First, put parentheses around prepositional phrases; then double underline verbs and verb phrases and single underline their subjects. Finally, put a broken line beneath dependent clauses. Start by marking the first paragraph and checking your answers. Remember that *ing* verbs alone and the *to* _____ forms of verbs are never real verbs in sentences. Also note that we have identified a few changes to the excerpt with brackets [ ] and ellipses (. . .). For more about their use, see Section 36.

The success of some recent Korean start-ups suggests that Korean culture is becoming increasingly more tolerant of Korean Americans. Daniel Shin, a Korean American from McLean, Virginia, with a Wharton Business degree, moved to Korea in 2010 to found Ticketmonster, a website that offers discounts on various products, similar to Groupon. Just twenty months after its founding, according to *Inc.* magazine, Ticketmonster had seven hundred employees and $25 million per month in revenue. In 2011, Shin sold Ticketmonster to the Internet coupon site LivingSocial for a reported $380 million. At the time, Shin was twenty-six years old.

Shin had the foresight to see an industry gap in Korea and jump in with Ticketmonster. But he did butt heads with more conservative Korean business types. Shin told *Inc.* magazine that [one] executive . . . said he would disown a son of his who dropped a successful corporate life to embark on a start-up.

Exercise 13.7 Sentence Writing

Write ten sentences of your own that contain both single-word verbs and verb phrases. Try writing about whether you would rather have the security of "a successful corporate life," "embark on a start-up" of your own, or do something completely different. Then double underline your verbs and verbs phrases and single underline their subjects for additional practice.

14. Using Standard English Verbs

The next two sections are for those who need to practice using Standard English verbs. Many of us grew up doing more speaking than writing. But in college and in the business and professional worlds, knowledge of Standard Written English is essential.

The following tables show the forms of four verbs as they are used in Standard Written English. These forms might differ from the way you use these verbs when you speak. Memorize the Standard English forms of these important verbs. The first verb—*talk*—is one of the regular verbs, verbs that all end the same way according to a pattern; most verbs in English are regular. The other three verbs charted here—*have, be,* and *do*—are irregular and are important because they are used not only as main verbs but also as helping verbs in verb phrases.

Don't go on to the exercises until you have carefully reviewed Table 14.A, B, c, and D.

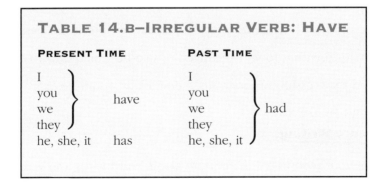

TABLE 14.A–REGULAR VERB: TALK

PRESENT TIME		PAST TIME	
I		I	
you	talk	you	
we		we	talked
they		they	
he, she, it	talks	he, she it	

TABLE 14.B–IRREGULAR VERB: HAVE

PRESENT TIME		PAST TIME	
I		I	
you	have	you	
we		we	had
they		they	
he, she, it	has	he, she, it	

TABLE 14.c—IRREGULAR VERB: BE

PRESENT TIME		PAST TIME	
I	am	I	was
you		you	
we	are	we	were
they		they	
he, she, it	is	he, she, it	was

TABLE 14.d—IRREGULAR VERB: DO

PRESENT TIME		PAST TIME	
I		I	
you	do	you	
we		we	did
they		they	
he, she, it	does	he, she, it	

Sometimes you may have difficulty with the correct endings of verbs because you haven't heard them correctly. Note how the *s* sound and the *ed* sound at the end of certain words can blur into a similar sound at the beginning of the next word. Consequently, an *ed* or *s* ending may not be clearly pronounced, as in "They tri*ed* to finish their essays," but it needs to be there when written. Read the following sentences aloud, making sure that you exaggerate every sound:

1) He seems satisfied with his new job.

2) She likes saving money for the future.

3) It takes strength of character to control spending.

4) Todd brings salad to every party that he attends.

5) I used to know all of the state capitals.

6) They were supposed to sign both forms.

7) He recognized the suspect and excused himself from the jury.

8) The chess club sponsored Dorothy in the school's charity event.

Now read some other sentences aloud from this text, making sure that you say all the *s* and *ed* endings. Reading aloud and listening to others will help you learn verb endings automatically.

EXERCISES

In these pairs of sentences, use the *present* form of the verb in the first sentence and the *past* form in the second. All the verbs follow the pattern of the regular verb *talk* except the irregular verbs *have, be,* and *do.* Keep referring to Tables 14.A–D if you're not sure which form to use. Check your answers often.

Exercise 14.1

1. (end) Many new movies _____ too suddenly. The movie I saw yesterday _____ before I had finished my medium popcorn.

2. (do) Denise _____ her homework at the dinner table. She _____ two hours of homework last night.

3. (be) I _____ now the president of the film club on campus. I _____ just a member of the club last semester.

4. (vote) Patrick _____ in every election. He even _____ with an absentee ballot in the presidential election of 2008.

5. (have) The twins _____ similar ideas about the environment. Last year, they _____ a fund-raiser for their local wildlife preserve.

6. (shop) We _____ for almost everything online. We _____ for groceries online last week.

7. (be) They _____ finally satisfied with their living room. They _____ embarrassed by it before the remodeling.

8. (pick) I _____ the location of our seats whenever we go to a concert. Yesterday, I also _____ our seats on the plane for our upcoming vacation.

9. (do) We _____ what we can for the birds in winter. A few years ago, we _____ our best to save a nearly frozen sparrow.

10. (have) My twin sisters _____ the same teacher now. They _____ different teachers last year.

Exercise 14.2

1. (be) She _____ a lawyer now. She _____ a law student last year.

2. (do)   They _____ their best work on the weekends. They _____
a great job last weekend.

3. (have)   I _____ a new education plan. I _____ originally a plan
that would have taken too long to complete.

4. (ask)   She _____ for help when she needs it. She _____ her tutor
for help with her latest essay.

5. (have)   I always _____ the flu at this time of year. I _____ the flu
last year right on schedule.

6. (learn) We _____ something about writing each week. Yesterday we
_____ how to write a thesis.

7. (be)   Most of us _____ right handed. Therefore, we _____ not
comfortable drawing with our left hands.

8. (do)   She _____ well on all of her assignments. She _____ very
well on the term project.

9. (play)   He _____ the piano now. He _____ the guitar as his first
instrument.

10. (be)   I _____ a natural comedian. However, last month I _____
too depressed to be funny.

Exercise 14.3

Circle the correct Standard English verb forms.

1. I (start, started) a new volunteer job last month, and so far I really (like,
likes) it.

2. The organization (offer, offers) relief boxes to victims of crime or natural
disasters around the world.

3. The other volunteers (is, are) all really nice, so we (has, have) a good
work environment.

4. Yesterday, we (finish, finished) a project that (need, needed) lots of boxes.

5. The supervisors who (run, runs) the organization always (do, does) their
best to explain the victims' situations to us.

6. And they (advise, advises) us to make sure that the boxes (comfort,
comforts) the victims as much as possible.

7. I can tell that the supervisors (enjoy, enjoys) their work; they (is, are) always happy to see the relief on the victims' faces.

8. My fellow volunteers and I (complete, completed) our latest project in just one week even though the supervisor (expect, expected) it to take us two weeks.

9. We (has, have) our supervisors to thank for a smooth-running organization.

10. And I (thank, thanks) my coworkers for being my friends.

Exercise 14.4

Choose the correct Standard English verb forms.

1. My cousin Isabel and I (has, have) a lot in common.

2. We both (play, plays) many different sports.

3. She (play, plays) soccer, softball, and basketball.

4. I (play, plays) tennis, badminton, and golf.

5. However, Isabel (practice, practices) more often than I (does, do).

6. The result (is, are) that she (win, wins) more often, too.

7. I (is, am) as skilled as she (is, am), but I (is, am) a little bit lazy.

8. Our parents (remind, reminds) us about practicing all the time.

9. Isabel really (follow, follows) their advice.

10. We both (has, have) talent, but I (is, am) not as disciplined as she (is, am).

Exercise 14.5

Choose the correct Standard English verb forms to show the past.

1. Last semester, my drawing teacher (gave, give, gives) us a challenging assignment.

2. He (hands, handed, hand) each of us half a photograph taped to a whole piece of paper.

3. We (have, had, has) to imagine the missing half of the picture and draw it.

4. My half-image (shows, show, showed) parts of a subway tunnel.

5. There (was, were, are) half a stairway with a railing and a few people walking to their trains.

6. With all my creative energy, I (imagines, imagine, imagined) the rest of the image.

7. Then I (fills, filled, fill) in a rogue skateboarder heading down the stairway on top of the railing.

8. I (does, did, do) a great job on the realistic details of his hair, clothes, position, and board.

9. The full picture—with my additions—(look, looks, looked) dangerous and exciting.

10. For its impact and skill, my drawing (receives, received, receives) a perfect score.

Exercise 14.6 Proofreading Practice

Correct any sentences in the following paragraph that do not use Standard English verb forms.

Yesterday, when I walk on campus to go to my classroom, I notice a problem that needs to be fixed. Every morning, there is a long line of students in their cars waiting to enter the parking lots because the light at the corner do not change fast enough. It change too slowly, so cars start to stack up on the side streets. Anybody who walk to school is affected, too. Drivers get desperate when they are stuck in traffic. Many of them don't watch where they're going and almost run over people who is walking in the crosswalks and driveways.

Exercise 14.7 Sentence Writing

Write ten sentences about an existing problem on your campus. Check your sentences to be sure that they use Standard English verb forms. Try exchanging papers with another student for more practice.

15. Using Regular and Irregular Verbs

Regular verbs end the same way in the past form and in verb phrases with helping verbs. Here is a table showing all of the forms of several *regular* verbs and listing the various helping verbs with which they are used. All other regular verbs follow the same patterns.

TABLE 15.A REGULAR VERBS				
BASE FORM	**PRESENT**	**PAST**	**PAST PARTICIPLE**	***ING* FORM**
(Use after *can, may, shall, will, could, might, should, would, must, do, does, did.*)			(Use after *have, has, had.* Some can be used after forms of *be.*)	(Use after forms of *be.*)
ask	ask (s)	asked	asked	asking
bake	bake (s)	baked	baked	baking
count	count (s)	counted	counted	counting
dance	dance (s)	danced	danced	dancing
decide	decide (s)	decided	decided	deciding
enjoy	enjoy (s)	enjoyed	enjoyed	enjoying
finish	finish (es)	finished	finished	finishing
happen	happen (s)	happened	happened	happening
learn	learn (s)	learned	learned	learning
like	like (s)	liked	liked	liking
look	look (s)	looked	looked	looking
mend	mend (s)	mended	mended	mending
need	need (s)	needed	needed	needing
open	open (s)	opened	opened	opening
start	start (s)	started	started	starting
suppose	suppose (s)	supposed	supposed	supposing
tap	tap (s)	tapped	tapped	tapping
walk	walk (s)	walked	walked	walking
want	want (s)	wanted	wanted	wanting

NOTE 15.A—When there are several helping verbs, the one closest to the verb determines which form of the main verb should be used: They *should* finish soon; they could *have* finished an hour ago.

NOTE 15.B—When do you write *ask, finish, suppose, use?* And when do you write *asked, finished, supposed, used?* Here are some guidelines that will help you decide.

Write *ask, finish, suppose, use* (or their *s* forms) when writing about the present time, repeated actions, or facts:

He *asks* questions whenever he *is* confused.

They *always finish* their projects on time.

I *suppose* you *want* me to help you *move.*

Birds *use* leaves, twigs, and feathers to build their nests.

Write *asked, finished, supposed,* used under three conditions.

1. **When writing about the past:**

   He *asked* the teacher for another explanation.

   She *finished* her internship last year.

   They *supposed* that there *were* others bidding on that house.

   I *used* to study piano.

2. **When some form of *be* (other than the word *be* itself) comes before the word:**

   He *was asked* the most difficult questions.

   She *is finished* with her training now.

   They *were supposed* to sign at the bottom of the form.

   My essay *was used* as a sample of clear narration.

3. **When some form of *have* comes before the word:**

   The teacher *has asked* us that question before.

   She will *have finished* all of her exams by the end of May.

   I *had supposed* too much without any proof.

   We *have used* many models in my drawing class this semester.

All of the verbs in Table 15.A are *regular.* That is, they're all formed in the same way—with an *ed* ending on the past form and on the past participle. But many verbs are irregular. Their past and past participle forms change spelling instead of just adding an *ed.* What follows is a table of many *irregular* verbs. Notice that the base, present, and *ing* forms end the same as regular verbs. Refer to this table when you aren't sure which verb form to use. Try to memorize new forms as you encounter them.

TABLE 15.B IRREGULAR VERBS

BASE FORM	PRESENT	PAST	PAST PARTICIPLE	*ING* FORM
(Use after *can, may, shall, will, could, might, should, would, must, do, does, did*.)			(Use after *have, has, had*. Some can be used after forms of *be*.)	(Use after forms of *be*.)
be	is, am, are	was, were	been	being
become	become (s)	became	become	becoming
begin	begin (s)	began	begun	beginning
break	break (s)	broke	broken	breaking
bring	bring (s)	brought	brought	bringing
buy	buy (s)	bought	bought	buying
build	build (s)	built	built	building
catch	catch (es)	caught	caught	catching
choose	choose (s)	chose	chosen	choosing
come	come (s)	came	come	coming
do	do (es)	did	done	doing
draw	draw (s)	drew	drawn	drawing
drink	drink (s)	drank	drunk	drinking
drive	drive (s)	drove	driven	driving
eat	eat (s)	ate	eaten	eating
fall	fall (s)	fell	fallen	falling
feel	feel (s)	felt	felt	feeling
fight	fight (s)	fought	fought	fighting
find	find (s)	found	found	finding
forget	forget (s)	forgot	forgotten	forgetting
forgive	forgive (s)	forgave	forgiven	forgiving
freeze	freeze (s)	froze	frozen	freezing
get	get (s)	got	got or gotten	getting
give	give (s)	gave	given	giving
go	go (es)	went	gone	going
grow	grow (s)	grew	grown	growing
have	have or has	had	had	having
hear	hear (s)	heard	heard	hearing
hold	hold (s)	held	held	holding
keep	keep (s)	kept	kept	keeping
know	know (s)	knew	known	knowing
lay (to put)	lay (s)	laid	laid	laying
lead (like "bead")	lead (s)	led	led	leading

TABLE 15.B– IRREGULAR VERBS (CONTINUED)

BASE FORM	PRESENT	PAST	PAST PARTICIPLE	ING FORM
leave	leave (s)	left	left	leaving
lie (to rest)	lie (s)	lay	lain	lying
lose	lose (s)	lost	lost	losing
make	make (s)	made	made	making
meet	meet (s)	met	met	meeting
pay	pay (s)	paid	paid	paying
read (pron. "reed")	read (s)	read (pron. "red")	read (pron. "red")	reading
ride	ride (s)	rode	ridden	riding
ring	ring (s)	rang	rung	ringing
rise	rise (s)	rose	risen	rising
run	run (s)	ran	run	running
say	say (s)	said	said	saying
see	see (s)	saw	seen	seeing
sell	sell (s)	sold	sold	selling
shake	shake (s)	shook	shaken	shaking
shine (give light)	shine (s)	shone	shone	shining
shine (polish)	shine (s)	shined	shined	shining
sing	sing (s)	sang	sung	singing
sleep	sleep (s)	slept	slept	sleeping
speak	speak (s)	spoke	spoken	speaking
spend	spend (s)	spent	spent	spending
stand	stand (s)	stood	stood	standing
steal	steal (s)	stole	stolen	stealing
strike	strike (s)	struck	struck	striking
swim	swim (s)	swam	swum	swimming
swing	swing (s)	swung	swung	swinging
take	take (s)	took	taken	taking
teach	teach (es)	taught	taught	teaching
tear	tear (s)	tore	torn	tearing
tell	tell (s)	told	told	telling
think	think (s)	thought	thought	thinking
throw	throw (s)	threw	thrown	throwing
wear	wear (s)	wore	worn	wearing
win	win (s)	won	won	winning
write	write (s)	wrote	written	writing

Be aware that verb forms from the past participle column can work as *adjectives* to describe their subjects when they come after *be* (or other linking verbs: *appear, seem, look, feel, get, act, become*). For more about sentence patterns and linking verbs, see Section 20. Here are several examples:

They are highly *educated*. ("Educated" follows a linking verb as an *adjective*.)

They educated themselves. ("Educated" is a *verb* that shows action here.)

You appear *shaken*.

He seems *contented*.

We feel *motivated*.

I was *embarrassed*. ("Embarrassed" is an *adjective* that describes my condition.)

I get *embarrassed* easily.

I became *embarrassed* at the party.

My friends embarrassed me accidentally. ("Embarrassed" is an *action verb*.)

As you can see, past participle forms can act as *adjectives* that may look like *real verbs* in sentences.

EXERCISES

Write the correct form of the verbs in the blanks. Refer to the columns and explanations on the preceding pages if you aren't sure which form to use after a certain helping verb. Check your answers after each exercise.

Exercise 15.1

1. (eat)   People _____ a lot when they go to the movies.

2. (eat)   I can _____ a whole bag of popcorn myself.

3. (eat)   When someone else is _____ popcorn, the crunching sound drives me crazy.

4. (eat)   Once I have _____ my dinner, I stay away from snacks.

5. (eat)   My sister _____ a worm when she was in kindergarten.

6. (eat)   My two-year-old nephew _____ everything; he is not picky.

7. (eat)   The apple in my lunch was half-_____.

8. (eat)   The people at the conference were _____ in silence.

9. (eat)   We _____ while we watched a documentary on television.

10. (eat)   If you want to pass a test, you should always _____ a good breakfast.

Exercise 15.2

1. (drive)   I always _____ my brother to school; in fact, I have _____ him to school for a whole year now.

2. (think)   The other day, I was _____ of new ways to get him there in the morning, but he _____ that they were all bad ideas.

3. (take)   He could _____ a school bus that stops nearby; instead he _____ me for granted.

4. (tell)   It all started when he _____ our mother that some of the other children were _____ him to stay out of their seats.

5. (write)   I _____ a note to the bus driver to see if she could help ease my brother's mind, but so far she hasn't _____ back.

6. (know)   When I was my brother's age, I _____ some tough kids at school, so I _____ how he must feel.

7. (teach)   But experiences like that _____ us how to get along with everyone; they sure _____ me.

8. (tear)   Now I am _____ between wanting to help him avoid the tough kids and wanting to _____ my hair out from having to take him to school every day.

9. (ride)   We have _____ together for so long that I might miss him if I _____ alone.

10. (make)   I have _____ up my mind. I will _____ the best of it while he still needs me. What else are big brothers for?

Exercise 15.3

1. (take, suppose)   My friend Brenda _____ a day off last week even though she was _____ to be working.

2. (do, earn)   She _____ not feel sick exactly; she just felt that she had _____ a day of rest.

3. (call, tell, feel)   So Brenda _____ her office and _____ her boss that she did not _____ well enough to work that day.

4. (think, be)   She never _____ that she would get caught, but she _____ wrong.

5. (leave, drive, see)   Just as Brenda was _____ the house to buy some lunch, her coworker _____ by and _____ her.

6. (feel, know, tell)   She _____ such panic because she _____ that he would _____ their boss that she looked fine.

7. (try, go)   Brenda _____ to explain herself when she _____ back to the office the next day.

8. (be, undo)   The damage had _____ done, however, and nothing could _____ it.

9. (wish, take)   Now Brenda _____ that she could _____ back that day.

10. (use, call, do)   She _____ to have a great relationship with her boss, but since the day she _____ in "sick," he _____ not trust her anymore.

Exercise 15.4

1. (use, put)   Many people _____ a direct deposit system that _____ their salary money directly into their bank accounts.

2. (do, do)   With such a system, the employer _____ not have to issue paychecks, and employees _____ not have to cash or deposit them.

3. (transfer, spend)   The employer's computer just _____ the money to the bank's computer, and the employee can _____ it as usual after that.

4. (be, like, choose)   Direct deposit _____ almost always optional, but so many people _____ the system that most people _____ it.

5. (do, want)   My uncle _____ not trust such systems; he _____ to have complete control over his cash.

6. (trust, be)   He barely even _____ banks to keep his money safe for him, so he _____ definitely suspicious of direct deposit.

7. (imagine, make)   I can _____ him as a pioneer in an old Western movie sleeping on a mattress stuffed with all of the money he has ever _____.

8. (talk, ask, worry)   I was _____ to my uncle about money the other day, and I _____ him why he always _____ about it so much.

9. (look, say, live, understand)   He just _____ at me and _____, "If you had ever _____ without money, you would _____."

10. (wonder, be)   I _____ about my uncle's past experiences and hope that he _____ never without money again.

Exercise 15.5

1. (lie, fall)   I was _____ out in the sun last Sunday, and I _____ asleep.

2. (be, do)   That _____ the worst thing I could have _____.

3. (wear, shield)   I was _____ a pair of big dark sunglasses, which _____ my eyes from the light.

4. (lie, wake, realize, happen)   I must have _____ there for over an hour before I _____ up and _____ what had _____.

5. (feel, start)   At first I _____ fine, but then my skin _____ to feel really tight and thin.

6. (pass, turn, begin)   As the minutes _____, my skin _____ bright red, and the pain _____.

7. (describe, experience)   I can't even _____ how much pain I _____.

8. (be, feel, see)   Almost worse than the pain _____ the embarrassment I _____ as I _____ my face in the mirror.

9. (look, tape, be, protect, wear)   Around my eyes, it _____ as if someone had _____ the shape of white glasses to my face, but that _____ just the skin that had been _____ by the sunglasses I was _____.

10. (have, feel)   The people at work _____ a big laugh the next day at my expense, but then they just _____ sorry for me.

Exercise 15.6 Paragraph Practice

In the following excerpt from the book *The World According to Bob,* James Bowen shares his experiences of finding a stray ginger cat named Bob, who changed his life. Remember that to be *regular*, a verb's *past forms* always end in "ed"—*walk, walked, have walked*—and that *irregular* verbs change forms instead—*choose, chose, have chosen.* Note that we have double-underlined Bowen's verbs and made minor changes to the excerpt for this exercise, including switching the American spelling of "realized" for the British "realised." Identify each of Bowen's verbs or verb phrases as regular or irregular by writing the abbreviation *reg.* or *irr.* over it.

They say that cats choose you, not the other way around. I realized that Bob had chosen me when he followed me to the bus stop . . . one day. We were far from home, so when I shooed him away and watched him disappear into the busy crowds, I imagined that was the last I would see of him. But as the bus pulled away, he appeared out of nowhere, leaped on board in a blur of ginger, and plonked himself down on the seat next to me. And that had been that.

Exercise 15.7 Sentence Writing

Write ten sentences about a time in the past when you met your own or someone else's pet (animal companion) for the first time. Use Bowen's excerpt as a sample, and refer to the "Irregular Verbs" in Table 15.B if you need help finding the correct forms to use with the helping verbs *have, has,* and *had.* Then double-underline your verbs, and identify each one as regular or irregular.

16. Maintaining Subject-Verb Agreement

As you have seen, the subject and verb in a sentence work together, so they must always agree. Different subjects need different forms of verbs. When the correct verb follows a subject, you have **subject-verb agreement.**

The following sentences illustrate how *s* verbs follow most singular subjects but not plural subjects.

One student studies.   Two students study.

The bell rings.   The bells ring.

A democracy listens to the people.   Democracies listen to the people.

One person writes the dialogue.   Many people write the dialogue.

The following sentences show how forms of the verb *be* (*is, am, are, was, were*) and the helping verbs *be, have,* and *do* are made to agree with their subjects. We have labeled only the verbs that must agree with the subjects.

This puzzle is difficult.   These puzzles are difficult.

I am amazed.   You are amazed.

He was studying.   They were studying.

That class has been canceled.   Those classes have been canceled.

She does not want to participate.   You do not want to participate.

The following words are always singular and take an *s* verb or the irregular equivalent (*is, was, has, does*):

one	anybody	each
anyone	everybody	
everyone	nobody	
no one	somebody	
someone		

Someone feeds my dog in the morning.

Everybody was at the party.

Each does her own homework.

Remember that prepositional phrases often come between subjects and verbs, see Section 8. You should ignore the nouns in these interrupting phrases, or you may mistake the wrong word for the subject and use a verb form that doesn't agree.

Someone (from the apartments) feeds my dog (in the morning).

Someone is the singular subject of this sample sentence, not the plural noun *apartments* in the prepositional phrase.

Everybody (on the list) (of celebrities) was (at the party).

Everybody is the singular subject, not the plural noun *celebrities* in the second prepositional phrase.

Each (of the twins) does her own homework.

Each is the singular subject, not the plural noun *twins* in the prepositional phrase.

However, the words *some, any, all, none,* and *most* are exceptions to this pattern of ignoring prepositional phrases. These five words can be singular *or* plural, depending on the objects that follow them in prepositional phrases. Again, we have labeled only the verbs that must agree with the subjects.

Some (of the *information)* is helpful.

Some (of the *facts)* are convincing.

Does any (of the *furniture)* come with the apartment?

Do any (of the *chairs* and *tables)* come with the apartment?

All (of her *work)* has been published.

All (of her *poems)* have been published.

None (of the *jewelry)* was missing.

None (of the *jewels)* were missing.

On July 4th, most (of the *country)* celebrates with a picnic or a party.

On July 4th, most (of the *citizens)* celebrate with a picnic or a party.

When a sentence has more than one subject joined by *and,* the subject is plural:

The teacher *and* the tutors eat lunch at noon.

A doughnut *and* a bagel were sitting on the plate.

However, when two subjects are joined by *or,* then the subject *closest* to the verb determines the verb form:

Either the teacher *or* the *tutors* eat lunch at noon.

Either the tutors *or* the *teacher* eats lunch at noon.

A doughnut *or* a *bagel* was sitting on the plate.

In most sentences, the subject comes before the verb. However, in some cases, the subject follows the verb, and subject-verb agreement needs special attention, as shown in the following examples:

Over the building flies a solitary flag. → A flag flies over the building.

Over the building fly several flags. → Several flags fly over the building.

There is a good reason for that deadline. → A good reason is there . . . .

There are good reasons for that deadline. → Good reasons are there . . . .

EXERCISES

Circle the correct verbs in parentheses to maintain subject-verb agreement in the following sentences. Remember to ignore prepositional phrases, unless the subjects are *some, any, all, none,* or *most.* Check your answers after the first exercise.

Exercise 16.1

1. A dog's name (affect, affects) its life as much as a person's name does.

2. Traditions for naming a dog (go, goes) all the way back to Ancient Greece.

3. Researchers at Stanford University (has, have) studied the ancient Greeks' methods for choosing and naming their dogs.

4. They discovered that in ancient Greece, short names for dogs (was, were) preferred over long names.

5. There (was, were) many common dog names that reinforced Greek ideals of strength, agility, and beauty.

6. Some common names for dogs with positive qualities (was, were) Blossom, Keeper, Happy, Jolly, Plucky, Trooper, and Swift.

7. A typical name for a dog with a negative quality (was, were) Lurcher, Spoiler, Hasty, Stubborn, Riot, Growler, or Yelp.

8. Researchers also (describe, describes) a Greek ritual for choosing the best puppy.

9. A mother and her puppies (was, were) separated, sometimes with a hazard between them.

10. The first of the puppies to be retrieved by the mother dog (was, were) thought to be the best.

Source: Smithsonian Magazine, July 9, 2012 *[http://www.smithsonianmag.com/smart-news/ how-ancient-greeks-named-their-puppies-1154943/]*

Exercise 16.2

1. An old rhyme about sneezing (give, gives) a sneeze on each day of the week special meaning.

2. The poem (sound, sounds) a lot like the one that (begin, begins) "Monday's child (is, are) full of woe."

3. This poem about sneezing also (connect, connects) Monday with a negative outcome.

4. It (say, says) that a sneeze on Monday (mean, means) "danger."

5. A Tuesday sneeze (forecast, forecasts) a meeting with a "stranger."

6. Wednesday and Thursday (is, are) days when sneezes (mean, means) we will receive a "letter" or "something better," respectively.

7. There (is, are) no TGIF celebrations for sneezes on Friday, for they (foretell, foretells) "sorrow."

8. But a sneeze on Saturday (mean, means) the visit of a loved one "tomorrow."

9. Sunday sneezes (is, are) left out of the poem altogether.

10. Such day-of-the-week rhymes from the past (seem, seems) to reveal a lot about us.

Source: Schott's Original Miscellany (Bloomsbury, 2003)

Exercise 16.3

1. There (is, are) new risks for kids in this technological age; these risks primarily (involve, involves) their wrists.

2. Many adults already (suffer, suffers) from carpal tunnel syndrome.

3. And now children (is, are) also coming down with similar conditions, called repetitive stress injuries (RSIs).

4. From the use of computers and video games (come, comes) unnatural body positions that (lead, leads) to health problems.

5. The child's wrists, neck, and back (start, starts) to hurt or feel numb after he or she (work, works) or (play, plays) on the computer for a long time.

6. The problem (start, starts) with computer furniture.

7. The chairs, desks, and screens (is, are) usually not at the proper height to be used comfortably by children.

8. Straining and repetition often (cause, causes) reduced circulation and even nerve damage.

9. Often RSI damage to the wrists (is, are) irreversible.

10. Experts in the field of RSI (warn, warns) parents to teach children how to avoid these injuries.

Source: *healthychildren.org* ("Repetitive Stress Injury")

Exercise 16.4

1. There (is, are) a web site that rates movies based on how accurately they (portray, portrays) the laws of physics.

2. "Insultingly Stupid Movie Physics" (is, are) the name of the site.

3. Examples of bad physics in movies (include, includes) bullets that (spark, sparks) on contact and laser beams that (is, are) visible to the naked eye.

4. The reviewers at Intuitor.com (give, gives) movies one of the following ratings: GP, PGP, PGP-13, RP, XP, or NR.

5. These labels (rank, ranks) the physics in a particular movie from "good physics" [GP] to "pretty good physics" [PGP] to "totally unbelievable physics" [XP], such as those in *Star Trek 2009, Armageddon,* and *Avatar.*

6. The recent classic films *Titanic, Casino Royale,* and *The Terminator* (has, have) all received GP or PGP ratings.

7. A movie that (get, gets) the PGP-13 rating—such as *King Kong* in 2005—is one that (has, have) flaws in portraying the laws of physics, but the movie (is, are) so convincing that it may lead children to believe that it (is, are) scientifically accurate.

8. The NR label (signify, signifies) that movies like *The Hulk* and *Spider-Man* (is, are) "not rated" because of their obvious focus on imaginative, not scientific, possibilities.

9. RP, the lowest of the site's ratings, (is, are) given to movies with such bad physics that they (make, makes) the reviewers "retch."

10. The RP rating (has, have) been given to *10,000 BC, The Abyss, Independence Day,* and to two of *The Matrix* movies.

Source: http://www.intuitor.com/moviephysics/

Exercise 16.5

1. A group of scientists (is, are) looking into the sensation that we (call, calls) déjà vu.

2. Déjà vu (is, are) the feeling that we (is, are) repeating an experience that (has, have) happened in exactly the same way before.

3. Part of the odd sensation (is, are) that we (is, are) aware of the illogical part of déjà vu while it (is, are) happening.

4. Scientists (has, have) developed a new profile of a person who (is, are) likely to experience this particular sensation.

5. People who (is, are) most prone to déjà vu (is, are) between fifteen and twenty-five years old.

6. Regardless of age, however, anyone who (experience, experiences) déjà vu probably (has, have) a vivid imagination.

7. Stress and fatigue (is, are) often factors because the mind (function, functions) differently under these conditions.

8. Education level and income also (determine, determines) a person's susceptibility to déjà vu.

9. The phenomenon of déjà vu (seem, seems) to require an open mind.

10. Since political leanings (affect, affects) open-mindedness, liberals (tend, tends) to have more déjà vu experiences than conservatives.

Source: Psychology Today, March/April 2005

Exercise 16.6 Proofreading Practice

Find and correct the ten subject-verb agreement errors in the following paragraph.

Unfortunately, tension between members of the public are common these days. When two people at a movie theater irritates each other or have a disagreement, the whole audience suffer. Everyone who is sitting around the troublemakers want to move immediately to another section. However, if anyone get up to sit somewhere else, then everyone else start to get nervous. So most people just waits until one of the two fighting people calm down. After that, the members of the audience forgets about the disturbance and enjoy the rest of the movie. The same pattern repeat itself in stadiums and ballparks, too.

Exercise 16.7 Sentence Writing

Write ten sentences in which you describe the shoes that you are wearing today. Have fun writing about their smallest details! Use verbs in the *present* tense since they are the ones that can go wrong if they don't agree. As you write your sentences, underline the verbs twice and their subjects once. Then check these two parts carefully to be sure they agree. Refer to the explanations whenever necessary.

For example, you might write, "One of the laces on my left shoe is broken." After ignoring the prepositional phrases in this example, "(of the laces)(on my left shoe)," the subject and verb that must agree are "one is." The word "broken" is a *verbal*, a verb used as an adjective to describe "one of the laces on my left shoe." See Section 18 for more about verbals.

And remember, whether you write about shoes or Shakespeare, your sentences will use similar patterns and structures. For example, in a literature class in the future, you might write, "One of the lines in Hamlet's speech is truncated" and know with confidence that your subject and verb agree.

17. Avoiding Shifts in Time

People often worry about using different time frames in writing. Let common sense guide you. If you begin writing a paper in past time, don't shift back and forth to the present unnecessarily; and if you begin in the present, don't shift to the past without good reason. In the following paragraph, the writer starts in the present and then shifts to the past, then shifts again to the present:

> In the novel *To Kill a Mockingbird,* Jean Louise Finch is a little girl who lives in the South with her father, Atticus, and her brother, Jem. Everybody in town calls Jean Louise "Scout" as a nickname. When Atticus, a lawyer, defended a black man against the charges of a white woman, some of their neighbors turned against him. Scout protected her father by appealing to the humanity of one member of the angry mob. In this chapter, five-year-old Scout turns out to be stronger than her father and a whole group of adult men.

All the verbs should be in the present:

> In the novel *To Kill a Mockingbird,* Jean Louise Finch is a little girl who lives in the South with her father, Atticus, and her brother, Jem. Everybody in town calls Jean Louise "Scout" as a nickname. When Atticus, a lawyer, defends a black man against the charges of a white woman, some of their neighbors turn against him. Scout protects her father by appealing to the humanity of one member of the angry mob. In this chapter, five-year-old Scout turns out to be stronger than her father and a whole group of adult men.

This sample paragraph discusses only the events that happen within the novel's plot, so it needs to maintain one time frame—the present, which we use to write about literature and repeated actions.

However, sometimes you will write about the present, the past, and even the future together. Then it may be necessary to use these different time frames within the same paragraph, each for its own reason. For example, if you were to give biographical information about Harper Lee, author of *To Kill a Mockingbird,* within a discussion of the novel, you might need to use all three time frames:

> *To Kill a Mockingbird* is Harper Lee's most famous work, and it received the Pulitzer Prize for fiction in 1961. It deals with the effects of prejudice unforgivingly from a child's point of view. Harper Lee grew up in Alabama, and she based elements in the book on experiences from her childhood. Like the character of Atticus Finch, Lee's father was a lawyer. She wrote *Mockingbird,* her first novel, in his law offices. In 2015, Lee published a second novel, *Go Set a Watchman,* which covers the later relationship of Atticus and Jean Louise and became a controversial publication for many reasons. Sadly, Harper Lee

died at the age of 89 in 2016, but *To Kill a Mockingbird* will remain one of the most moving and compassionate novels in American literature.

Source: http://www.biography.com/people/harper-lee-9377021

The previous paragraph uses past (*grew, based, was, wrote, received, published, became, died*), present (*is, deals, covers*), and future (*will remain*) in the same paragraph without committing the error of unnecessary shifting. A shift in time occurs when the writer changes time frames *inconsistently* or *for no reason*, confusing the reader (as in the first example given).

PROOFREADING EXERCISES

Read the following three paragraphs to identify which ones shift *unnecessarily* back and forth between time frames. In the paragraphs that do include shifts in time, change the verbs to maintain one time frame. One of the paragraphs is already correct, even though it includes multiple time frames, because those time frames make sense.

Exercise 17.1

Back in the early 1900s, Sears Roebuck sold houses through the mail. In the famous Sears catalog, these mail-order houses are listed along with the rest of the products. The house kits arrived in thousands of pieces, and people can put them together themselves, or they hire a builder to help them. In 1919, one company, Standard Oil, placed an order for an entire town's worth of homes for its employees. The house kits even include the paint that the homeowners use to paint the houses when they finish. The ability to order a whole house from the Sears catalog ended in 1940, but thousands of these houses are still standing in communities across America.

Source: CBS News Sunday Morning, May 18, 2003

Exercise 17.2

No one knows for certain who the model for Leonardo da Vinci's *Mona Lisa* was. However, recent studies have discovered some new information. Dutch scientists used a computer program that is capable of "emotion recognition" to find out how the model felt at the time of the painting. Their results show that she was primarily happy. But her expression also registers tiny bits of anger, fear, and disgust. Another expert, Japanese forensic scientist Dr. Matsumi Suzuki, has created an actual voice for *Mona Lisa*. Using measurements of her head and hands, Dr. Suzuki has determined that she was approximately five-and-a-half feet tall and had a deep voice. A recording of what Mona Lisa might have sounded like can be heard on the Web.

Source: Renaissance Magazine, Issue #50 (2006)

Exercise 17.3

Plastic surgery helps many people look better and feel better about themselves. Of course, there were stories of unnecessary surgeries and even heartbreaking mistakes. People make their own decisions about whether plastic surgery was right for them. Dogs, however, can't communicate what they wanted. Nevertheless, some people took their dogs in for cosmetic surgeries, such as tummy tucks and face-lifts. Just like humans, dogs sometimes needed surgery to correct painful or unhealthy conditions. A dog with a low-hanging tummy could get an infection from scratches that were caused by rocks on the ground. And another dog may need a face-lift to help it stay clean when it ate. Animal lovers were worried that some canine plastic surgeries were done without good reasons.

Source: Newsweek, March 21, 2005

18. Recognizing Verbal Phrases

As explained in the previous sections, the main job of verbs and verb phrases is to join with subjects to form clauses, both independent and dependent. However, some forms of verbs get to take a vacation from their normal job and play a different part of speech in a sentence. When a verb acts as a noun, adjective, or adverb—*not* a real verb—in a sentence, it is called a *verbal.*

A verbal can act as a noun subject:

Skiing is my favorite sport. (*Skiing* is a noun. Here, it is the subject of the sentence, not the verb. The real verb in the sentence is *is.*)

A verbal can act as a noun object:

I like *to ski* during the winter. (*To ski* is a noun object; it is *what I like.* I could similarly write, "I like *cocoa* during the winter." The real verb in both sentences is *like,* and the two objects are *to ski,* a verbal as a noun, and *cocoa,* a regular noun.) For more about sentence patterns with objects, see Section 20.

A verbal can act as an adjective:

My *bruised* ankle healed quickly. (*Bruised* is an adjective that describes the noun, *ankle.* The real verb in the sentence is *healed.*)

A verbal can also act as an adverb:

My ankle swelled quickly, *doubling* in size. (*Doubling* is an adverb, adding to the verb *swelled.*)

Verbals also link up with other words to form *verbal phrases.* To see the difference between a real verb phrase and a verbal phrase, look at these two sentences:

I was bowling with my best friends. (*Bowling* is the main verb in a verb phrase. Along with the helping verb *was,* it shows the action of the sentence.)

I enjoyed *bowling* with my best friends. (Here the real verb is *enjoyed.* *Bowling* is not the verb; it is the object, and it links up with a prepositional phrase to form a verbal phrase—*bowling with my best friends*—which is the whole *activity* I *enjoyed.*)

Look at the following sentences that use all of the verbs listed in Table 18.A as verbals and verbal phrases:

Running is great exercise. (real verb = is)

She spent two hours *thinking of a title for her essay.* (real verb = spent)

We had such fun *baking those cherry vanilla cupcakes.* (real verb = had)

TABLE 18.A—THREE KINDS OF VERBALS

1. *ing* verbs used without helping verbs, such as *running, thinking, and baking*
2. verbs in the *to* ___ form, such as *to walk, to eat,* and *to educate*
3. *ed, en,* or *t* forms (past participles) such as *tossed, taken,* and *lost*

I like *to walk around the zoo by myself.* (real verb = like)

To eat exotic foods takes courage. (real verb = takes)

They wanted *to educate themselves.* (real verb = wanted)

He served us a *tossed* salad with artichoke hearts. (real verb = served)

Taken in Spanish, the class made even more sense to me. (real verb = made)

I found my *lost* watch on the windowsill. (real verb = found)

EXERCISES

Each of the following sentences contains at least one verbal or verbal phrase. Double underline the real verbs or verb phrases and put brackets around the verbals and verbal phrases. Locate the verbals first (**winning, graded, to sleep . . .**) and include any word that go with them (**winning a race, graded online, to sleep through the night**). Remember that real verbs will never be inside verbal phrases, but other verbals or prepositional phrases might be. Check your answers after each set to make the most progress.

Example: They tried [to help] by [cooking a meal of [frozen] leftovers].

Exercise 18.1

1. Mark Twain lived to become one of the most admired Americans of his time.

2. Traveling across the U.S. and to countries around the world, Twain formed unwavering opinions, both favorable and unfavorable, of the people and places he visited.

3. Twain began to write his autobiography in the last years before he died in 1910.

4. Hoping to be honest and thorough, he decided to dictate his thoughts as they struck him.

5. However, he knew that it might be impossible to be as honest as he wanted to be.

6. Being truthful meant including statements that could hurt or upset the people that he knew, and he knew almost everyone.

7. Twain thought of a way to avoid causing that potential pain or embarrassment.

8. He decided not to publish his autobiography until 100 years after his death.

9. In that way, Twain did not need to hold back any of his strong opinions.

10. In 2010, the first volume of *The Autobiography of Mark Twain* was finally released, making it one of the most anticipated books of all time.

Source: http://www.nytimes.com/2010/07/10/books/10twain.html

Exercise 18.2

1. The idea of home-schooling children has become more popular recently.

2. Some families decide to teach children at home instead of enrolling them in schools with other students.

3. Many school districts have special independent-study "schools," offering such families the structure and materials that they need to provide an appropriate curriculum to study at home.

4. There are many different reasons for choosing home-schooling and independent-study programs.

5. For instance, child actors and potential Olympic athletes often must study independently to fit school into their busy schedules.

6. The independent-study format allows parents and special teachers to instruct young actors filming and young athletes training around the world.

7. Home-schooling can also benefit gifted children and students with long-lasting medical issues.

8. Independent-study programs help students from kindergarten through high school to do all of their reading, writing, and studying on their own.

9. Students do meet with independent-study school teachers regularly to turn in homework and receive new assignments.

10. These teachers ensure students' progress by checking the completion of assignments and clarifying any points of confusion.

Source: http://www.cde.ca.gov/sp/eo/is/cefindependentst.asp

Exercise 18.3

1. Philippe Halsman was a well-known portrait photographer working in the twentieth century.

2. Halsman's photographs were good enough to appear on the cover of *Life* magazine 101 times.

3. Capturing the essence of famous people on film was Halsman's specialty.

4. The list of celebrities that Halsman was asked to photograph included Marilyn Monroe, Albert Einstein, and Winston Churchill.

5. Halsman found that taking good pictures of such powerful people was not easy.

6. He often tried to find new ways to loosen them up.

7. In 1952, Halsman asked one of his elite clients to jump in the air while being photographed.

8. Halsman loved the results, and he started a series of jumping pictures.

9. Who doesn't like to see famous people like Richard Nixon jumping up like a little boy in a photograph?

10. Halsman gathered the best of the jumping photographs in a book called *Philippe Halsman's Jump Book.*

Source: Smithsonian, October 2006

Exercise 18.4

1. Some travelers want to know how to behave in other countries.

2. *Behave Yourself!* is a book written to help such people.

3. It outlines what to do and what not to do in different countries around the world.

4. In Austria, for example, cutting your food with a fork is more polite than cutting it with a knife.

5. In Egypt, nodding the head upward—not shaking the head from side to side—means "no."

6. In the Netherlands, complimenting people about their clothes is not a good idea.

7. An Italian diner will fold lettuce into a bite-size piece with the fork and knife instead of cutting it.

8. A common mistake that people make in many countries is to stand with their hands on their hips.

9. This posture and pointing at anything with the fingers are thought to be very rude and even threatening.

10. Travelers should study any country before visiting it in order to avoid confusing or offending anyone.

Source: Behave Yourself! (Globe Pequot, 2005)

Exercise 18.5

1. John Steinbeck, author of *The Grapes of Wrath,* was the first native of California to receive the Nobel Prize for literature.

2. Calling his hometown of Salinas "Lettuceberg," Steinbeck's writing made the area famous.

3. At the time, not everyone liked the attention brought by his portrayals of life in *Cannery Row* and other works.

4. Steinbeck's father was the treasurer of Monterey County for ten years, working also for the Spreckels company.

5. John Steinbeck tried to find satisfaction in his birthplace, enrolling in and quitting his studies at Stanford University many times.

6. Finally, Steinbeck moved to New York, distancing himself from his California roots.

7. Steinbeck won the Nobel Prize in 1962, revealing the literary world's esteem for his work.

8. Not writing anything of the caliber of the Salinas stories while living in New York, Steinbeck did return to California before he died in 1968.

9. In 1972, the Salinas library changed its name, to be known thereafter as the John Steinbeck Library.

10. The house Steinbeck was born in became a restaurant and then a full-fledged museum chronicling the life of Salinas' most celebrated citizen.

Source: California People (Peregrine Smith, 1982)

Exercise 18.6 Paragraph Practice

Double underline the real verbs or verb phrases, and put brackets around the verbals and verbal phrases in the following paragraphs about how rain helped to form the Earth as we know it. This excerpt is from the book *Rain: A Natural and Cultural History,* by Cynthia Barnett. Note that we have used ellipses (. . .) to show where we have shortened the excerpt. For more about the use of ellipses in quotations, see Section 36.

As even-tempered as it turned out to be, Earth started off 4.6 billion years ago as a red-faced and hellish infant. The universe had been unfolding for about 10 billion years. A new star, the sun, had just been born. Its afterbirth—cold gas and dust and heavier minerals and flaming rocks—was flying about, beginning to orbit. The heavy debris gravitated to the sun, where temperatures were well suited for rock and metal to condense. That's why the four planets closest in, known as the terrestrials, are all made of essentially the same stuff.

For its first half-billion years, Earth was a molten inferno some 8,000 degrees Celcius—hotter than today's sun. Scientists call this violent era the Hadean, from the Greek word *Hades,* or hell. Time and again, the young Earth built up a crust, only to see it incinerated by storms of flaming meteors. . . .

Only when air cools do water molecules begin to stick together, latching on to the gritty particles. When billions of them have condensed, they form tiny liquid droplets. Billions of droplets, in turn, become clouds in the sky. This is the beauty of water vapor: It falls back to Earth as rain. . . .

About half a billion years after it started, the blitzkrieg began to wind down. As the last flaming chunks fell to the surface or hurtled away, the planet finally had a chance to cool. The water vapor could condense.

At long last, it began to rain.

Exercise 18.7 Sentence Writing

Write ten sentences that contain verbal phrases. Use the ten verbals listed here to begin your verbal phrases: *thinking, folding, skiing, marking, to take, to get, to paste, to exercise, planned, given.* The last two may seem particularly difficult to use as verbals. You'll find sample sentences listed in the Answers. But first, try to write your own sentences containing verbals so that you can compare the two.

19. Correcting Misplaced or Dangling Modifiers

To modify something means to change whatever it is, usually by adding to it. You might modify a normal car, for example, by adding a special roof rack. In English, **modifiers** are words, phrases, and clauses working as adjectives and adverbs to *add* information to part of a sentence. To do its job properly, a modifier must be in the right spot—as close to the structure it modifies as possible. Putting a roof rack *underneath* a car instead of on the roof where it belongs would cause the roof rack to be *misplaced.* In the following example, the verbal phrase *Flying from tree to tree* is too far away from the word that it modifies, *the birds,* so the phrase seems to say that the children are *flying from tree to tree* instead. Therefore, like a misplaced roof rack under a car, *flying from tree to tree* is a **misplaced modifier** in this sentence:

> *Flying from tree to tree,* the children watched the birds in the park.

To correct this misplaced modifier, we move it so that it's right next to the birds:

> The children watched the birds *flying from tree to tree* in the park.

In the next example, there is no word for the phrase *At the age of eighteen* to modify:

> *At the age of eighteen,* my family finally bought a dog.

Obviously, the family was not eighteen when it bought a dog. And the dog was not eighteen. *At the age of eighteen* is a **dangling modifier** without any word to modify. To correct this dangling modifier, we can turn it into a dependent clause with its own subject and verb to clarify who was eighteen:

> *When I was eighteen,* my family finally bought a dog.

Now the meaning of the whole sentence is clear. Here's another sentence with a dangling modifier:

> The train arrived at our station after a two-hour nap.

Can you identify the dangling modifier? You're right if you think it is *after a two-hour nap.* Did the train or the station take a two-hour nap? Who did? Here is a correction that adds the subject and verb *I took* to clarify who took a nap:

> The train arrived at our station after I took a two-hour nap.

EXERCISES

Carefully rephrase any of the following sentences that contain misplaced or dangling modifiers. Note that misplaced and dangling modifiers often make sentences sound comical because of the confusion about what's happening. Some of the sentences are already correct and do not need revision. Compare your revisions to the answers after each exercise to make the most progress.

Exercise 19.1

1. I noticed an iPad on the ground walking to my car.
2. They located the auditorium by asking a security guard for directions.
3. Full of 360-degree loops, people will wait for hours to ride the new roller coaster.
4. Being just six years old, the flight attendant helped the little boy find his seat.
5. As soon as the tutor stopped talking, the students started asking questions.
6. We have found several travel bargains shopping on the Internet.
7. Hidden by the long curtains, Angelica finally spotted her lost keys.
8. After getting help from a specialist, her knee began to improve.
9. With a low-cost data plan, I can't use my phone very often to go online.
10. Faded from direct sunlight, students couldn't read the bulletin board.

Exercise 19.2

1. Loaded with explosions and special effects, the new movie is a hit.
2. Before asking for an extension, the teacher gave us a few extra days to turn in our papers.
3. They spotted a hawk and its babies looking through their binoculars.
4. After I finished my audition, the director released everyone else.
5. I called the doctor on the roof.
6. We sat on the lawn and waited for further instructions on how to prune the roses.

7. Screeching to a stop, I got on the bus and grabbed a seat.

8. Without pickles, I can't eat a hamburger.

9. Given as a token of friendship, that ring means a lot to me.

10. We had to write a paragraph about the weather in our notebooks.

Exercise 19.3

1. Lying under the table for a week, they finally found their lost credit card.

2. She located the door to the auditorium walking down the hall.

3. They bought a hammer at the hardware store.

4. After taking an aspirin, my doctor told me to drink extra water.

5. He always brings a calculator to school in his backpack.

6. Our mail carrier tripped and fell on a crack in the sidewalk.

7. Arguing nonstop, the road trip was not as much fun as we hoped it would be.

8. Now that she has finished her math classes, she can focus on her major.

9. Seeing her new granddaughter's picture for the first time, our mother cried.

10. Smiling nicely at everyone, the students immediately liked their substitute teacher.

Exercise 19.4

1. Taken before surgery, that medicine can help your recovery.

2. Filled with the perfect amount of air, I enjoyed the way the new tires made my car handle on the road.

3. After three weeks of waiting, the textbooks that I bought online finally arrived.

4. He cooked all of his meals in his slippers.

5. The class watched the video with the door open.

6. While driving past the park, a ball bounced into the street between two parked cars.

7. Torn into tiny pieces, I didn't even want the scraps of that quiz paper near me.

8. I will take the test again tomorrow.

9. Trying to look happy, the runner-up applauded too loudly.

10. Walking in the cracks of the sidewalk, I saw an army of ants.

Exercise 19.5

1. Feeling the thrill of a day at the amusement park, my blisters didn't bother me.

2. Full of touching scenes, my friends and I saw the new tearjerker.

3. My classmates and I always turned our essays in on time.

4. Practicing for an hour a day, her piano has improved.

5. Gasoline prices fluctuate with politics.

6. Sitting on a bench all day, an idea came to her.

7. On the road to their cousins' house, they discovered a new outlet mall.

8. He felt the pressure of trying to get a good job from his parents.

9. I enjoy talking to new people at parties.

10. Written in chalk, the notes on the board were hard to read.

Exercise 19.6 Proofreading Practice

Find and correct any misplaced or dangling modifiers in the following paragraph.

I love parades, so last year my family and I traveled to Pasadena, California, to see one of the biggest parades of all—the Tournament of Roses Parade on New Year's Day. It turned out to be even more wonderful than I expected.

Arriving one day early, the city was already crowded with people. Lots of families were setting up campsites on Colorado Boulevard by nightfall. We didn't want to miss one float in the parade, so we found our own spot and made ourselves at home. When the parade began, I had as much fun watching the spectators as the parade itself. I saw children pointing at the breathtaking horses and floats sitting on their fathers' shoulders. Decorated completely with flowers or plant material, I couldn't believe how beautiful the floats were and how good they smelled.

The crowd appreciated all the sights and sounds of the parade. Marching and playing their instruments with perfect precision, everyone especially enjoyed hearing the school bands. They must have practiced for the whole year to be that good.

My experience didn't end with the parade, however. After the last float had passed by, I found a twenty-dollar bill walking down Colorado Boulevard. Now hanging on my wall at home, I framed it as a souvenir of my trip to the Rose Parade.

Exercise 19.7 Sentence Writing

Write five sentences that contain misplaced or dangling modifiers; then revise those sentences to put the modifiers where they belong or to clarify their meaning. Use the examples in the explanations as models. For more practice, exchange papers with another student and correct each other's misplaced or dangling modifiers.

20. Following Sentence Patterns

Sentences are built according to a few basic **sentence patterns.** For proof, read each of the following sets of words and rearrange them to form a complete statement that is not a question:

apples a ate raccoon the

have classes many together taken we

your in am partner I lab the

walking her will to be she job new

look in wonderful you scrubs

There are only one or two possible combinations for each set of words due to English sentence patterns. Either *A raccoon ate the apples,* or *The apples ate a raccoon,* and so on. But in each case, the verb or verb phrase usually makes its way into the middle of the statement, and the nouns and pronouns take their places before the verbs as subjects and after verbs and prepositions as objects.

To understand sentence patterns, you need to know that every verb performs one of three jobs. Note that the focus is on the **bolded** verbs below.

The Three Jobs of Verbs

1) Verbs can **show actions:**

A raccoon **ate** the apples.

We have **taken** many classes together.

She will be **walking** to her new job.

2) Verbs can **link subjects with nouns, pronouns, or adjectives** that describe them:

I **am** your partner in the lab.

You **look** wonderful in scrubs.

3) Verbs can **help other verbs** form verb phrases:

We **have** taken many classes together. (Without the help of *have,* the main verb would be *take* or *took.*)

She **will be** walking to her new job. (Without *will be,* the main verb would be *walks* or *walked.*)

Look at these sentences for more examples of verbs performing these three jobs. We have also marked their subjects for clarity:

Mel **submitted** a scholarship application. (The verb *submitted* shows Mel's action.)

His accomplishments **are** impressive. (The verb *are* links the subject, *accomplishments,* with an adjective, *impressive.*)

He **has** worked as a volunteer every semester. (The verb *has* helps the main verb *worked* in a verb phrase that shows that he continues to do so.)

Knowing the three jobs that a verb can perform will help you gain an understanding of the **three basic sentence patterns:**

SUBJECT + ACTION VERB + OBJECT PATTERN

Some action verbs must be followed by an object—a person, place, thing, or idea— that receives the action.

    S   AV   Obj
Sylvia completed her degree. (*Sylvia completed* makes no sense unless it is followed by the object that she completed—*her degree.*)

SUBJECT + ACTION VERB (+ NO OBJECT) PATTERN

At other times, the action verb completes the meaning and needs no object after it.

    S   AV
She celebrated at home with her family. (*She celebrated* makes sense alone.

It does not need the two prepositional phrases—*at home* and *with her family,* which simply tell where and how she celebrated.)

SUBJECT + LINKING VERB + DESCRIPTION PATTERN

A special kind of verb that does *not* show an action is called a *linking verb.* The linking verb acts like an equal sign in a sentence: "I am student" means "I = a student" means "A student = I." These verbs link the subject with a word that describes the subject. The description can be a noun, a pronoun, or an adjective. Learn to recognize the most common linking verbs: *is, am, are, was, were, seem, feel, appear, become,* and *look. E*ven the verbs *taste* and *smell* can be linking verbs at times.

    S   LV   Desc
Sylvia is a natural writer. (*Sylvia* equals *a natural writer.*)

    S   LV   Desc
Sylvia seems very happy. (*Very happy* describes *Sylvia.*)

> **NOTE 20.A**—As explained in Section 13, a verb phrase includes a main verb and its helping verbs. Note that helping verbs can help main verbs in any of the sentence patterns.

       S   AV

Sylvia is moving to Seattle. (Here the verb *is* does not link Sylvia with a description but helps the main verb *moving,* an action verb with no object followed by the prepositional phrase *to Seattle.*)

Table 20.A outlines the sentence patterns using short, easy-to-memorize examples:

TABLE 20.A THREE BASIC SENTENCE PATTERNS

S   +   AV   +   Obj

Stephanie adopted a dog.

S   +   AV   +   (no object)

The dog travels (with her).

S   +   LV   +   Desc

The dog is a cute mix.

His eyes look sweet and thoughtful.

These basic patterns are the grammatical backbone for most of the clauses used in English sentences. Knowing them can help you control your sentences and improve your phrasing.

EXERCISES

First, put parentheses around any prepositional phrases in the following sentences. Next, underline the verbs or verb phrases twice and their subjects once. Then mark the correct sentence pattern above the words: S + AV + Obj, S + AV, or S + LV + Desc. Remember that these patterns never mix or overlap. For example, you won't find "She took tall," which mixes an action verb (AV) with a description of the subject (Desc). However, if there are two clauses, each one may have a different pattern. Check your answers after each set to make the most progress.

Exercise 20.1

1. Sleep is an important part of life.
2. Animals and humans use sleep as a vacation for their brains and bodies.
3. Some facts about sleep might surprise people.
4. Large animals require less sleep than small animals do.
5. A typical cat will sleep for twelve hours in a day.
6. An ordinary elephant will sleep for only three hours.
7. Smaller animals use their brains and bodies at higher rates.
8. Therefore, they need many hours of sleep.
9. The reverse is true for large animals.
10. Humans fall between cats and elephants for their sleep requirements.

Exercise 20.2

1. Erasto Mpemba is a big name in science.
2. In the early 1960s, he observed an odd phenomenon.
3. At the time, he was a high school student in Tanzania.
4. Mpemba made ice cream for a school project.
5. He boiled the milk and mixed it with the other ice cream ingredients.
6. Then he put this boiling hot mixture directly into the freezer.
7. He discovered that the hot liquid froze very fast.
8. Mpemba told his teachers and fellow students about his discovery.
9. They laughed at the idea of hot liquid freezing quickly.
10. Now all scientists call this phenomenon the "Mpemba effect."

Sources: Current Science, September 8, 2006, and *physicsweb.org,* April 2006

Exercise 20.3

1. In late September 2006, the Stade de France in Paris hosted an unusual spectacle.
2. Hundreds of actors, stunt people, and extras reenacted the famous chariot race from the classic 1959 film *Ben-Hur.*
3. The same show included live gladiator fights and a galley ship assault.
4. Promoters also encouraged participation from the audience.
5. Many of the 60,000 audience members attended in traditional Roman costumes.
6. The stadium sold toga-like robes in advance along with the tickets.
7. Obviously, the live chariot race was the highlight of the show.
8. Participants in the dangerous race rehearsed for nine months.
9. The chariot race lasted for fifteen minutes.
10. It was the final event of the night.

Source: npr.org, Weekend Edition Saturday, September 23, 2006

Exercise 20.4

1. Horatio Greenough was a sculptor in the 1800s.
2. Greenough created a controversial statue of George Washington.
3. The statue weighed twelve tons, but its weight was not the reason for the controversy.
4. The controversial aspect of the statue involved Washington's clothes.
5. The statue portrayed Washington in a toga-like garment.
6. His stomach, chest, and arms were bare and very muscular.
7. One part of the toga draped over the statue's raised right arm.
8. The bare-chested statue of Washington stood in the rotunda of the Capitol for only three years.
9. Officials moved the statue many times.
10. In 1962, it arrived in its final home at the American History Museum.

Source: Smithsonian, February 2005

Exercise 20.5

1. Charles Osgood is a writer, TV host, and radio personality.

2. He is also the editor of a book about letters.

3. The book's title is *Funny Letters from Famous People.*

4. In his book, Osgood shares hilarious letters from history.

5. Thomas Jefferson wrote to an acquaintance about rodents eating his wallet.

6. Benjamin Franklin penned the perfect recommendation letter.

7. Franklin did not know the recommended fellow at all.

8. Beethoven cursed his friend bitterly in a letter one day.

9. In a letter the following day, Beethoven praised the same friend excessively and asked him for a visit.

10. Osgood ends the book with a letter by Julia Child; it includes her secrets for a long life.

Source: Funny Letters from Famous People (Three Rivers Press, 2004)

Exercise 20.6 Paragraph Practice

Label the sentence patterns in the following paragraph from the book *The First Men on the Moon: The Story of Apollo 11,* by David M. Harland. It helps to put parentheses around prepositional phrases first to isolate them from the words that make up the sentence patterns—the subjects, the verbs, and any objects after action verbs or any descriptive words after linking verbs (*is, was, were, seem, appear,* and so on). This paragraph describes Neil Armstrong's first moments on the moon.

Armstrong released his grip on the handrail of the ladder and stepped fully off the foot pad. Walter Cronkite proudly told his CBS audience that a 38-year-old American was now standing on the surface of the Moon. When Armstrong scraped his foot across the surface, he noticed that the dark powdery material coated his overshoe. "The surface is fine and powdery. I can kick it up loosely with my toe. It adheres in fine layers like powdery charcoal to the sole and sides of my boots." Although his boots only slightly impressed the surface, the material preserved the imprint of his boots very well. "I only go in a small fraction of an inch—maybe one-eighth of an inch—but I can see the prints of my boots and the treads in the fine, sandy particles."

Exercise 20.7 Sentence Writing

Using Neil Armstrong's descriptions of the moon's surface as models, write ten sentences describing the weather today and how it feels to be living in it. Keep the sentences short to allow your sentence patterns to flow naturally. Then find and label the sentence patterns you have used. For extra practice, exchange papers with another student and label each other's sentence patterns.

21. Avoiding Clichés, Awkward Phrasing, and Wordiness

CLICHÉS

A **cliché** is an expression that has been used so often it has lost its originality and effectiveness. Whoever first referred to the most important result of something as "the bottom line" had thought of an original way to express it, but today that expression is worn out. Most of us use occasional clichés when speaking, but in writing, clichés are missed opportunities to express an idea or detail in your own way.

Here are a few examples of clichés. Think of more you could add to the list:

too little too late

truth be told

a team player

last but not least

this day and age

different as night and day

out of this world

white as a ghost

sick as a dog

tried and true

at the top of his lungs

the thrill of victory

one in a million

a loose cannon

easier said than done

better late than never

Clichés lack freshness because the reader knows what's coming next. Can you complete these expressions?

the agony of . . .

breathe a sigh of . . .

lend a helping . . .

odds and . . .

raining cats and . . .

been there . . .

worth its weight . . .

Clichés are expressions that too many people use. Try to avoid them in your writing.

AWKWARD PHRASING

Unlike clichés, the problem of **awkward phrasing** comes from writing sentence structures that *no one* else would use because they break basic sentence patterns, omit necessary words, or use combinations of words without clear meaning. Like clichés, awkward sentences might *sound* acceptable when spoken, but not when written. Here is an example:

> There should be greater efforts (in communication) (between students and their academic advisors).

Who is doing *what* here? Efforts should be? The words that could form a much better clause are hiding in prepositional phrases: *students, communication,* and *advisors.* Here is the sentence again after revising it to eliminate awkward phrasing:

> Students and their advisors should communicate more often.

Basically, awkward phrasing results in sentences that leave readers wondering:

> During the experiment, the following of key principles was essential to ensure the success of it.

Similar to the previous example, these sixteen words don't actually say very much because the phrasing of *the following. . . was essential to ensure* makes little sense. What do you think it is trying to say? Here is a revision to clarify one possible meaning:

> We followed key principles to ensure the success of the experiment.

WORDINESS

Good writing is concise writing. Effective writers don't use twenty words if they can say it better in ten. "In today's society" isn't as clear as "today," and it's a cliché. "At this point in time" could be "presently" or "now." For proof, look at a piece of writing that you recently enjoyed reading. You'll find that most of its sentences are relatively short.

One kind of **wordiness** comes from saying something twice. There's no need to write "in the month of August" or "9 a.m. in the morning" or "my personal opinion." August *is* a month, 9 a.m *is* morning, and everyone's opinion *is* personal. All you need to write is "in August," "9 a.m.," and "my opinion."

Another type of wordiness comes from using words that add nothing to the meaning of the sentence. "The point is that we can't afford it" says no more than "We can't afford it." Here is another wordy sentence:

The company doing the construction worked on that building, off and on, for a period of six years.

And here it is after eliminating the extra words:

The construction company worked on that building for six years.

Of course, naming the *construction company* and *that building* would be even better. Including precise details in your sentences is often the best way to avoid wordiness.

WORDY WRITING	CONCISE WRITING
advance planning	planning
an unexpected surprise	a surprise
at a later date	later
basic fundamentals	fundamentals
green in color	green
but nevertheless	but (or nevertheless)
combine together	combine
completely empty	empty
down below	below
end result	result
fewer in number	fewer
free gift	gift
in order to	to
in spite of the fact that	although
large in size	large
new development	development
on a regular basis	regularly
past history	history
rectangular in shape	rectangular
refer back	refer
repeat again	repeat
serious crisis	crisis
sufficient enough	sufficient (or enough)
there in person	there
two different kinds	two kinds
very unique	unique

PROOFREADING EXERCISES

The following student paragraphs contain examples of clichés, awkward phrasing, and wordiness. Revise the paragraphs so that they are concise examples of Standard Written English. When you're done, compare your revisions with the sample answers.

Exercise 21.1

I've been trying to help my small son finish his first-grade homework every night, but that's easier said than done. Of course, I think that he is the smartest kid in the world, but getting him to show it takes a lot of hard work. When I do get him to sit down in front of his workbooks, he will work for a few minutes on them and then run off as soon as my back is turned. I try to tell him that when I was his age, I got in big trouble if I didn't do my homework. Unfortunately, my son's teacher just doesn't give him a sticker for that day if he doesn't do his. Stickers don't do the trick as motivators. I hope with all my heart that my son will learn the value of keeping up in school.

Exercise 21.2

In today's society, many shoppers at the supermarkets are on the lookout for organic meats, fruits, and vegetables. In fact, they don't draw the line at fresh foods; these same shoppers' eyes light up whenever they see an organic label on a box, can, or any other package. I know this for a fact since I work as an employee at the supermarket in the middle of the busiest section of town. It's not only people with a lot of money that want the foods grown without pesticides and hormones. It's just about everybody that walks in the door. I guess that what's going on is that people are taking a good long look at their lives and caring about their children's eating habits too. I do have to admit that the organic eggs I buy taste pretty good when you get right down to it. Knowing that the eggs come from happy, free-ranging chickens makes me feel good about eating them. Of course, the bottom line for some people will always be price. If organic foods cost more than traditionally grown foods, some of the shoppers are going to keep passing them by on the supermarket shelves.

Exercise 21.3

I have a friend who used to be one of those struggling actors who couldn't find a steady job, but now she has become a professional house sitter, and it has really paid off in more ways than one. First of all, she joined a house sitters' organization that is supposed to find out about all of the house-sitting opportunities that are available at any one time and match house sitters up with each of them. Then she landed her first house-sitting job at a house in Malibu. You're not going to believe this, but she got paid to live in a house on the beach in Malibu and even got her meals and movie rentals for free. All she had to do to do the job she was paid for was to watch out for the house and feed one cat. The cat was even an indoor cat. Now my friend is house sitting in Sedona, watching a house for friends of the same people who own the Malibu house. Well, I'll tell you, I want a job like that and am thinking seriously about trying it out for myself.

22. Correcting for Parallel Structure

Your writing will be clearer and more memorable if you use **parallel structure**. That is, when you write two pieces of information or any kind of list, put the items in similar form. Look at this sentence, for example:

My favorite movies are comedies, romantic, and sci-fi fantasies.

The sentence lacks parallel structure. The second item in the list, an adjective, doesn't match the other two, which are nouns. Here's a revision to make them parallel:

My favorite movies are comedies, love stories, and sci-fi fantasies.

Now the items are parallel; they are all nouns. Or you could write the following:

I like movies that make me laugh, cry, and think.

In this new sentence, the three items are parallel verbs within one dependent clause. Here are a few more examples. Note how much easier it is to read the sentences with parallel structure.

WITHOUT PARALLEL STRUCTURE	WITH PARALLEL STRUCTURE
I like hiking, skiing, and to go for a jog.	I like hiking, skiing, and jogging. (all *"ing"* verbals)
The office has run out of pens, paper, ink cartridges, and we need more toner, too.	The office needs more pens, paper, ink, and toner. (all nouns)
They decided that they needed a change, that they could afford a new house, and wanted to move to Arizona.	They decided that they needed a change, that they could afford a new house, and that they wanted to move to Arizona. (all dependent clauses)

The parts of an outline should always be parallel. Following are two brief outlines about food irradiation. The parts of the outline on the *left* are not parallel. The first subtopic (I.) is a question; the other (II.) is just a noun. And the supporting points (A., B., C.) are written as nouns, verbs, and even clauses. The parts of the outline on the *right* are parallel. Both subtopics (I. and II.) are plural nouns, and all details (A., B., C.) are action verbs followed by objects.

NOT PARALLEL	PARALLEL

Food Irradiation
  I. How is it good?
    A. Longer shelf life
    B. Using fewer pesticides
    C. Kills bacteria
  II. Concerns
    A. Nutritional value
    B. Consumers are worried
    C. Workers' safety

Food Irradiation
  I. Benefits
    A. Extends shelf life
    B. Requires fewer pesticides
    C. Kills bacteria
  II. Concerns
    A. Lowers nutritional value
    B. Alarms consumers
    C. Endangers workers

Using parallel structure will make your writing more effective. Note the parallelism in these well-known quotations:

A place for everything and everything in its place.

Isabella Mary Beeton

Ask not what your country can do for you; ask what you can do for your country.

John F. Kennedy

EXERCISES

In the following exercises, rephrase any sentences that do not contain parallel structures. Some sentences are correct.

Exercise 22.1

1. Preparing for emergencies involves two steps: planning for anything and to gather certain supplies.

2. When planning for emergencies, ask yourself the following questions.

3. What kinds of emergencies have occurred or might occur in your area?

4. Where would you go, and what method of transportation would you use to get there?

5. Have you made a list of phone contacts within the area and outside it, too?

6. Do the adults, teenagers, and do the children in the family carry those phone numbers with them?

7. Are the most important supplies ready at hand, including water, food, flashlight, radio, and are there batteries as well?

8. Have you assembled your own first-aid kit, or maybe you have bought a ready-made one?

9. Do you stay prepared by reading and understanding your important insurance policies; also, do you remember to update them?

10. By planning for anything and if you stock up on the right supplies, you can prepare yourself and your family for emergencies.

Exercise 22.2

1. Taking driving lessons was exciting, but I also found it nerve-wracking.

2. At first, I learned how to start the car, steer it, and eventually how to make the car stop smoothly.

3. Between driving lessons, I studied the manual, watched videos about driving, and I even practiced the hand signals that people use in emergencies.

4. My instructors taught me, tested me, and were encouraging to me.

5. Each of my teachers had a special tip or two to share about driving.

6. Finally, my teachers decided that I had learned enough, and I was probably ready to take the test for my driver's license.

7. I arrived at the testing location, waited in the lobby for a few minutes, and then I heard someone call my name.

8. During the test, I changed lanes, made right and left turns, and even showed that I could parallel park like a professional driver.

9. The man who tested me said that I knew the rules and kept telling me that I must have had good teachers.

10. I got my driver's license and sent a box of chocolates to my driving school to thank everyone who helped me.

Exercise 22.3

1. The Internet is full of information about new gadgets and using the latest technology.

2. People want to have the coolest phones, the clearest photos, and travel accessories that are the best quality.

3. One of these high-tech inventions is a new kind of wedding ring.

4. The ring doesn't use technology to help people do something more easily or living more comfortably.

5. Instead, it helps people avoid doing something, and that is not to forget their anniversary.

6. The "Remember Ring" is designed for people who love gadgets, but they tend to forget special occasions.

7. It includes several hi-tech features: a perpetually charging battery, a clock run by a microchip, and a tiny element that heats up.

8. The built-in heating element activates at a preprogrammed time and reminding the wearer about an upcoming anniversary.

9. One day before the anniversary, the ring starts to heat up to 120 degrees for ten seconds once every hour.

10. The Remember Ring comes in seven styles in both white gold and the regular yellow kind.

Source: news.cnet.com, June 10, 2013

Exercise 22.4

Rephrase the following list to improve the use of parallel structures. The list includes instructions on how to begin searching for ancestors—in other words, how to create a "family tree." Try to maintain similar phrasing at the beginning of the instructions and in any pairs or lists within them.

1. To begin, decide which person or the family you want to focus on.

2. Making a blank chart that includes spaces for all of a person's important information will help.

3. Then visit a relative who knows a lot of family history and hopefully someone who saves papers and mementos.

4. You should plan to spend a lot of time with any such valuable resource.

5. It is best to gather information from one individual at a time and about one person.

6. Ask about every part of the person's life—marital status, children, believing in religion, working, and travel.

7. As you talk with your resources, thank them for providing you with valuable information.

8. Visit the attics or even going into the dusty old cupboards of anyone who has documents relating to your family.

9. Don't forget the local records office in the town where a relative grew up.

10. To make your family tree come together faster, you can purchase books that provide preprinted worksheets and family tree templates.

Exercise 22.5

Revise the following sentences to make them a list of clear suggestions using parallel structures. You may want to add transitions like *first* and *finally* to help make the steps clear.

1. Experts give the following tips to get the most out of a visit to the doctor.

2. Avoid getting frustrated after a long wait in the reception area or if you have to wait a long time in the exam room.

3. You should always answer the doctor's questions first; then asking the doctor your own questions might be a good idea.

4. It's smart to inquire about a referral to a specialist if you think you need one.

5. Finding out if there are other treatments besides the one the doctor first recommends can't hurt.

6. Ask about any tests that the doctor orders, and you might wonder what the results mean, so you probably want to get in touch with the doctor after the results come back.

7. Prescriptions are often given quickly and with little explanation, so ask about side effects and optional medicines if one doesn't work.

8. When discussing these things with your doctor, try not to be nervous.

9. The final step is to be prepared to wait in a long line at the pharmacy.

10. If you follow these suggestions when visiting a doctor, you will be more informed and also you can feel involved in your own treatment.

Exercise 22.6 Proofreading Practice

Proofread the following paragraph about William Shakespeare, and revise it to correct any errors in parallel structure.

The world knows relatively little about the life of William Shakespeare. Stanley Wells' book *Is It True What They Say about Shakespeare?* addresses the questions that people continue to have about the famous poet and playwright. Because of Shakespeare's talent and the reputation that his works have earned, everyone wants to know when he was born, the schools he went to, his travels, who his friends or lovers were, the way he looked, as well as the method and date he wrote each of his poems and plays. Wells starts with the basic question, "Is it true that . . .?" Throughout the book, he identifies commonly held beliefs about Shakespeare, discusses the historical evidence, and then he judges each belief to be "true," "untrue," or something in between. Wells even examines the numerous theories that someone else wrote the works of Shakespeare, but there is no evidence that he finds strong enough to convince him of their validity.

Exercise 22.7 Sentence Writing

Write ten sentences that include parallel structures. You may choose your own subject, or you may describe the process you go through (or tips that you could give someone else) when studying for an important test. Be sure to include pairs and lists of objects, actions, locations, or ideas.

23. Using Pronouns

Nouns name people, places, things, and ideas—such as *students, school, computers,* and *literacy.* **Pronouns** take the place of nouns to avoid repetition and to clarify meaning. The pronouns *they* or *them* could replace *students* and *computers;* the pronoun *it* could replace *school* and *literacy.* Personal pronouns that replace people's names or descriptions vary depending on gender and number.

Of the many kinds of pronouns, personal pronouns cause the most difficulty because they often include two ways of identifying the same person (or people) as either a subject or an object. Although only one form is technically "correct" in a given situation, modern usage sometimes relaxes these rules about subject and object pronouns.

SUBJECT GROUP	OBJECT GROUP
I	me
we	us
you	you
he	him
she	her
they	them
it	it

To follow standard rules, use a pronoun from the **Subject Group** in two instances:

1) Before a verb as a subject (even if a verb is missing at the end):

> *He* is my cousin. (*He* is the subject of the verb *is.*)

> *He* is older than *I.* (Here a second verb is missing at the end, but it is implied. The sentence means "*He* is older than *I am.*" *I* is the subject of the understood verb *am.*)

Whenever you see *than* used to compare two items in a sentence, ask yourself whether a verb has been left off the end of the sentence. Add the verb, and you'll automatically use the correct pronoun. Instead of informally writing, "She's taller than *me,*" write, "She's taller than *I am*" if you want to use the proper pronoun.

2) After a linking verb (*is, am, are, was, were*) as a pronoun that renames the subject:

> The ones who should apologize are *we.* (*We are the ones who should apologize.* Therefore, the pronoun from the Subject Group is used.)

> The winner of the lottery was *she.* (*She was the winner of the lottery.* Therefore, the pronoun from the Subject Group is used.)

Modern usage allows some exceptions to this rule, however. For example, it's common to hear people say *It's me* instead of the grammatically correct *It is I*.

Use pronouns from the **Object Group** for all other purposes. In the following sentence, *me* is not the subject, nor does it rename the subject. It is the object in a prepositional phrase (see Section 8). Therefore, it comes from the Object Group.

> My boss went to lunch with Jenny and *me*.

In sentences with pairs like *Jenny and me*, a good way to tell whether to choose a pronoun from the Subject Group or the Object Group is to ignore the extra name and the word *and*. When we ignore the paired word, the choice becomes clear: *My boss went to lunch with ~~Jenny and~~ (I, **me**)*. You would never say, *My boss went to lunch with I*.

> ~~My father and~~ (me, **I**) play chess on Sundays.
>
> *(Her,* **She***)* ~~and her friends~~ rented a movie.
>
> It is up to (we, ***us****)* ~~students~~ to find a solution.
>
> The coach asked ~~Craig and~~ (I, **me**) to carry the trophy.

Pronoun Agreement and Reference

Just as subjects and verbs must agree, pronouns should agree with the nouns they replace or refer to. If the noun is singular (ex. *parrot*), the pronoun referring to it should also be singular (*it* or *its*): The *parrot* sat on *its* perch. Likewise, if the noun is plural (parrots), the pronoun referring to it should be plural (*their*): The *parrots* sat on *their* perches. Here are two more examples:

> Each classroom has its own chalkboard.

The pronoun *its* refers to the singular noun *classroom* and therefore is singular.

> Both classrooms have their own chalkboards.

The pronoun *their* refers to the plural noun *classrooms* and therefore is plural.

The same methods to maintain subject and verb agreement also apply to **pronoun agreement.** For instance, ignore any prepositional phrases that come between a word and the pronoun that refers to it.

> That *box* of supplies arrived with a huge dent in *its* side.
>
> *Boxes* of supplies often arrive with huge dents in *their* sides.
>
> The *player* with the best concentration usually beats *her* opponent.
>
> *Players* with the best concentration usually beat *their* opponents.

When a pronoun refers to more than one word joined by *and*, the pronoun is plural:

> The *teacher and* the *tutors* eat *their* lunches at noon.

However, when a pronoun refers to more than one word joined by *or*, then the word closest to the pronoun determines its form:

> Either the teacher *or* the *tutors* eat *their* lunches in the classroom.

> Either the tutors *or* the *teacher* eats *his* lunch in the classroom.

It is tempting to avoid gender bias by using pairs of pronouns that include both singular forms—*he or she, his or her, him or her*. The results are wordy and awkward:

> As an actor, *he or she* must share *his or her* emotions with the audience.

> If anyone calls, tell *him or her* that I'll be back soon.

> Somebody left *his or her* backpack in the language lab.

Here are a few better ways to eliminate gender bias and wordiness *without* using pairs of pronouns:

> As actors, *they* must share *their* emotions with the audience. (Use plurals.)

> Tell *anyone* who calls that I'll be back soon. (Rephrase to omit extra pronouns.)

> Somebody left *a* backpack in the language lab. (Use articles—*a, an, the.*)

Finally, to be effective, a **pronoun** must have one clear **reference** in a sentence:

> Before synching my phone with my computer, I deleted everything on *it*.

> Did you delete everything on your *phone* or on your *computer*? The pronoun "*it*" could refer to either one, making the reference unclear. Here's a revision that clarifies the pronoun reference:

> I deleted everything on my *phone* before synching *it* with my computer.

EXERCISES

Exercise 23.1

Circle the correct pronouns in the following sentences. Remember the trick of ignoring extra words in a pair to help you choose the correct pronoun. Refer to the examples whenever necessary, and check your answers after each set to make the most progress.

1. My friend Kate and (I, me) took another field trip to a museum last week.

2. I usually enjoy these museum visits more than (she, her).

3. Last time, however, (she and I, me and her) both enjoyed it.

4. Since Kate is less of an art lover than (I, me), at first she didn't feel comfortable just standing and looking at a painting or a sculpture.

5. The first two times that (she and I, her and me) had gone museum-hopping, the gallery and choice of collection were made by (I, me).

6. The one who made the choices this time was (she, her).

7. Kate may not get into art as much as (I, me), but she sure picked a great place to visit—a beautiful new gallery on a nearby university campus.

8. Since no one else chose this gallery, Kate and (I, me) had the sun-filled rooms lined with paintings all to ourselves.

9. They were lovely in the natural light, and one huge painting even drew (she and I, her and me) to sit by it for a long time before moving on.

10. When Kate comes with (I, me) again, I will leave all decisions up to (she, her).

Exercises 23.2–23.5

Circle the correct pronoun or pair of pronouns. If the correct answer is **he or she,** **his or her,** or **him or her,** revise the sentence to avoid gender bias **and** wordiness. Check your answers as you go through the exercise.

1. I live a long way from the city center and don't own a car, so I use public transportation and rely on (its, their) stability.

2. Based on my experiences, I'd say the city's system of buses has (its, their) problems.

3. Each of the bus routes that I travel on my way to work falls behind (its, their) own schedule.

4. Many of the other passengers also transfer on (his or her, their) way to work.

5. One day last week, each of the passengers had to gather (his or her, their) belongings and leave the bus, even though it had not reached a scheduled stop.

6. Both the driver and the mechanic who came to fix the bus offered (his, their) apologies for making us late.

7. Once the bus was fixed, the passengers were allowed to bring (his or her, their) things back on board.

8. Everyone did (his or her, their) best to hide (his or her, their) annoyance from the driver because he had been so nice.

9. As every passenger stepped off the bus at the end of the line, the driver thanked (him or her, them) for (his or her, their) patience and understanding.

10. Sometimes it is the people within a system that makes (it, them) work after all.

Exercise 23.3

1. The teacher gave my classmates and (I, me) very specific instructions for the essay.

2. My brother was surprised to learn that Bruce Lee was taller than (he, him).

3. (She and he, Her and him) are working on the same topic for their speeches.

4. Each of the dentists received (his or her, their) gift bags full of toothbrushes and dental floss.

5. Mobile phone companies are usually very competitive in (its, their) pricing.

6. I confess that the person responsible for ordering those flowers was (I, me).

7. Everyone in the audience had (his or her, their) opinion of the performances and expressed it with (his or her, their) applause.

8. Only the jury knows all of the factors involved in (its, their) decision.

9. No one understands your feelings better than (I, me).

10. I talked to my academic counselor; it was (she, her) who called this morning.

Exercise 23.4

1. My friend asked, "Are you taking as many classes as (I, me) this semester?"

2. When it comes to organic farming methods, no one knows more than (she, her).

3. At work, I always answer the phone correctly by saying, "This is (she, her)" when someone asks, "May I speak to the manager?"

4. A little boy and girl were opening (his or her, their) presents when you arrived.

5. We asked the parking enforcement office to waive (its, their) fees for the event.

6. Everyone must use (his or her, their) own password to enter the network.

7. Purchase orders can be signed by my boss or (I, me).

8. The winners of the scholarships were Justin and (she, her).

9. Those two actors have given the best performance of (his or her, their) lives.

10. The judge sent the lawyers and (we, us) jurors a message.

Exercise 23.5

1. The university representative gave my friends and (I, me) a brochure of the campus.

2. Each of the students will buy (his or her, their) own materials for the jewelry class.

3. The top players in last year's poker tournament have finished (his or her, their) first game in this year's competition.

4. I can't remember—was it you or (I, me) who asked for a raise first?

5. Due to the holiday, everyone was allowed to turn (his or her, their) essay in late.

6. It was (she, her) who loaned him the money for a vacation.

7. There is no one more interested in bats and other flying creatures than (he, him).

8. You and (I, me) drive the same kind of car, but mine is an automatic.

9. I can't believe that the tutors helped you and (I, me) for over an hour.

10. According to Max and (she, her), the deadline for applications is today.

Exercise 23.6 Proofreading Practice

The following paragraph contains several incorrect or unclear pronouns. Find and correct the errors.

Rude drivers have one thing in common. Whether male or female, they all believe that they know how to drive better than anyone else. The other day, as my friends and me were driving to school, we stopped at an intersection. A very old man who used a cane started to walk across it in front of my friends and I just before the light was ready to change. So we waited. But while we waited for him, an impatient driver behind us started to honk his horn since he couldn't see him. I wondered, "Does he want us to hit him, or what?" Finally, it was clear. He pulled his car up beside ours, opened his window, and yelled at us before he sped away. The old man reached the other side safely, but he hardly noticed.

Exercise 23.7 Sentence Writing

Write ten sentences in which you compare two people or celebrities in terms of athletic ability or artistic creativity. Then check that your pronouns are grammatically correct, that they agree with the words they replace, and that they have clear references.

24. Avoiding Shifts in Person

To understand what **person** means when using pronouns, imagine a conversation between three people. The *first person* would speak using "I." That person would call the *second person* "you." And when those two talked of a *third person*, they would use "he," "she," or "they." Here are more pronoun forms arranged by person:

First person—*I, me, mine, we, us, ours*

Second person—*you, yours*

Third person—*he, him, his, she, her, they, them, theirs, one, anyone, it, its*

Although it is possible, and at times necessary, to use all three groups of pronouns in a paper, most writers try not to shift from one group to another without a good reason. Such errors are called **shifts in person**.

The following paragraph includes unnecessary shifts in person:

Few people know how to manage *their* time. *We* don't need to be efficiency experts to realize that *everyone* could get a lot more done by budgeting *his* or *her* time more wisely. Nor do *you* need to work very hard to become more organized.

To correct the shifts in person, you could use only *first-person* pronouns:

Few of *us* know how to manage *our* time. *We* don't need to be efficiency experts to realize that *we* could get a lot more done by budgeting *our* time more wisely. Nor do *we* need to work very hard to become more organized.

Or you could address the reader directly and use only *second-person* pronouns:

You are not alone if you don't know how to manage *your* time. *You* don't need to be an efficiency expert to realize that *you* could get a lot more done by budgeting *your* time more wisely. Nor do *you* need to work very hard to become more organized.

Finally, you could correct the shifts by using only *third-person* pronouns:

Few people know how to manage *their* time. *One* does not need to be an efficiency expert to realize that *everyone* could get a lot more done by budgeting *his* or *her* time more wisely. Nor does *anyone* need to work very hard to become more organized. (Note that "*his* or *her*" could then be deleted to avoid using this wordy pair of pronouns. See Section 23.)

PROOFREADING EXERCISES

Read the following three paragraphs to identify which ones include pronouns that shift *unnecessarily* between *first*, *second*, and *third person*. In the paragraphs that do include many shifts in person, revise the phrasing to eliminate unnecessary shifting. One of the paragraphs is already correct; one of them shifts unnecessarily many times, and one of them contains only one needless pronoun shift. The first paragraph (Exercise 24.1) is an excerpt from the book *Fashion 101: A Crash Course in Clothing*, by Erica Stalder.

Exercise 24.1

Coats are high fashion nowadays, but did you know that most coat styles made their first appearance as military apparel? Your rain-proof multitasking trench coat? It was first seen on British soldiers in WWII. Your friend's cool-looking bomber jacket? It came straight from the US Air Force, which designed the garment specifically for pilots. Whether trudging through 35-degree temperatures in Virginia during the Civil War or fighting in snow-bitten Armenia in January of 1914 during WWI, soldiers have always relied on serious outerwear to get the job done, and designers have always looked to the military for ideas about how to create functional clothing. Of course, not all coat styles originated from the armed forces. We have Native Americans to thank for the parka. Whether you're suiting up to battle the elements or adding a final touch to an outfit, take a moment to really look at—and appreciate—the history and style behind your outermost layer.

Exercise 24.2

I was reading about superstitions for my psychology class, and I learned that a lot of these beliefs concern brooms and sweeping. One superstition says that, whenever you change your residence, you should get a new broom. People should not take their old brooms with them because the brooms might carry any bad luck that was swept up at the old place and bring it to the new one. Also, if you sweep dirt out an open door, make it the back door so that the bad luck will depart forever. If you sweep dirt out the front way, the same bad luck will come right back in again. Finally, I learned never to walk across a fallen broomstick unless I never want to get married, for that is the fate for anyone who steps over a broomstick. I bet most people would be surprised by how many things can go wrong when you pick up a broom.

Exercise 24.3

Most of us in America could use more vacation time. We hear about citizens of other countries getting several weeks—and sometimes even months—off every year. There are long-standing traditions in some European, South American, and Asian countries, for example, that almost require workers to rest their bodies, recharge their energies, and lift their spirits. But in the United States, we have to fight for and often forfeit our one-week or two-week vacations. In fact, if we complain too loudly about needing a break, we could be the newest person on the unemployment line. It's time for all of us to stand up for our right to sit down in the shade—or walk out in the sun—and take some rest.

Sentence Structure Progress Test

One sentence in each pair contains an error in sentence structure or phrasing. Read both sentences carefully to find a clear fault in one of them. Then write the letter of the *correct* sentence in the blank. This test will help you gauge your progress and identify areas of sentence structure that you could still know better. Be confident, and check your answers only after trying your best.

1. _____ **A.** I found a twenty-dollar bill looking through my backpack.

      B. Looking through my backpack, I found a twenty-dollar bill.

2. _____ **A.** The math tutor asked Jake and me to collect the papers.

      B. The math tutor asked Jake and I to collect the papers.

3. _____ **A.** We designed an experiment to see how quickly bananas ripen in various situations.

      B. A bunch of green bananas were all that we needed for the experiment.

4. _____ **A.** Today, collecting celebrity dolls and action figures is a popular hobby for both adults and children.

      B. Today, both adults and children collects celebrity dolls and action figures.

5. _____ **A.** In many sports, the compensation of professional female athletes need immediate attention.

      B. In many sports, the gap between male and female salaries is huge.

6. _____ **A.** Some people love to participate in group activities; others avoid them and work better independently.

      B. Truth be told, I don't mind if a person is a team player or a loose cannon; I get along with everyone.

7. _____ **A.** As young adults, most of us learn that you can't have everything.

      B. Many of us also realize that we don't need everything to be happy.

8. _____ **A.** As soon as registration ends and students have added all of the classes that they need.

B. The atmosphere on campus lightens, and the process of learning begins again.

9. _____ **A.** The campus bookstore sells textbooks in-store and online.

B. It is convenient to buy textbooks online, but I like to look through a book before I buy them.

10. _____ **A.** The chess club is going to pack their boxes on Wednesday and move to its new space on Friday.

B. I've heard that the table tennis club plans to use the chess club's old space.

11. _____ **A.** The critique of our sculpture projects lasted much longer than a critique usually does.

B. The comments that we shared during peer review were the most helpful.

12. _____ **A.** Although high school reunions are common topics for satire.

B. There must be a good reason why people still look forward to them.

13. _____ **A.** The morale at the small company I work for is low at the moment.

B. We recently learned that either the employees or the owner have to take a small pay cut until sales improve.

14. _____ **A.** An effective logo must convey the essence of a brand and captures the interest of the public in an instant.

B. My typography teacher complimented my teammates and me on the successful logo we created for our imaginary brand of stapler.

15. _____ **A.** Hazardous driving conditions during the recent storm was responsible for a decrease in traffic throughout the city.

B. Hazardous driving conditions during the recent storm were responsible for a decrease in traffic throughout the city.

Sentence Structure Practice

The following excerpt is the first paragraph from the "Forward" of a book titled *Press Start to Play,* a collection of short stories about gaming, edited by Daniel H. Wilson and John Joseph Adams. In his "Forward" to Wilson and Adams' book, author Ernest Cline explores some of the reasons why human beings need and love to play games.

Using *all* of the identification methods that you have practiced in Part Two, mark the sentence structures within this excerpt's seven sentences. Label their (prepositional phrases), subjects, verbs and verb phrases, [verbals] and [verbal phrases], as well as any dependent clauses. Finally, identify **sentence types** as **simple, compound,** or **complex** by comparing these sentences to the examples in Tables 10.A and 10.B. Note that this excerpt does not contain any **compound-complex** sentences. We have numbered the sentences and made minor changes for the purpose of this exercise.

1) Since their invention half a century ago, video games have come to play a vital role in modern human civilization. 2) I think that this is because we modern humans were never designed to live as we do now—sitting in traffic, working in offices, shopping in stores. 3) We are, by design, hunter–gatherers. 4) Millions of years of evolution have wired our brains with an inherent need to hunt, gather, explore, solve puzzles, form teams, and conquer challenge after challenge in order to survive. 5) For most people, day-to-day life no longer requires many of those experiences or challenges, and so those primal, instinctive needs inside us have no natural outlet. 6) To keep our minds and bodies healthy, we simulate those old ways in the midst of our modern, technological lives, where everything on the planet has already been hunted and gathered. 7) Thankfully, the technology that created this problem also gave us its solution: video games.

Punctuation

WHAT IS THE LEAST YOU SHOULD KNOW ABOUT PUNCTUATION?

Punctuation is a written code. As part of this code, each piece of punctuation works with the words and sentence structures covered in Parts One and Two to clarify meaning. You learned very early as a writer to capitalize the first letter and put a period, question mark, or exclamation point (. ? !) at the end of an independent clause to create a sentence. The main uses of commas (,) and semicolons (;) you learned when you studied independent clauses, dependent clauses, and sentence types in Section 10 and the ways to avoid run-on sentences in Sections 9 and 12. You may be less familiar, however, with the uses of colons (:), dashes (—), quotation marks (" "), and italics/underlines (__). To preview how punctuation works with words and sentence structures to create meaning, take the Punctuation Preview Test that follows.

Punctuation Preview Test

Think of this preview test as an opportunity to discover how much you already know about punctuation, rather than as a test to be graded. A full explanation follows each of the answers, but first try your best. One sentence in each pair contains an error in punctuation or capitalization. Read both sentences carefully to find a clear fault in one of them. Then write the letter of the *correct* sentence in the blank:

1. _____ **A.** Whenever I turn left, the steering wheel makes a noise.

   B. The steering wheel makes a noise, whenever I turn left.

2. _____ **A.** Why do so many sci-fi movies involve the Statue of liberty in some way?

   B. Many sci-fi movies—including *Independence Day, A.I.,* and the original *Planet of the Apes*—feature the Statue of Liberty.

3. _____ **A.** They returned from Canada on March 3, 2015 and started training immediately.

   B. On March 3, 2015, they returned from Canada and started training immediately.

4. _____ **A.** In terms of office supplies, I need: paper, ink cartridges, and correction fluid.

   B. The office supplies that I need are paper, ink cartridges, and correction fluid.

5. _____ **A.** "Will we make it to the theater by 7:00?" I asked my Uber driver.

   B. I asked my Uber driver, "Will we make it to the theater by 7:00"?

6. _____ **A.** Have you read *Harry Potter And The Deathly Hallows?*

   B. The seventh book in the series was *Harry Potter and the Deathly Hallows.*

7. _____ **A.** The teacher gave us two options: write an essay or give a speech.

   B. Our two options were to write an essay, or give a speech.

8. _____ **A.** I love to take classes in the Spring because the campus looks so beautiful.

   B. Because the campus looks so beautiful, I love to take classes in the spring.

9. _____ **A.** I have strengthened the thesis of my essay, my paragraphs still need work.

          B. Although my paragraphs still need work, I've strengthened the thesis of my essay.

10. _____ **A.** The Rolling Stones, one of the most famous rock bands in the world played in Cuba for the first time in March 2016.

          B. In March 2016, Cubans enjoyed their first concert by the Rolling Stones, one of the most famous rock bands in the world.

11. _____ **A.** Last semester, students who took more than four classes received free parking permits.

          B. Students, who took more than four classes last semester, received free parking permits.

12. _____ **A.** Fans of global entertainment love to visit Seoul, South Korea, and Mumbai, India.

          B. Two forms of entertainment, K-Pop and Bollywood attract fans from across the globe.

13. _____ **A.** How much does it cost to remodel and rebuild a dugout?

          B. I wonder if we can raise enough money for a new dugout?

14. _____ **A.** Ivan and Becky, two of the new trainees, learned quickly during their first shift.

          B. It took other trainees longer to get accustomed to our checkout system, products and procedures.

15. _____ **A.** Some greeters in retail stores say "Welcome" or "Hello", but they don't sound sincere.

          B. It must be difficult to greet so many customers with "Welcome" or "Hello" and sound sincere every time.

25. Periods, Question Marks, Exclamation Points, Semicolons, Colons, Dashes

Use a period (.) at the end of sentences that make statements or mild commands and after some abbreviations.

> Heavy rain will cause delays on Interstate 80. (statement)
>
> Take a different route if you can. (mild command)
>
> Fwy.　Sept.　in.　pgs.　ft.　Ave.　Tues. (abbreviations)

Use a question mark (?) after direct questions but not after indirect questions.

> Has online registration already started? (direct question)
>
> I wonder if online registration has already started. (indirect question)

In a sentence with quotation marks, put the question mark *outside* the quote marks if the sentence itself is a question but *inside* if the quotation or title is a question.

> Have you actually said, "I quit"? (The sentence is a question.)
>
> I asked my boss, "Do you want me to quit?" (The quotation is a question.)
>
> Did they play "Should I Stay or Should I Go?" (Sentence and song title are both questions.)

Use an exclamation point (!) after expressions or quotations that convey strong emotions or loud sounds. Exclamations appear most often in informal writing.

> I need a break from reality! Let's see a movie.
>
> When the heavy box landed, I heard a loud crack!

The same rules about using quotation marks with question marks apply to using them with exclamation points.

> Someone yelled, "I can't believe I got an A!" (Quotation is an exclamation.)
>
> I finally memorized "The Road Not Taken"! (Poem title is not an exclamation.)

Use a semicolon (;) between two independent clauses in a sentence when they are *not* joined by one of the *conjunctions* called *fanboys* (for, and, nor, but, or, yet, so).

> My brother co-signed for a loan; now I have a car of my own.
>
> She volunteered her house as a polling place; however, its rooms were too small to qualify.

To be sure that a semicolon is correct, try replacing it with a period and capital letter.

My brother co-signed for a loan. Now I have a car of my own.

She volunteered her house as a polling place. However, its rooms were too small to qualify.

Aside from its main use to separate two independent clauses, a semicolon can also act as a "**super comma**" within a list to separate items that already contain commas.

I enjoy cooking, my hobby; biking, my passion; and screen-printing, my job.

Use a colon (:) after a set-up clause—a complete statement that sets up an expectation in the reader's mind. Imagine that the colon is a *fence*, and you're setting the reader up to *look over the fence*. Then, after the colon, include the word, list, explanation, or quotation that the reader is expecting.

The company announced its Employee of the Month: Lee Jones.

That car comes in the following colors: red, black, blue, and white.

I gave my boss a simple explanation: I need more time with my family.

Hamlet asks the ultimate question: "To be, or not to be?"

The previous examples all contain complete set-up clauses before the colons. Now look at a few sentences that do *not* require colons because they do *not* include complete set-up clauses.

The company announced that Lee Jones is its Employee of the Month.

That car comes in red, black, blue, and white.

I explained to my boss that I need more time with my family.

Hamlet asks, "To be, or not to be?"

Note that, in the last example, the signal phrase *Hamlet asks* leads directly into the quotation without including the words *the ultimate question* to complete the set-up clause. Therefore, no colon—just a comma—comes between them. See Section 36 for more about punctuating quotations introduced by signal phrases.

Use dashes (—) in place of other punctuation to emphasize information or to isolate phrasing that includes its own punctuation. Dashes are optional and should be used sparingly. They can replace commas, semicolons, or colons.

Lee Jones—Employee of the Month—quit yesterday. (Dashes replace commas.)

I love Bollywood movies—my sister hates them. (Dash replaces a semicolon.)

We have exciting news for you—we're moving! (Dash replaces a colon.)

The new club members—Jan, Ted, and Anne—arrived. (Dashes isolate a list.)

EXERCISES

Exercises 25.1 and 25.2

Add the necessary end punctuation (periods, question marks, and exclamation points) to the following sentences. Any punctuation marks used *within* the sentences are correct and do not need to be changed. Pay attention to the other punctuation marks, however, to help you understand their uses while you are adding the end punctuation.

Exercise 25.1

1. Do you know how many resources go into making the jeans that we all love to wear

2. Here are a couple of the details: the dyeing process uses about a pound of harsh chemicals and 15 dye baths to create a single pair of jeans

3. Would you believe that it also takes 2,500 gallons of water to finish that one pair

4. Of course, each movement of the jeans through the process requires electricity

5. Luckily, textile scientists in Switzerland have come up with a "greener" method of jeans production

6. The result is called Advanced Denim, and its environmental benefits are staggering

7. The scientific and environmental communities are excited, and who wouldn't be

8. This new denim requires only one trip through a dye vat and finishes the fabric with eco-friendly substances

9. The Advanced Denim process uses 30 percent less energy and over 90 percent less water than traditional denim

10. Can you imagine the positive effects it could have when multiplied by the 2 billion pairs of jeans produced each year

Source: Science Daily, June 19, 2012

Exercise 25.2

1. Have you noticed that light bulbs don't last as long as they used to

2. Some seem to burn out after only a month or two

3. Would you believe that one light bulb has lasted for 110 years

4. Well, it's true—believe it or not

5. At a fire station in Livermore, California, the same bulb has been burning since 1901

6. The now famous light bulb is treated like a celebrity by the firefighters

7. They are proud of its history, and who wouldn't be

8. The famous bulb doesn't get cleaned or covered by any type of shade; no one wants to risk damaging it or making it burn out after so many years

9. The Livermore Light Bulb, as it's called, has even made it into the *Guinness Book of World Records* as the longest running light bulb

10. Anyone who wants to see this famous bulb in action can visit its 24-hour Web cam online

Source: www.centennialbulb.org

Exercises 25.3 and 25.4

Add any necessary semicolons, colons, and dashes to these sentences. The commas and end punctuation do not need to be changed. Some sentences are already correct.

Exercise 25.3

1. Have you ever heard of Vinnie Ream?

2. This young woman a very controversial figure in Washington, D.C. began her career as a sculptor in 1863 at the age of sixteen.

3. Miss Ream was a student of the famous sculptor Clark Mills he is perhaps best known for his statue of Andrew Jackson located across from the White House.

4. Vinnie Ream started to work with Mills in his studio in the basement of the Capitol building soon members of Congress were volunteering to sit for Miss Ream, and she sculpted busts of them.

5. Her fame and reputation grew in the late 1860s that's when she was awarded a $10,000 commission to create a life-size statue of Abraham Lincoln.

6. Vinnie Ream had known Lincoln in fact, before his assassination, President Lincoln would allow Miss Ream to sit in his office within the White House and work on a bust of him as he carried out the business of running the country.

7. Ream's intimate observation of Lincoln at work affected her design of Lincoln's posture and facial expression for her statue of him.

8. Vinnie Ream's relationships and the works she produced were not accepted by everyone Ream's youth and physical beauty led to much of this harsh criticism.

9. Some people questioned her motives others even questioned her abilities.

10. Ream prospered in spite of the jealous accusations of others and often demonstrated her sculpting abilities in public to prove that she did her own work.

Source: Smithsonian, August 2000

Exercise 25.4

1. Thunderstorms are spectacular demonstrations of nature's power.

2. Do you know where the safest places are during a thunderstorm?

3. One relatively safe place is inside a building that has plumbing pipes or electrical wires those channels can absorb the electrical energy unleashed by lightning.

4. Of course, once inside such a building, people should stay away from the end sources of plumbing and wiring faucets, hoses, phone receivers, and computer terminals.

5. Buildings without pipes or wires are not safe shelters during lightning strikes these might include pergolas, dugouts, and tents.

6. Outside, lightning can move over the ground therefore, you should be aware of a position that emergency officials call the "lightning squat."

7. This emergency position involves curling up into the smallest ball you can while balancing on the balls of your feet and covering your ears.

8. That way, there is less of you in contact with the ground if lightning strikes.

9. Lightning is electrical energy consequently, it can travel far from the actual storm clouds.

10. In fact, lightning has struck as far as twenty miles away from the storm that caused it.

Source: Current Health, October 2003

Exercise 25.5

Add the necessary periods, question marks, exclamation points, semicolons, colons, and dashes. Any commas in the sentences are correct and should not be changed.

1. What do math and origami Japanese paper folding have to do with each other

2. Erik Demaine and other origami mathematicians would answer, "Everything"

3. If you have never heard of the field of origami mathematics, you're not alone

4. Origami math is a relatively new field back in 2003, Demaine won a "genius" award partly due to his work with origami and its applications in many fields

5. The MacArthur Foundation awarded Demaine more than just the title "genius" it awarded him half a million dollars

6. At twenty, Demaine was hired as a professor by the Massachusetts Institute of Technology he became the youngest professor MIT has ever had

7. Erik Demaine has his father to thank for much of his education Martin Demaine home-schooled Erik as the two of them traveled around North America

8. Erik was always intensely interested in academic subjects during his travels, he and his father would consult university professors whenever Erik had questions that no one else could answer

9. Erik Demaine continues to investigate one area in particular the single-cut problem

10. This problem involves folding a piece of paper then making one cut the result can be anything from a swan to a star, a unicorn, or any letter of the alphabet

Source: New York Times, February 15, 2005

Exercise 25.6 Paragraph Practice

We have removed periods, question marks, exclamation points, semicolons, colons, and dashes in the following excerpt from the book *101 Things I Learned in Architecture School,* by Matthew Frederick. Add missing pieces of punctuation (. ? ! ; : —) where they belong. Capital letters show where new sentences begin. Note that the second paragraph is one sentence that needs a pair of dashes to enclose a lengthy list. Any punctuation already in the excerpt is correct and should not be changed.

Manage your ego If you want to be recognized for designing a good or even great building, forget about what *you* want the building to be instead ask, "What does the *building* want to be" A design problem has to be addressed on its own terms the needs of the client, the nature of the site, the realities of the building program, and many others These factors point toward an inherent order that must be acknowledged before self-expression can enter the design process

Strive to accommodate and express universal concerns in your work the human quest for meaning and purpose, the variegated play of light and shadow on a textured wall, the interweaving of public and private relationships, the structural and aesthetic opportunities inherent in building materials and you will find an interested audience.

Exercise 25.7 Sentence Writing

Imitate the excerpt in Exercise 25.6 with ten sentences of your own in which you give advice about something school-related that *you* know how to do well. Use periods, question marks, exclamation points, semicolons, colons, and dashes correctly.

26. Commas Used to Separate Elements

Commas guide the reader through your sentence structures in the same way that signs guide people on the highway. Imagine what effects misplaced or incorrect road signs would have. From now on, try not to use a comma without a good reason for it.

Commas serve two purposes in the written code of punctuation: they *separate* elements or *enclose* elements. This section covers the first function of commas—to separate one part of a sentence from another. The next section will explain how commas are used to enclose sentence structures.

Use a comma to separate two independent clauses joined by one of the conjunctions called *fanboys* (*for, and, nor, but, or, yet, so*).

We all brought our final drafts to class, *and* the teacher congratulated us.

My art history book will be very expensive, *but* I'll look for a good deal online.

If you use a comma without a *fanboys* between two independent clauses, the result is an error called a **comma splice.**

Dogs are people's best friends, people are cats' best friends. (comma splice)

Dogs are people's best friends, *and* people are cats' best friends. (corrected)

Before using a comma, be sure one of the *fanboys* actually connects two independent clauses and not just two words or phrases. The following sentence contains only one independent clause with two verbs. Because no subject follows the *fanboys*, the sentence does not require a comma:

My dog curled up under my chair *and* waited for me to finish my essay.

Now compare the previous sentence with this one that does require a comma:

My cat was hungry, *and* she meowed for me to finish my essay.

Use commas to separate items in a series, date, or address.

Students in literature classes read *short stories, poems,* and *plays*.

Today I *walked to school, biked to work,* and *took a train to the movies.*

Some writers leave out the comma before the *and* connecting the last two items in a series, but this comma is needed to separate all of the items clearly and equally.

> My favorite sandwiches are *tuna, turkey,* and *ham and cheese.*
>
> My favorite composers are *Mozart, Beethoven, Chopin,* and *Shubert.*

In a full date or an address including city and state or country, put a comma after each item, including the last.

> He was born on *August 21, 1961,* in *Clitheroe, England,* but later moved to Paris.
>
> Our old house at *212 Eden Street, Denver, Colorado,* has become a bakery.

When only the month and year are used in a date, no commas are needed.

> My aunt graduated from Yale in *May 2011.*

Use a comma to separate an introductory word, phrase, or dependent clause from the beginning of a sentence. The complete sentence begins *after* the introduction.

> *Finally,* he received a check from his insurance company. (introductory word)
>
> *During her last performance,* the actress lost her voice. (introductory phrase)
>
> *When I finish my homework,* I feel so satisfied. (dependent clause)

Use a comma to separate a tag question, contrast, comment, or description from the end of a sentence. The complete sentence ends *before* the tag.

> The new restrictions don't begin until January, *do they?* (tag question)
>
> Customers usually ask for a refund, *not an exchange.* (tag contrast)
>
> My professor said he was "ruminating," *whatever that means.* (tag comment)
>
> We spent all day at the beach, *filled with tourists and sunshine.* (description)

As these examples show, a tag is a kind of afterthought. Note that most prepositional phrases and dependent clauses at the ends of sentences are not tags and do *not* require commas.

> "Ruminate" means to think *about something.* (prepositional phrase)
>
> I feel so satisfied *when I finish my homework.* (dependent clause)

EXERCISES

Add commas according to the specific directions for each exercise. Any other punctuation already in the sentences is correct. Refer to the examples whenever necessary, and check your answers often.

Exercise 26.1

Add commas to the following sentences to separate two independent clauses joined by a *fanboys*. Remember that some *fanboys* link other parts of a sentence, not independent clauses, and may *not* require commas. Look for the *fanboys* that have a subject and verb before *and* after them to find the ones that join independent clauses.

1. The young actor named Sabu began his career in 1937 and he became famous for his unique background and abilities.

2. He had an amazing rapport with animals and an athletic and energetic acting style.

3. An American filmmaker discovered Sabu as a young boy in Southern India and asked him to be in a film about elephants.

4. In real life, Sabu understood elephants very well for his father owned and trained elephants.

5. *The Elephant Boy* was Sabu's first film and it made him an instant celebrity.

6. He went on to star in fantasy films like *The Thief of Bagdad* and *Arabian Nights.*

7. The special effects in these two films matched today's standards and in some ways exceeded them.

8. In his most celebrated role, Sabu played Mowgli in the live-action 1942 film of Rudyard Kipling's *The Jungle Book.*

9. Sabu's version of *The Jungle Book* was made decades before Disney's animated versions but it captured the essence of the mysterious jungle even more vividly with real actors and animals.

10. In one scene, Sabu rode into the village on a galloping water buffalo and calmly slid off the animal to deliver his dialogue.

Source: http://www.imdb.com/name/nm0754942/

Exercise 26.2

Add commas to the following sentences to separate items in a series, date, or address. Some sentences may not need any commas.

1. I finished high school on June 23 2015 after moving here from Houston Texas.

2. My favorite English teacher was young enthusiastic and highly motivated.

3. We read essays stories poems novels and research articles in her class.

4. My group even opted to read a play memorize all of its parts and perform it for everyone.

5. One of Ms. Kern's best assignments involved writing a complaint letter.

6. She taught us how to argue fairly and how to modify what she called the "tone of voice" in our writing.

7. We each wrote a letter of complaint about a product a service or an experience that was unsatisfactory to us.

8. Then we sent copies of our letter to the company's business address to our home address and to Ms. Kern's school address.

9. Ms. Kern assured us that we would receive a response from the company if we described our dissatisfaction clearly asked for a reasonable solution and used a respectful tone.

10. My company replied to my letter with a note of apology a bumper sticker and an impressive gift card to use at any of the company's stores.

Exercise 26.3

Add commas after introductory words, phrases, or dependent clauses in the following sentences. Some sentences may not need any commas.

1. As if people don't have enough to worry about Melinda Muse wrote a book called *I'm Afraid, You're Afraid: 448 Things to Fear and Why.*

2. In her book Muse points out the dangers of common places, objects, foods, months, days, and activities.

3. If people go to Vegas regularly they should worry because paramedics can't reach people as quickly in large crowds or huge buildings.

4. Another dangerous spot is the beauty parlor; people can suffer a stroke from leaning their heads back too far into the shampoo sink.

5. In the comfort of our homes unwashed new clothes may transfer dangerous chemicals to people's eyes, skin, and lungs.

6. Among the foods to avoid grapefruit juice can interfere with certain medications' effectiveness.

7. Thanks to Independence Day celebrations and outdoor picnics July ranks highest of all the months in accidental injuries and food poisonings.

8. Being linked with more suicides and heart attacks than any other weekday Mondays are the most dangerous days of the week.

9. Believe it or not singing in a choir can even permanently damage people's ears.

10. After reading *I'm Afraid, You're Afraid* it's possible to be afraid of almost everything.

Source: I'm Afraid, You're Afraid: 448 Things to Fear and Why (Hyperion, 2000)

Exercise 26.4

Add commas before tag questions, contrasts, comments, or descriptions in the following sentences. Some sentences may not need any commas.

1. The United States introduced the Susan B. Anthony dollar in 1979 making her the first woman on a circulating coin.

2. No one deserved this honor more than Susan B. Anthony having led the fight for women's voting rights in America.

3. The Anthony dollar quickly became unpopular however.

4. People disliked certain features of the coin not the person on the coin.

5. This dollar coin was too much like a quarter nearly the same size and color with the same rough edge around it.

6. People mistakenly put Anthony dollars in machines that called for quarters.

7. In 1999, the government stopped issuing Susan B. Anthony dollars preferring to introduce a new golden dollar coin instead.

8. The new coin portrayed the image of a famous American woman just as the Anthony dollar did.

9. The Sacagawea "golden dollar" has suffered from its own lack of popularity unfortunately.

10. Women haven't had much luck as images on coins have they?

Source: http://womenshistory.about.com/od/anthonysusanb/a/anthony.htm

Exercise 26.5

Use commas to separate all of the necessary elements in the following sentences.

1. Fish may be considered "brain food" but I've never liked it.

2. While everyone is saying how delicious a big salmon steak is or how yummy the shrimp tastes you'll find me grimacing and munching on the bread.

3. Part of the problem with fish is the smell but my friends who love to eat fish also love the smell of fish cooking.

4. I always thought that was strange but it makes sense doesn't it?

5. If someone hates the taste of onions that person probably also hates the smell of onions cooking.

6. Come to think of it my husband hates to eat sweets and doesn't like the smell of them either.

7. When we walk into a bakery together he practically has to hold his nose the way I would in a fish market.

8. To me that's odd but my aversion to fish must seem weird to someone who loves it.

9. Our daughter adores the taste of bacon but she hates the smell of bacon frying.

10. So I guess there are always exceptions.

Exercise 26.6 Paragraph Practice

Use commas to separate all of the necessary elements in the following paragraph. Try to identify the elements you are separating. Check your answers often to make the most progress.

There I was in the pilot's seat of a small airplane. I had signed up for a course in flying at the aviation school but I didn't really expect to get my pilot's license. Learning the instruments took the most time. Once we began training in the cockpit the instructor told us what to do and we did it. When I turned the yoke to the right the plane banked right. When I turned it to the left the plane went left. Actually it was very similar to driving a car only much more fun. I'm exaggerating about it being easy of course. My favorite type of practice involved landings bringing the plane in softly and safely. After many hours of supervised flying my time to solo came and I was nervous but excited. I covered my checklist on the ground took off without any problems and landed smoothly in the middle of the runway. On a cold day in October 2014 I became a licensed pilot. Now I can work toward my next dream of becoming a private pilot for a rock star.

Exercise 26.7 Sentence Writing

For more practice using commas to separate elements in sentences, combine the following sets of details in different ways to create sentences that include two independent clauses with *fanboys* or an introductory element, a list, or a tag. Refer to the examples in the explanations whenever necessary. Feel free to reorder these details and add to or alter the phrasing. If you include a list, be sure to use parallel structure (see Section 22). You'll find sample combinations in the Answers, but try not to look at them before writing some of your own.

I like to watch golf and tennis.
I love to play baseball and soccer.

Tutors do not correct students' essays.
They can explain how to clarify ideas.

They will also show how to add stronger details.

They may even offer tips on improving organization.

My parents grew up in the 1960s.

Most cars in the 1960s had seatbelts.

There were no car seats for children.

Air bags had not been introduced yet.

27. Commas Used to Enclose Elements

The second function of **commas** is to enclose "scoopable" elements in sentences. **Scoopable elements** are extra words, phrases, and clauses that can be scooped out of the middle of a sentence because they are not necessary to understand its meaning. Have you noticed that a comma (,) is shaped like the tip of an ice cream scoop? Let this similarity help you remember to use commas to enclose *scoopable* elements. Use two commas, like the ones used here, to show where each scoopable element begins and ends.

Use commas to enclose the name of a person being spoken to in a sentence.

> Did you know, *Danielle*, that you left your backpack at the library?
>
> We regret to inform you, *Mr. Davis*, that your policy has been canceled.

Use commas to enclose transitions or expressions that interrupt the flow of the sentence (such as *however, moreover, therefore, of course, by the way, on the other hand, I believe,* or *I think*).

> I know, *of course*, that I have missed the deadline.
>
> They will try, *therefore*, to use the rest of their time wisely.
>
> Today's exam, *I think*, was only a practice test.

Read the previous examples *aloud*, and you'll hear how these expressions surrounded by commas stand out as interruptions. Sometimes such expressions flow smoothly in the sentence and do not need commas around them.

> *Of course* he checked to see if there were any rooms available.
>
> We *therefore* decided to stay out of it.
>
> *I think* you made the right decision.

Remember, when a word like *however* comes between two independent clauses, a semicolon should separate them, as explained in Section 25. In such sentences, *however* functions as an introductory word for the second independent clause, as explained in Section 26 about commas that separate elements.

> Voter turnout was low; *however*, the election results were definitive.
>
> She has started to like architecture; *therefore*, she plans to change her major.
>
> I spent hours studying for the test; *finally*, I felt prepared.

Thus, you've seen words like *however, therefore,* and *finally* used in several ways:

1. as introductory words or tag comments, using a comma to separate them from the rest of the sentence

2. as "scoopable" words that interrupt the flow of the sentence, using two commas to enclose them

3. as words that flow smoothly within the sentence using no punctuation

4. as transitions between two independent clauses, using a semicolon before and a comma after them.

Use commas to enclose extra or unnecessary information in the middle of a sentence. These are the most common forms of "scoopables."

Here's an example of a sentence that includes additional information about its subject:

Maxine Taylor, who organized the fund-raiser, will introduce the candidates.

The clause *who organized the fund-raiser* is scoopable information in the sentence. Without it, we know the name of the subject and what she is going to do: "Maxine Taylor will introduce the candidates." Therefore, the additional information is enclosed by commas to show that it is scoopable. Now read the following sentence:

The person who organized the fund-raiser will introduce the candidates.

Of the two—*the person* and *who organized the fund-raiser*—can you tell which information is more specific? You're right if you think *who organized the fund-raiser* is more specific. Without it, the subject is unclear: "The person will introduce the candidates." The reader has no idea *which person* it will be. The clause *who organized the fund-raiser* is required to identify the person, so there are no commas around it. Here's another example:

A film version of <u>Hamlet</u>, Shakespeare's famous play, won an Oscar in 1949.

The additional identification *Shakespeare's famous play* is scoopable. It could be left out without making the subject unclear: "A film version of <u>Hamlet</u> won an Oscar in 1949." Therefore, two commas enclose the scoopable information to show that it piece of extra identification. Here is the same sentence with the information reversed:

A film version of Shakespeare's famous play <u>Hamlet</u> won an Oscar in 1949.

In this sentence, the title of the movie is not additional but *necessary*. Without it, the sentence would read, "A film version of Shakespeare's famous play won an Oscar in 1949." The reader would not know which *one* of Shakespeare's many famous plays won the Oscar in 1949. Therefore, the title Hamlet is necessary, and commas should not be used around it.

Occasionally, scoopable elements show up at the end of the sentence, and when they do, the period acts as the end of the scoop. We might even call these "scoopable tags." See Section 26 for more about using commas with tags.

We drove to Las Vegas with Siobhan, our good friend from Ireland.

EXERCISES

Use commas to enclose any "scoopable" elements in the following sentences. Some sentences may not need commas. Refer to the explanations and examples whenever necessary. Check your answers often to make the most progress.

Exercise 27.1

1. The first person who guessed correctly won a trip to the Grand Canyon.

2. Professor Jones who guessed correctly won a trip to the Grand Canyon.

3. Cookies that contain nuts may be harmful to people with allergies.

4. My cookie recipe which does not contain nuts is safe for people with allergies.

5. Students who take the train to school catch a shuttle from the station to campus.

6. Melissa who takes the train to school catches a shuttle from the station to campus.

7. The teacher explained the answer to the question that everyone missed.

8. The teacher explained the answer to question 14 which everyone missed.

9. The gorilla an animal on many endangered species lists has an average lifespan of 30 to 50 years.

10. Koko the gorilla who became famous for learning to communicate through sign language turned 45 years old in July 2016.

Source: koko.org (for Koko information)

Exercise 27.2

1. We hope of course that people will honor their summons for jury duty.

2. Of course we hope that people will honor their summons for jury duty.

3. People who serve as jurors every time they're called deserve our appreciation.

4. Thelma and Trevor Martin who serve as jurors every time they're called deserve our appreciation.

5. We should therefore be as understanding as we can be about the slow legal process.

6. Therefore we should be as understanding as we can be about the slow legal process.

7. A legal system that believes people are innocent until proven guilty must offer a trial-by-jury option.

8. The U.S. legal system which believes people are innocent until proven guilty offers a trial-by-jury option.

9. With that option, we hope that no one will receive an unfair trial.

10. With that option, no one we hope will receive an unfair trial.

Exercise 27.3

1. The story of Dracula the frightening Prince Vlad Tepes has been fascinating people across the world for hundreds of years.

2. He was held as a prisoner in Bran Castle a medieval fortress in Transylvania in the 15th century.

3. Bran Castle also called Dracula's Castle has become a popular tourist attraction.

4. For the past forty years, people who traveled to Romania have been visiting the museum at Bran Castle.

5. The towers and Transylvanian charm of the castle have also made it the perfect setting for many Dracula movies.

6. The owners of Dracula's Castle have changed throughout the years.

7. It was given to Marie Queen of Romania in 1920.

8. But the political landscape changed, and the castle became national property in 1948.

9. A law that was passed in 2005 returned Bran Castle to the ancestors of the Romanian royal family.

10. Queen Marie's grandson Dominic von Habsburg now owns the castle, along with his two sisters Maria Magdalena and Elizabeth.

Source: Renaissance Magazine, Issue #51 (2006)

Exercise 27.4

1. Arthur S. Heineman a California architect designed and built the world's first motel in the 1920s.

2. He chose the perfect location the city of San Luis Obispo which was midway between Los Angeles and San Francisco.

3. Heineman an insightful man of business understood the need for inexpensive drive-in accommodations on long motor vehicle trips.

4. Hotels which required reservations and offered only high-priced rooms within one large structure just didn't fulfill the needs of motorists.

5. Heineman envisioned his "Motor Hotel" or Mo-Tel as a place where the parking spaces for the cars were right next to separate bungalow-style apartments for the passengers.

6. Heineman's idea was so new that when he put up his "Motel" sign several residents of the area told him to fire the sign's painter who couldn't even spell the word *hotel.*

7. Heineman had the sign painter place a hyphen between *Mo* and *Tel* to inform the public of a new kind of resting place.

8. Heineman's Milestone Mo-Tel the world's first motel opened in San Luis Obispo in 1925.

9. Before Heineman's company the Milestone Interstate Corporation could successfully trademark the name "Mo-Tel," other builders adopted the style and made *motel* a generic term.

10. Some of the original Milestone Mo-Tel building now called the Motel Inn still stands on the road between Los Angeles and San Francisco.

Source: Westways, May/June 2000

Exercise 27.5

1. I bought a book *The Story of the "Titanic"* because I am interested in famous events in history.

2. This book written by Frank O. Braynard is a collection of postcards about the ill-fated ocean liner.

3. The book's postcards four on each page can be pulled apart and mailed like regular ones.

4. The postcards have images of *Titanic*-related people, places, and events on one side.

5. The blank sides where messages and addresses go include brief captions of the images on the front of the cards.

6. The book's actual content the part written by Braynard offers a brief history of each image relating to the *Titanic*.

7. One of my favorite cards shows the ship's captain Edward Smith and its builder Lord Pirrie standing on the deck of the *Titanic* before it set sail.

8. Another card is a photograph of *Titanic* passengers on board the *Carpathia* the ship that rescued many survivors.

9. There is also a picture of two small children survivors themselves who lost their father in the disaster but were later reunited with their mother.

10. The most interesting card a photo of the ship's gymnasium shows that one of the pieces of exercise equipment for the passengers was a rowing machine.

Source: The Story of the "Titanic" (Dover, 1988)

Exercise 27.6 Paragraph Practice

Use commas to enclose any extra or unnecessary ("scoopable") elements in the following paragraph. Remember to add a pair of commas, one to begin the scoop and another to end it, unless the scoopable element ends at the period.

Do you know Ryan that there is a one-unit library class that begins next week?

It's called Library 1 Introduction to the Library and my friends recommended it.

The librarians who teach it will give us an orientation and a series of assignment sheets. Then whenever we finish the assignments we turn them in to the librarians for credit. Ms. Kim the librarian that I spoke with said that the course materials cover really valuable library skills. These skills such as finding books or articles in our library and using the Internet to access other databases are the ones universities will expect us to know. I therefore plan to take this class, and you I hope will take it with me.

Exercise 27.7 Sentence Writing

Combine the following sets of sentences in different ways with scoopables in mind. Try to combine each set in a way that needs commas and in a way that doesn't need commas. In other words, try to make an element "scoopable" in one sentence and not "scoopable" in another. You may reorder the details and change the phrasing as you wish. Sample responses are provided in the Answers, but try to write your own before looking at them.

> Persis Frank is a great boss.
> A great boss recognizes hard work and rewards dedicated employees.
> She plans to buy herself an expensive watch.
> It is sold by Tag Heuer.
> Tag Heuer is her favorite brand.

> Only two people were in the store when the commercial was filmed.
> One was the manager.
> The other was an actor.

TABLE 27.A USES OF THE COMMA

1. Use a comma to separate two independent clauses joined by one of the *fanboys (for, and, nor, but, or, yet, so)*.
2. Use a comma to separate items in a series, date, or address.
3. Use a comma after an introductory word, phrase, or dependent clause.
4. Use a comma before a tag question, contrast, comment, or description.
5. Use commas around the name of a person being spoken to.
6. Use commas around interrupting words and expressions.
7. Use commas around extra, unnecessary ("scoopable") information.

COMMA REVIEW EXERCISE

Add the missing commas, and identify which one of the seven comma uses applies in the brackets at the *end* of each sentence (see Table 27.A again for the numbered list). Each of the seven sentences illustrates a different rule.

I am writing you this note Melanie to ask you to do me a favor. [ ] Before you leave for work today would you take the chicken out of the freezer? [ ] I plan to get started on the appetizers drinks and desserts as soon as I wake up. [ ] I will be so busy however that I might forget to thaw out the chicken. [ ] It's the first time I've cooked all the food for a party by myself and I want everything to be perfect. [ ] The big oval baking pan the one that is in the cupboard above the refrigerator will be the best place to keep the chicken as it thaws. [ ] Wish me luck seriously! [ ]

28. Quotation Marks and Italics/Underlines

Knowing the code of punctuation is crucial when you include **quotations** of other people's words and ideas or the titles of other people's work.

Use quotation marks around direct quotations (the exact words of a speaker or writer) but not around paraphrases or indirect quotations. For more about "Choosing and Using Quotations," see Section 36.

> In his first speech as president, Franklin D. Roosevelt said the famous words, "The only thing we have to fear is fear itself." (a direct quotation)

> In his first speech as president, Franklin D. Roosevelt reassured the nation and told people not to be afraid. (a paraphrase)

> The officer said, "Please show me your driver's license." (a direct quotation)

> The officer asked to see my driver's license. (an indirect quotation)

If the writer or speaker continues for two or more sentences, use just one set of quotation marks around them.

> She said, "One of your brake lights is out. You need to take care of the problem right away."

If the quotation begins the sentence, the words telling who is speaking (called the signal phrase) are set off with a comma unless the quotation ends with a question mark or an exclamation point. See Section 36 for more about signal phrases.

> "I didn't even know it was broken," I said.

> "Do you have any questions?" she asked.

> "You mean I can go!" I answered excitedly.

> "Yes," she said, "consider this just a warning."

Notice that most of the previous quotations begin with a capital letter. But when a quotation is interrupted by a signal phrase, the second part doesn't begin with a capital letter unless the second part is a new sentence.

> "If you knew how much time I spent on the essay," the student explained, "you would agree that it deserves an A."

> "An artist might work on a painting for years," the teacher replied. "That doesn't mean that the result will be a masterpiece."

Use quotation marks to identify the titles of short works: poems, essays, articles, chapters, songs, short stories, web pages, and TV or radio episodes.

We read Dickinson's poem "I'm Nobody! Who Are You?" in my speech class.

"One Ordinary Day, with Peanuts" is an eerie short story by Shirley Jackson.

My favorite Woodie Guthrie song is "This Land Is Your Land."

Jerry Seinfeld's troubles in "The Puffy Shirt" episode are some of the funniest moments in TV history.

"The Writer's Almanac" is a web page with daily updates about famous writers and other interesting information.

Use italics or underlines to identify the titles of long works: books, newspapers, magazines, plays, albums or CDs, web sites, movies or DVDs, and TV or radio series.

Italicize the appropriate titles whenever you write using a computer.

The Host is a film based on the novel by Stephanie Meyer, author of *Twilight*.

I read about the latest discovery of dinosaur footprints on *CNN.com*.

Many people found the series finale of *Lost* to be a perfect ending.

My mother loves to read the archives on *The Writer's Almanac* web site.

When *handwriting* a paper, use <u>underlines</u>, the low-tech equivalent of italicizing.

<u>The Host</u> is a film based on the novel by Stephanie Meyer, author of <u>Twilight</u>.

I read about the latest discovery of dinosaur footprints on <u>CNN.com</u>.

Many people found the series finale of <u>Lost</u> to be a perfect ending.

My mother loves to read the archives on <u>The Writer's Almanac</u> web site.

EXERCISES

Correctly punctuate quotations and titles in the following sentences by adding quotation marks or italics/underlines.

Exercise 28.1

1. A film crew was setting up in the park by my house, and I saw a sign that said, Extras holding.

2. I found someone who didn't look too busy and asked, Are you looking for extras?

3. Yes, she answered, if you want to be in a crowd scene, just fill out the paperwork and sit over there.

4. I didn't even think twice and told her, Sure, I'd love to be in it.

5. I found out from another extra that we were filming the pilot for a new TV comedy series along the lines of Desperate Housewives.

6. When I asked what I was supposed to do, he said, They'll give you a picket sign, and you'll wave it. That's it.

7. I held my sign that said, No more cuts to education! and waved it when I was told to.

8. While it was happening, I kept telling myself, You're going to be on TV—just try not to look stupid.

9. I heard someone ask, Did anyone else hear that the title of the series is going to be Tangle Square?

10. We all shook our heads; then I added, But that's an interesting title, if it's true.

Exercise 28.2

1. I am reading a book called Don't: A Manual of Mistakes & Improprieties More or Less Prevalent in Conduct and Speech.

2. The book's contents are divided into chapters with titles such as At Table, In Public, and In General.

3. In the section about table don'ts, the book offers the following warning: Don't bend over your plate, or drop your head to get each mouthful.

4. The table advice continues by adding, Don't bite your bread. Break it off.

5. This book offers particularly comforting advice about conducting oneself in public.

6. For instance, it states, Don't brush against people, or elbow people, or in any way show disregard for others.

7. When meeting others on the street, the book advises, Don't be in a haste to introduce. Be sure that it is mutually desired before presenting one person to another.

8. In the section titled In General, there are more tips about how to get along in society, such as Don't underrate everything that others do, and overstate your own doings.

9. The Don't book has this to say about books, whether borrowed or owned: Read them, but treat them as friends that must not be abused.

10. And one can never take the following warning too much to heart: Don't make yourself in any particular way a nuisance to your neighbors or your family.

Exercise 28.3

1. Emilie Buchwald once noted, Children are made readers on the laps of their parents.

2. Have you read Mark Twain's book The Adventures of Tom Sawyer?

3. I took a deep breath when my counselor asked, How many math classes have you had?

4. Let's start that again! shouted the dance teacher.

5. Last night we watched the Beatles' movie Help! on DVD.

6. Books, wrote Jonathan Swift, are the children of the brain.

7. Voltaire stated in A Philosophical Dictionary that Tears are the silent language of grief.

8. Why do dentists ask questions like How are you? as soon as they start working on your teeth?

9. Did you say, I'm sleepy or I'm beeping?

10. My favorite essay that we have read this semester has to be The Pie by Gary Soto.

Exercise 28.4

1. Women's Wit and Wisdom is the title of a book I found in the library.

2. The book includes many great insights that were written or spoken by women throughout history.

3. England's Queen Elizabeth I noted in the sixteenth century that A clear and innocent conscience fears nothing.

4. Nothing is so good as it seems beforehand, observed George Eliot, a female author whose real name was Mary Ann Evans.

5. Some of the women's quotations are funny; Alice Roosevelt Longworth, for instance, said, If you don't have anything good to say about anyone, come and sit by me.

6. If life is a bowl of cherries, asked Erma Bombeck, what am I doing in the pits?

7. Some of the quotations are serious, such as Gloria Steinem's statement, The future depends on what each of us does every day.

8. Maya Lin, the woman who designed Washington D.C.'s Vietnam Veterans Memorial, reminded us that, as she put it, War is not just a victory or a loss. . . . People die.

9. Emily Dickinson had this to say about truth: Truth is such a rare thing, it is delightful to tell it.

10. Finally, columnist Ann Landers advised one of her readers that The naked truth is always better than the best-dressed lie.

Exercise 28.5

1. In Booker T. Washington's autobiography Up from Slavery, he describes his early dream of going to school.

2. I had no schooling whatever while I was a slave, he explains.

3. He continues, I remember on several occasions I went as far as the schoolhouse door with one of my young mistresses to carry her books.

4. Washington then describes what he saw from the doorway: several dozen boys and girls engaged in study.

5. The picture, he adds, made a deep impression upon me.

6. Washington cherished this glimpse of boys and girls engaged in study.

7. It contrasted directly with his own situation: My life had its beginning in the midst of the most miserable, desolate, and discouraging surroundings.

8. I was born, he says, in a typical log cabin, about fourteen by sixteen feet square.

9. He explains, In this cabin I lived with my mother and a brother and sister till after the Civil War, when we were all declared free.

10. As a slave at the door of his young mistress's schoolhouse, Booker T. Washington remembers, I had the feeling that to get into a schoolhouse and study in this way would be about the same as getting into paradise.

Source: Great Americans in Their Own Words (Mallard Press, 1990)

Exercise 28.6 Paragraph Practice

Correctly punctuate quotations and titles in the following paragraph by adding quotation marks or underlining (*italics*).

We were allowed to choose a book to review in our journals last week. The teacher specified that it should be a short nonfiction book about something of interest to us. I found a great book to review. It's called Tattoo: Secrets of a Strange Art. Albert Parry breaks the contents down into chapters about tattoo legends, techniques, and purposes. A few of the chapter titles are The Art and Its Masters, The Circus, Identification, and Removal. The book also includes illustrations and photographs of tattoo designs and tattooed people and animals throughout history, including Miss Stella: The Tattooed Lady, The Famous Tattooed Cow, and Georgius Constantine. Parry describes Constantine's tattoos in the following way: the most complete, elaborate, and artistic tattooing ever witnessed in America or Europe. Parry continues, There was almost no part of his body, not a quarter-inch of the skin, free from designs. Needless to say, since I love tattoos, I loved Parry's book about them.

Source: Tattoo: Secrets of a Strange Art (Dover, 2006)

Exercise 28.7 Sentence Writing

Write ten sentences that list and discuss your favorite films, books, TV shows, characters' expressions, and so on. Be sure to punctuate quotations and titles correctly. Refer to the explanations and examples whenever necessary.

29. Capital Letters

Capital letters are an essential part of the code of punctuation. Without capitals, we couldn't start a sentence or distinguish between the generic name of a plant (fern) and the specific name of friend (Fern).

Capitalize the first word of every sentence.

> Peaches and nectarines taste best when they are cold.
>
> I think every piece of fruit is work of art.

Capitalize the first word of a sentence-length quotation.

> The college president asked, "What can we do for our students today?"
>
> "The lab's tools are a little dangerous," Zoe said, "but I am always careful." (The *but* is not capitalized because it does not begin a new sentence.)
>
> "I love my art classes," she added; "Maybe I'll change my major." (*Maybe* is capitalized because it begins a new sentence within the quoted material.)

Capitalize the first, last, and main words in a title. Don't capitalize prepositions (*in, of, at, with, about . . .*), fanboys (*for, and, nor, but, or, yet, so*), or articles (*a, an, or the*). See Section 40 for more about titles.

> I found a copy of Darwin's book *The Origin of Species* at a yard sale.
>
> Our class read the essay "How to Write a Rotten Poem with Almost No Effort."
>
> *Shakespeare in Love* is a tribute to the life and work of William Shakespeare.

Capitalize names of specific people, places, languages, and nationalities.

English	Shah Rukh Khan	Cesar Chavez
Inuit	Danish	Hindi
Ryan White	Croatia	Shanghai

Capitalize names of months, days of the week, and special days, but not the seasons.

March	the Fourth of July	spring
Monday	Valentine's Day	summer
Earth Day	Labor Day	fall

Capitalize a title of relationship if it takes the place of the person's name. If *my* (or *your, her, his, our, their*) is in front of the word, no capital is used.

I asked Mom to call you.	*but*	I asked my mom to call you.
We visited Aunt Sophie.	*but*	We visited our aunt.
They spoke with Grandpa.	*but*	They spoke with their grandpa.

Capitalize names of particular people or things, but not general terms.

I admire Professor Washborne.	*but*	I admire my professor.
We saw the famous Danube River.	*but*	We saw the famous river.
Are you from the South?	*but*	Is your house south of the mountains?
I will take Philosophy 4 and English 100.	*but*	I will take philosophy and English.
She graduated from Sutter High School.	*but*	She graduated from high school.
They live at 119 Forest St.	*but*	They live on a beautiful street.
We enjoyed the Long Island Aquarium.	*but*	We enjoyed the aquarium.

E X E R C I S E S

Add all of the necessary capital letters to the sentences that follow.

Exercise 29.1

1. i have always wanted to learn another language besides english.
2. recently, i have been watching a lot of films from india.
3. some people call them "bollywood movies."
4. whatever they are called, i love to watch them.
5. one part of these movies that i love is their main language: hindi.
6. i have to use english subtitles to understand the dialogue most of the time.
7. but sometimes i can catch what's happening without the subtitles.

8. because of my intense interest in hindi-language films, i plan to take a hindi class.

9. i have already bought a book that explains the devanagari writing system.

10. now i will enroll in a class and learn hindi as a second language.

Exercise 29.2

1. when people think of jazz, they think of *down beat* magazine.

2. *down beat*'s motto may be "jazz, blues & beyond," but some people think that the magazine has gone too far "beyond" by including two guitarists in the *down beat* hall of fame.

3. the two musicians in question are jimi hendrix and frank zappa.

4. jimi hendrix was inducted into the hall of fame in 1970.

5. *down beat* added frank zappa to the list in 1994.

6. since then, readers and editors have been debating whether hendrix and zappa belong in the same group as duke ellington, john coltrane, and miles davis.

7. those who play jazz guitar have some of the strongest opinions on the subject.

8. russell malone, mark elf, and john abercrombie all agree that hendrix and zappa were great guitarists but not jazz guitarists.

9. others like steve tibbetts and bill frisell don't have any problem putting hendrix on the list, but tibbetts isn't so sure about including zappa.

10. it will be interesting to see who *down beat*'s future inductees will be.

Source: Down Beat, July 1999

Exercise 29.3

1. many consider *the diary of anne frank* to be one of the most important books of the twentieth century.

2. anne frank wrote her famous diary during the nazi occupation of holland in world war ii.

3. the building in amsterdam where the frank family and several others hid during the two years before their capture is now a museum and has been recently renovated.

4. visitors to the anne frank house can stand before her desk and see pictures of movie stars like greta garbo on her wall.

5. they can climb the stairs hidden behind a bookcase that led to the annex where anne lived with her mother, edith; her father, otto; and her sister, margot.

6. one of the others hiding with the franks was peter van pels, who was roughly the same age as anne.

7. anne writes of her relationship with peter in her diary.

8. visitors to the museum can enter the room where peter gave anne her first kiss just a few months before the nazis discovered their hiding place in 1944.

9. anne's family and peter's were both sent to concentration camps in germany.

10. only anne's father lived to see the anne frank house open as a museum for the first time on may 3, 1960.

Source: Smithsonian, October 2001

Exercise 29.4

1. i recently saw the movie *v for vendetta,* and i wanted to learn more about it.

2. i found out that it's based on an extensive series of comic books.

3. they were written by alan moore and illustrated by david lloyd.

4. the original episodes of *v for vendetta* were published in black and white within a british comic series called *warrior.*

5. once the series caught on in the united states, dc comics began to publish it.

6. at that time, the creators added color to the drawings.

7. the letter v in the title *v for vendetta* stands for the main character, a mysterious costumed figure who calls himself v.

8. however, many other connections between the letter v and the roman numeral 5, which is written as a v, come up throughout the story.

9. v wears a mask that people in the united kingdom refer to as a guy fawkes mask.

10. guy fawkes was an english historical figure famous for his involvement in the gunpowder plot, which failed on the fifth of november in 1605.

Exercise 29.5

1. when my art teacher asked the class to do research on frida kahlo, i knew that the name sounded familiar.

2. then i remembered that the actress salma hayek starred in the movie *frida,* which was about this mexican-born artist's life.

3. frida kahlo's paintings are all very colorful and seem extremely personal.

4. she painted mostly self-portraits, and each one makes a unique statement.

5. one of these portraits is called *my grandparents, my parents, and i.*

6. kahlo gave another one the title *the two fridas.*

7. but my favorite of kahlo's works is *self-portrait on the borderline between mexico and the united states.*

8. in an article i read in *smithsonian* magazine, kahlo's mother explains that after frida was severely injured in a bus accident, she started painting.

9. kahlo's mother set up a mirror near her daughter's bed so that frida could use herself as a model.

10. in the *smithsonian* article from the november 2002 issue, kahlo is quoted as saying, "i never painted dreams. i painted my own reality."

Exercise 29.6 Paragraph Practice

We have removed capital letters in these paragraphs from the book *50 Years in the Mouse House: The Lost Memoir of One of Disney's Nine Old Men,* by Eric Larson. Add the capital letters necessary to identify the specific people, places, titles (in italics), organizations, and technologies in the excerpt. No other changes are necessary.

as walt and i walked away from the story meeting that day, he seemed relieved that at last the *sleeping beauty* picture was going to get underway. "i want a moving illustration," he said. i felt his sincerity. to me his words summed it all up: to walt nothing was impossible.

"we're in no hurry," walt would say. "we'll take the time the picture needs."

i looked around me and counted the men i would be privileged to work with . . . men who could make the *beauty* dream come true, for it was planned from the beginning that *sleeping beauty* would be a sharp departure from any picture we had made: in color, styling, rendering, and in character design and development. And it was to be in dramatic cinemascope proportions with music from tchaichovksy's *sleeping beauty ballet* recorded by the berlin symphony orchestra conducted by george bruns.

Exercise 29.7 Sentence Writing

Write ten sentences about an animated movie that you have seen or about animation as a style of filmmaking. Capitalize any specific names, films (in italics), characters, and locations that you use in your sentences.

Punctuation Progress Test

To the following sentences, add necessary punctuation: periods, question marks, exclamation points, semicolons, colons, dashes, commas, quotation marks, italics/ underlines, and capital letters. Sentences may require several different pieces of punctuation or capital letters. Note that apostrophes have already been added to contractions and possessives. Check your answers carefully, but first try your best.

1. we couldn't leave san antonio texas without visiting its most famous site the alamo

2. my teacher asked have you seen the earliest episodes of the simpsons

3. the taylors remodeled their garage now their son uses it as an apartment

4. when leslie my older sister got a speeding ticket she went to traffic school

5. we have refunded your money ms jones and have sent you a confirmation

6. the nutrition class that i need is offered in two ways online or in person

7. the united parcel service better known as ups is hiring on campus today

8. even though i am enjoying my latin class i wish i had taken chinese instead

9. you always forget the month of my birthday you think it's in july

10. pink normally a calming color can have the opposite effect when it's neon

11. stopping by woods on a snowy evening is a famous poem by robert frost

12. buying a new car online takes time patience and luck

13. my friend read the play the taming of the shrew in her gender studies class

14. that textbook the history of textiles is expensive isn't it

15. the foreign film club needs people to pass out flyers let's volunteer

Punctuation Practice

Add the necessary punctuation marks to the following paragraph: commas, semicolons, colons, dashes, quotation marks, periods, question marks, and exclamation points. Note that we have added capital letters to the starts of sentences and to phrasing that requires quotation marks.

Most people know what buyer's remorse means Buyer's remorse is the feeling of regret that immediately follows a purchase it affects many wary shoppers especially when they order online When these shoppers purchase items in an actual store they are fine They know that if they don't like something the store will take it right back for a refund However once they hit the Place order button on their computer or phone they immediately begin to doubt themselves The difference seems to involve the amount of time that it takes for an online order to arrive That extra time gives shoppers a chance to ask themselves Is this item really worth the shipping costs and trouble it will take to return it To cure online buyers' remorse many companies who sell primarily online offer free deliveries and returns and they have shortened the transit time to offer same-day or even one-hour deliveries on many items

Writing

WHAT IS THE LEAST YOU SHOULD KNOW ABOUT WRITING?

"Unlike medicine or the other sciences," William Zinsser points out, "writing has no new discoveries to spring on us. We're in no danger of reading in our morning newspaper that a breakthrough has been made in how to write [clearly]. . . . We may be given new technologies . . . to ease the burdens of composition, but on the whole we know what we need to know."

One thing is certain: people learn to write by *writing*—not by reading long discussions about writing. Therefore, the explanatory sections in Part Four are as brief as they can be, and they include samples by both professional and student writers.

Understanding the basic structures and learning the essential skills covered in these sections will help you become a better writer.

Writing as Structure

Aside from the basics of word use, sentence structure, and punctuation, what else do you need to understand to write better? Just as sentences are built according to accepted patterns, so are the larger "structures" in writing—paragraphs and essays, for example.

Think of writing as a system of structures, beginning small with words that connect to form phrases, clauses, and sentences. Then sentences connect to form paragraphs and essays. Each level has its own set of "blueprints." To communicate clearly in writing, words must be chosen and spelled correctly. Sentences must have a subject, a verb, and a complete thought. Paragraphs must be indented and should contain a main idea supported with sufficient detail. Essays should explore a valuable topic in several coherent paragraphs, usually including an introduction, a body, and a conclusion.

Not everyone approaches writing as a structure, however. It is possible to write better without thinking about structure at all. A good place to start might be to write what you care about and to care about what you write. You can make an amazing amount of progress by simply being *genuine*, being who you are naturally. No one has to tell you to be yourself when you speak, but you might need encouragement to be yourself in your writing.

First-Person and Third-Person Approaches

You may have identified—and your professors may have pointed out—two main approaches to writing: the first-person approach (using *I, me, we, us*) and the third-person approach (using *one, he, she, it, they, them*). Note that the second-person pronoun—*you*—serves a special purpose, not commonly required in college papers. Writers often use *you* to guide the reader through a process or to teach the reader how to do something, just as we use *you* in this book to teach "the least you should know about English." Unless you are writing a "how-to" paper of some kind, it's best to avoid using *you*. Let's focus, then, on first person vs. third person.

What are the benefits of the first-person approach? First-person pronouns allow you to express yourself directly ("I agree with Isaac Asimov.") and to connect with readers by including them in your observations. Here is an example from Browning's essay about the concept of "home" in Section 31: "Nesting. Why do we do it, why does it matter? Why do we care so much?" The first-person approach establishes a direct connection between the writer, the information, and the reader.

How does the third-person approach compare? The third-person point of view presents information about people and ideas more objectively. For example, you'll find this sentence in Vanderbilt's excerpt about traffic in Section 32: "So much time is spent in cars in the United States, studies show, that drivers (particularly men) have higher rates of skin cancer on their left sides. . . ." The third-person approach creates a comfortable distance between the writer, the information, and the reader.

Most writers don't consciously restrict themselves to one approach, but in some cases they do. As an example, Geoff Colvin adheres to the third-person approach in his excerpt about Mozart in Section 36. However, it is possible to use more than one approach when necessary. Professional writers often successfully blend first and third person, as Christia Spears Brown does in her excerpt about parenting babies and gender stereotypes in Exercise 10.6: "*We* don't know much about [babies] as individuals, but *we* do know *their* gender." Sometimes, writers even combine first, second, *and* third person, as James Bowen does in his memoir from Exercise 15.6: "*They* say cats choose *you*, not the other way around. *I* realized that Bob had chosen me . . . ." Being aware of your options will help you grow as a writer.

Learning to write well is important, and confidence is the key. The Writing sections will help you build confidence, whether you are expressing your own ideas or presenting and responding to the ideas of others. Like the Sentence Structure sections, the Writing sections are best taken in order. However, each one discusses an aspect of writing that you can review on its own at any time.

Basic Structures

30. THE PARAGRAPH

A **paragraph** is unlike any other structure in English. It has its own visual profile: the first line is indented about five spaces, and sentences continue to fill the space between both margins until the paragraph ends (which may be in the middle of the line):

_____

_____

_____

_____

_____

_____.

As a beginning writer, you may forget to indent your paragraphs, or you may break off in the middle of a line within a paragraph, especially when writing in class. You must remember to indent whenever you begin a new paragraph and fill the space between the margins until it ends. (Note: In business writing, paragraphs are not indented but double-spaced in between.)

Defining a Paragraph

A **paragraph** usually develops one idea, often phrased as a topic sentence from which all the other sentences in the paragraph radiate. The topic sentence does not need to begin the paragraph, but it most often does, and the other sentences support it with specific details. (For more on topic sentences and organizing paragraphs, see Section 34.) Paragraphs usually contain several sentences, though no set number is required. A paragraph can stand alone, but more commonly paragraphs are part of a larger composition, an essay. There are different kinds of paragraphs, based on the jobs they do.

Types of Paragraphs

SAMPLE PARAGRAPHS IN AN ESSAY

Introductory paragraphs begin essays. They provide background information about the topic and usually include the thesis statement or main idea of the essay. (See Section 34 for information on how to write a thesis statement.) Here is the introductory paragraph of a brief student essay about the impact of movies in our lives:

> We all love a good movie, whether it is action, drama, romance, or comedy, we just can't get enough of it. Movies are as important in our lives as food, it seems. And like food, we usually take them for granted. Why is that? The way I see it, movies can be like fast food or full, satisfying meals. Either way, we enjoy them.

In this opening paragraph, the student introduces the main idea that "Movies are as important in our lives as food" but that "we take them for granted" and sets up a two-part organization for the essay to show how some movies are "like fast food" and others "full, satisfying meals."

Body paragraphs are those in the middle of essays. Each body paragraph contains a topic sentence and presents detailed information about one idea or aspect that relates directly to the essay's thesis. (See Section 34 for more information on organizing body paragraphs.) Here are the body paragraphs of the same essay:

> In the same way that we eat fast food on the run, a good movie can take us on a journey. We don't question it; we just go, and we eat it with gusto. These movies focus on action and fantasy because they give us that edge in life. They take us to a dream or even nightmare place that we don't want to wake up from. They put us directly into the superhero's or alien hunter's shoes. In other words, they give us ordinary people that kick in life that we might not have. Like french fries, these films keep us wanting more until, eventually, we get sick of them.
>
> When we are not looking for mindless adventure, we set our eyes to something more serious and satisfying—movies that fortify us like a good meal. Documentaries and crime movies come to mind. We want these movies to inform, challenge, or expand our thoughts. Documentaries can bring us up to date on a world problem, our favorite rock band, or an important person that we might not know about. Crime stories and mysteries have us questioning every part of a complex puzzle, using logic and critical thinking. At the end of these films of substance, we earn the satisfaction of having learned or solved something new.

Notice that each body paragraph develops one of the two types of movies brought up in the thesis statement.

Concluding paragraphs are the final paragraphs in essays. They bring the discussion to a close and share the writer's final thoughts on the subject. Here is the conclusion of the sample essay:

> Most people enjoy a little bit of everything when it comes to movies. But I think the majority of us prefer the journey of fast-food films, full of action and fantasy. Whether we're slouching on the couch or sitting upright in front of a huge movie screen, these movies make us want to be there, saving the earth and stopping the bad guys. These films take us with them, and we go, no questions asked.

In this concluding paragraph, the student shares his final thoughts about the impact of movies, which ones seem to please us the most, and why.

SAMPLE OF A SINGLE-PARAGRAPH ASSIGNMENT

Single-paragraph writing assignments may be given in class or as homework. They test your understanding of the unique structure of a paragraph. They often ask you to react to a reading or provide details about a limited topic. Here is a sample paragraph-length reaction following the class's reading of an essay called "What Is Intelligence, Anyway?" by Isaac Asimov. In his essay, Asimov explains that there are other kinds of intelligence besides just knowledge of theories and facts. This student shares Asimov's ideas about intelligence and uses personal experiences to support her reaction:

> I agree with Isaac Asimov. Intelligence doesn't only belong to Nobel Prize winners. I define "intelligence" as being able to value that special skill a person has been born with. Not everyone is a math genius or a brain surgeon. For example, ask a brain surgeon to rotate the engine in a car. It isn't going to happen. To be able to take a certain skill that someone has inherited and push it to its farthest limits I would call "intelligence." Isaac Asimov's definition is similar to mine. He believes that academic questions are only correctly answered by academicians. He gives the example of a farmer. Questions on a farming test would only be correctly answered by a farmer. Not everyone has the same talent; we are all different. When I attend my math classes, I must always pay attention. If I don't, I end up struggling with what I missed. On the other hand, when I'm in my music classes, I really don't have to work hard because reading music, playing the piano, and singing all come easily to me. I see other students struggling with music the way I do with math. This is just another example of how skills and talents differ. Some people are athletic; others are brainy. Some people can sing; others can cook. It really doesn't matter what the skill might be. If it's a talent, to me that's a form of intelligence.

These shorter writing assignments help students practice presenting information within the limited structure of a paragraph. If this had been an essay-length reaction, the writer would have included more details about her own and other people's types of intelligence. And she may have wanted to quote from Asimov's essay and discuss his most important points at length.

31. THE ESSAY

Like the paragraph, an **essay** has its own profile, usually including a title and several paragraphs.

Title

_____

_____

_____

_____

_____.

_____

_____

_____

_____

_____.

_____

_____

_____

_____

_____.

_____

_____

_____

_____

_____.

_____

_____

_____.

While the paragraph is the single building block of text used in almost all forms of writing (essays, magazine articles, letters, novels, newspaper stories, e-mails, and so on), an essay is a larger, more complex structure.

The Five-Paragraph Essay and Beyond

The student essay analyzed in Section 30 illustrates the different kinds of paragraphs within essays. Many people like to include five paragraphs in an essay: an introductory paragraph, three body paragraphs, and a concluding paragraph. However, an essay can include any number of paragraphs. Three is a comfortable number of body paragraphs to start with—it is not two, which makes an essay seem like a comparison even when it isn't; and it is not four, which may be too many subtopics for the beginning writer to organize clearly.

An essay should be long enough to explore and support its topic without leaving unanswered questions in the reader's mind. As you become more comfortable with the flow of your ideas and gain confidence in your ability to express yourself, you can write longer essays. As with many skills, learning about writing begins with basic structures that expand and combine to include all possibilities.

Defining an Essay

There is no such thing as a typical essay. Essays may be serious or humorous, but the best of them present thought-provoking information or opinions. Try looking up the noun *essay* in a dictionary right now. Some words used to define an essay might need to be explained themselves:

An essay is *prose* (meaning it is written in the ordinary language of sentences and paragraphs).

An essay is *nonfiction* (meaning it deals with real people, factual information, actual opinions and events).

An essay is a *composition* (meaning it is created in parts that make up the whole, several paragraphs that explore a single idea, issue, or topic).

An essay is *personal* (meaning it shares the writer's unique perspective, even if only in the choice of topic, method of analysis, and details).

An essay is *analytical* and *instructive* (meaning it examines the workings of a subject and shares the results with the reader).

An essay may be *argumentative* (meaning it tries to convince the reader to accept an opinion or take action).

Notice that many aspects of a written essay involve creating, sharing, and exploring. The word *essay,* used as a *verb,* comes from a French word that means "to try or attempt." Think of each new essay as an opportunity to express yourself and to experiment with your ideas.

A Sample Professional Essay

For an example of a brief piece of writing that fits the above definition, read the following essay, in which professional writer Dominique Browning explains how hard it is to define the word *home*.

WANDERING HOME

Every morning for weeks this spring I was awakened at five by the gentle, persistent cooing of a dove. Such a soft, lovely song, yet each day it was able to penetrate my dreams and lure me from my bed onto the balcony. I would search through the treetops for a glimpse of her until the damp chill sent me back indoors, and then finally one day I spotted her. She had built a nest on the trellis right over my door, wedged in amid a looping tangle of wisteria. I didn't dare go out onto the balcony again, for fear of disturbing her. Several days later the cooing stopped, and I suppose she became serious about laying and hatching her eggs, or why else would she sit so still and silent in her new home?

Nesting. Why do we do it, why does it matter? Why do we care so much? This has been on my mind lately, because I recently met a real wanderer, someone who is defiantly, dogmatically, devotedly nomadic. He isn't selfishly drifting; homeless by choice, he has spent the past 20 years living all over the world, doing good. Home for him is a provisional thing. I was so struck by the marked contrast to the way my friends and I have hunkered down, sent out roots, gathered treasure, gotten anchored. Maybe got stuck, who knows? I have always thought of making a home as one of those basic desires, but why should it be?

It is too easy to say home is where the heart is, where your loved ones sleep. Your loved ones can go with you, wherever you roam, and your loved ones can just as well be scattered to all corners of the world. We grow up (most of us) and ruthlessly leave behind the first homes of our childhood. And we often leave with the thought that the home we make for ourselves will be markedly different from the one made by our parents.

Some of us end up finding home in the town where we were raised. Some of us have ancestral homes, where generations of the family have been raised—places dear enough to draw everyone back. Some of us simply choose a place, or, if we are lucky, we feel the place chooses us. For some of us, a home is as large as a country—"I'm at home in France," one friend will say, or "I felt like I had come home when I got to Ireland"—and for others, a home is as small as the four walls of a room. Some of us move restlessly from house to house; others are restless within the house, rearranging the furniture, circling toward some approximation of beauty, serenity. And then some of us are so settled that our bodies creak to leave the sofa.

Maybe home is one of those subjects over which much of the world is divided: those who care about it passionately and those who don't give it a second thought. Maybe some of us are the fixed points of the compass: we're home, so others can twirl in circles around the globe. Some of us need the foundation of a home because our thoughts, dreams, emotions are constantly wheeling, wandering. And for some of us, there is the great adventure of making a home—you know, that thing about the world in a grain of sand or, dare I say, a smear of paint, a dab of plaster, the twinkle of a chandelier, the gleam of that old pearwood commode. The adamant wanderer finally confessed to having a warehouse full of stuff collected over the years, so even a nomad isn't immune to fantasies of home, however delayed the gratification of making one might turn out to be.

As for the dove: after a few quiet weeks, I noticed on the ground beneath her nest what I first took to be a bright curl of Styrofoam and of course turned out to be the fragment of an eggshell. One down. One untimely flight, one tiny lost soul. But still the dove sits, home for the time being.

Now that you have learned more about the basic structures of the paragraph and the essay, you are ready to practice the skills necessary to write them.

Writing Skills

32. WRITING IN YOUR OWN VOICE

All writing speaks on paper. And the person listening is the reader. Some beginning writers forget that writing and reading are two-way methods of communication, just like spoken conversations between two people. When you write, your reader hears you; when you read, you also listen.

When speaking, you express a personality in your choice of phrases, your movements, and your tone of voice. Family and friends probably recognize your voice mail messages without your having to identify yourself. Would they also be able to recognize your writing? They would if you extended your **voice** into your writing.

Writing should not sound like talking, necessarily, but it should have a personality that comes from the way you decide to approach a topic, to develop it with details, to say it *your* way.

The beginning of this book discusses the difference between spoken English, which follows the looser patterns of speaking, and Standard Written English, which follows accepted patterns of writing. Don't think that the only way to add voice to your writing is to use the patterns of spoken English. Remember that Standard Written English does not have to be dull or sound academic. Look at this example of Standard Written English that has a distinct voice, part of the book *Traffic: Why We Drive the Way We Do (and What It Says about Us)* by Tom Vanderbilt:

Traffic has even shaped the food we eat. "One-handed convenience" is the mantra, with forkless foods like Taco Bell's hexagonal Crunchwrap Supreme, designed "to handle well in the car." I spent an afternoon in Los Angeles with an advertising executive who had, at the behest of that same restaurant chain, conducted a test, in actual traffic, of which foods were easiest to eat while driving. The main barometer of success or failure was the number of napkins used. But if food does spill, one can simply reach for Tide to Go, a penlike device for "portable stain removal," which can be purchased at one of the more than twelve hundred (and growing) CVS drugstores that feature a drive-through window. . . . Car commuting is so entrenched in daily life that National Public Radio refers to its most popular segments as "driveway moments," meaning that listeners are so riveted to a story they cannot leave their cars. . . . So much time is spent in cars in the United States, studies show, that drivers (particularly men) have higher rates of skin cancer on their left sides—look for the opposite effect in countries where people drive on the left.

Vanderbilt's examination of traffic's effect on us illustrates Standard Written English at its liveliest—from its sentence structures to its precise use of words. But more importantly, Vanderbilt's clear voice speaks to us and involves us in his fascination with traffic. You can involve your reader, too, by writing in your own voice. Here is an example of a student response to a brief assignment that asked her to describe a person who had recently made an impression on her.

Sitting at the kids' play area of my local mall one afternoon last week, I glanced over at another parent paying closer attention to his Blackberry than to his son. Enclosed in an oval-shaped ring with cushioned benches lining the edges, shoppers' kids ran around and played as their parents caught their breaths. In the middle of the play area lay an array of toys: boats, turtles, and small mounds of plastic for kids to crawl on and cylinders for them to crawl through. The workaholic looked up occasionally, making sure his son was still there. His thick brimmed glasses sat loosely on the bridge of his nose. His straight, jet-black hair was about a month overdue for a cut. In his late thirties, he was obviously concentrating more on his career and business than on his family in its youth. As I watched my own daughter run and play, I looked over to see the workaholic diligently typing away. I wasn't sure if he was checking e-mail, responding to e-mail, or updating his calendar, but his small brown eyes squinted, and this gave a pained look to his face; half deep in thought, the other half confused and stressed. Alternately leaning forward and slouching back, he caused his khaki pants to wrinkle and crease. His plaid shirt, unevenly tucked in, was held in place by an old and fading brown belt. His professional successes hadn't translated into any sense of style. Even on what might have been a rare day off, he couldn't escape the electronic leash that dominated his life. While his son grew up right in front of his eyes, his vision seemed way out of focus.

Notice that both professional and student writers can engage readers by telling stories (narration) and painting pictures with words (description). Narration and description require practice, but once you master them, you will strengthen and clarify your voice and increase interest in your writing.

Narration

Narrative writing tells a story or stories from the writer's personal experience. Since most of us like to tell stories, it is a good place to begin writing in your own voice. Effective narration allows readers to experience events with the writer. Since we all see the world differently and feel unique emotions, the purpose of narration is to take readers with us through our experiences. As a result, the writer gains a better understanding of the events, and readers get to live other lives momentarily.

A Sample Student Essay

Listen to the *voice* of a recently blind student writer who uses narration and description to present his new relationship with the cane that helps him maintain his independence:

Streetscaper

Being blind, one of the tools that I use to navigate in public is my identification cane. Every cane looks the same, but each one is unique to the blind. This cane is an extension of my finger; whatever I touch resonates to my brain the information it receives. My cane is fifty-eight inches long, which is just up to my chin. The longer length is good for landscaping the city. Most of the cane is white with a red tip. The white reflects light at pedestrians like a light saber. As I swipe it back and forth at night, the flashes of light pierce through the pedestrian field of vision.

My cane signals to all around that I am a master Jedi fighting the dark forces. In Egyptian, Jedi means magician. My cane is like a wand. Anything I point it at disappears. I can make a crowd of people part like the Red Sea. With a wave of my cane, I evoke the benevolence in people. Like a street evangelist, I magically transform the brute barbarians of the street into good Samaritans who offer help when I need it. Like the Salvation Army volunteer who chimes a bell at passersby, I swipe the ceramic tip of my cane on the pavement to

call the forces of good. It is vital that I have light
beings around when I need them, especially when there
are dark forces that try to hold me back from navigating
through streets.

   The darkness can hypnotize me into not being mobile,
like a snake charmer does to a cobra. My cane can break
this darkness if I believe in the magic it possesses. At
one point in my life, I was afraid of my cane because of
the responsibility that came with it. Now I cannot be
without it.

Description

Descriptive writing paints pictures with words that appeal to the reader's five senses—sight, sound, touch, taste, and smell. The writer of the description often uses comparisons (figures of speech) to help readers picture one thing by imagining something else. For example, in Section 31, Browning compares some people to "the fixed points of the compass," and Vanderbilt describes the stain-remover Tide to Go as a "penlike device" in his excerpt about traffic to help the reader *picture* the object.

   Here is an example of a descriptive paragraph in which a student describes her car door's remote control device by comparing it to a robot:

MY ROBOT

   My car door's remote control looks like a small robot's head. The front of it resembles a human face to me. It has two droopy eyes, a nose, and a mouth—but the eyes cannot see, the nose cannot smell, and the mouth cannot open because of a strip of shiny old tape that covers my robot's face like an uncomfortable mask and secures it to a flat piece of leather on my key chain. The chain holds my little robot like a prisoner, but it still has a mind of its own. Like a small child, it can be capricious. Sometimes it does what I want it to do, but other times it does what it wants to do. Its brain shows that it's working by blinking a red light on its forehead. And even though my little robot looks old and tired, it usually works when I need it the most.

You may have noticed that many of the examples in this section use both narration and description. In fact, most effective writing—even a good résumé or biology lab report—calls for clear storytelling and vivid word pictures to engage the reader.

Writing Exercises

The following two exercises will help you develop your voice as a writer. For now, don't worry about topic sentences or thesis statements or any of the skills we'll teach you in the sections to come. Narration and description have their own logical structures. A narrated experience is a story with a beginning, a middle, and an end. And we describe things from top to bottom, side to side, and so on. You will find more Writing Exercises throughout this section.

Writing Exercise 1
NARRATE AN EXPERIENCE TO ILLUSTRATE A FAMOUS SAYING

The following is a list of well-known expressions. No doubt you have had an experience that proves at least one of these to be true. To *illustrate* means to prove with an example. Write a short essay that narrates a story from your own life to illustrate one of these sayings. See if you can tell which of the sayings "Wandering Home" in Section 31 and "Streetscaper" in this Section (32) illustrate. You might want to identify the expression you have chosen in your introductory paragraph. Then use vivid details to bring the beginning, middle, and end of the story to life. Finish with a brief concluding paragraph to share your final thoughts on the experience.

> Experience is the best teacher.
>
> When life gives you lemons, make lemonade.
>
> No two people are alike.
>
> If at first you don't succeed, try, try again.
>
> Money can't buy happiness.

Writing Exercise 2
DESCRIBE A PICTURE WORTH 250 WORDS

Describe a picture that you respond to in a powerful way—one that you are drawn to, one that you *like*. It could be an advertisement, a well-known historical image, a famous drawing or painting, or a moment from a popular movie. Print a copy of the picture and observe it carefully. Your goal is to help the reader *visualize* the picture and convey the impression it makes. Try to use details and comparisons that appeal to the reader's senses in some way. Look back at the examples for inspiration. Be sure to attach the copy of your picture to your description so that the reader can see exactly what you're describing.

33. Finding a Topic

You will most often be given a **topic** or subject to write about; however, when the assignment asks you to choose your own topic without any further assistance, try to go immediately to your interests.

Look to Your Interests

If the topic of your paper is something you know about and—more important— something you *care* about, then the whole process of writing will be smoother and more enjoyable for you. If you collect coins, if you can draw, or even if you just enjoy going to the movies, bring that knowledge and enthusiasm into your papers.

Take a moment to think about and jot down a few of your interests now (no matter how unrelated to school they may seem), and then save the list for use later when deciding what to write about. One student's list of interests might look like this:

buying and selling on eBay

playing poker on weekends

skiing in the mountains in winter

shopping at flea markets

Another student's list might be very different:

playing the piano

going to concerts

watching "Bollywood" movies

drawing pictures of my friends

Still another student might list the following interests:

bowling in a league

participating in my book club

traveling in the summer

buying lottery tickets

These students have listed several worthy topics for papers. And because they are personal interests, the students have the details needed to support them. With a general topic to start with, you can use several ways to gather the details you will need to support it in a paragraph or an essay.

Focused Free Writing (or Brainstorming)

Free writing is a good way to begin. When you are assigned a paper, try writing for ten minutes, putting down all your thoughts on one subject—"traveling in the summer," for example. Don't stop to think about organization, sentence structures, capitalization, or spelling—just let details flow onto the page. Free writing will help you see what material you have and will help you figure out what aspects of the subject to write about.

Here is an example:

I like to draw pictures of my friends but sometimes they don't like it when I draw them. The nose is to big they think or the hair isn't just right. Once in awhile I get it perfect, but not that often. I like to style my drawings like cartoons kind of. Its almost like you'll see little baloons like in a cartoon strip with little sayings in them. I'm not a big talker myself, so I can express myself with my friends thru my drawings of them. Again, some of them like it and some of them don't.

Now the result of this free writing session is certainly not ready to be typed and turned in as a paragraph. But what did become clear in it was that the student could probably compare the two types of friends—those who like to be drawn and those who don't.

Clustering

Clustering is another way of putting ideas on paper before you begin to write an actual draft. A cluster is more visual than free writing. You could cluster the topic of "book clubs," for instance, by putting it in a circle in the center of a piece of paper and then drawing lines to new circles as ideas or details occur to you. The idea is to free your mind from the limits of sentences and paragraphs to generate pure details and ideas. When you are finished clustering, you can see where you want to go with a topic.

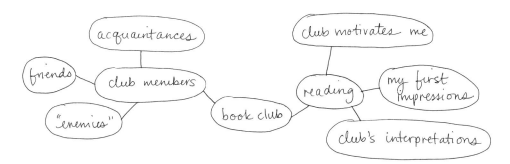

Talking with Other Students

It may help to talk to others when deciding on a topic. Many teachers divide their students into groups at the beginning of an assignment. Talking with other students helps you realize that you see things just a little differently. *Value* the difference—it will help your written voice that we discussed earlier, emerge.

Writing Exercise 3
LIST YOUR INTERESTS

Make a list of four or five of your own interests. Be sure that they are as specific as the examples listed in Section 33. Keep the list for later assignments.

Writing Exercise 4
DO SOME FREE WRITING

Choose one of your interests, and do some focused free writing about it. Write for ten minutes with that topic in mind but without stopping. Don't worry about anything such as spelling or sentence structures while you are free writing. The results are meant to help you find out what you have to say about the topic *before* you start to write a paper about it. Save the results for a later assignment.

Writing Exercise 5
PRACTICE CLUSTERING IDEAS

Choose another of your interests. Put it in the center of a piece of paper, and draw a cluster of details and ideas relating to it following the sample in this section. Take the cluster as far as it will go. Then choose one aspect to cluster again on its own. This way you will arrive at specific, interesting details and ideas—not just the first ones that come to mind. Save the results of all your efforts.

34. ORGANIZING IDEAS

Most important to keep in mind, no matter what you are writing, is the idea you want to get across to the reader. Whether you are writing a paragraph or an essay, you must have in mind a single idea that you want to express. In a paragraph, such an idea is called a *topic sentence;* in an essay it's called a *thesis statement,* but they mean the same thing—an idea you want to get across.

Thesis Statements

We will begin with a discussion of **thesis statements**. Let's choose one of the student interests listed in Section 33. "Buying and selling on eBay" is just a general topic; it doesn't make a point. What about eBay? Why do you like it? What does it do for you or for others? What point about eBay would you like to present to your reader? You might write a sentence like this:

> Buying and selling on eBay is fun and educational.

This sentence is a start, but it's not focused enough to develop. You might move into more specific territory and write one of the following sentences:

> I've learned a lot about business and geography by buying and selling on eBay.
>
> or
>
> Buyers and sellers learn a lot about business and geography through their transactions on eBay.

Now you have said something specific in two different ways. The first sentence uses the first-person pronoun *I*. The second sentence discusses "buyers" and "sellers" in general and uses *their*, a third-person pronoun, to refer to them. Some writing instructors may ask you to avoid writing in the first person, and others may encourage you to use it. (See the introduction to Part Four for more discussion of these approaches.) Whichever approach you use, when you write in one sentence the point you want to present to your reader, you have begun writing a thesis statement.

You may have a general idea in mind when you begin to write, but the support for it will evolve as you write. You can develop your thesis in various ways, but behind whatever you write will be your ruling thought, your reason for writing a particular essay, your thesis.

For any writing assignment, after you have done some free writing or clustering to explore your topic, the next step is to write a thesis statement. As you write your thesis statement, keep two rules in mind:

1. A thesis statement must be *a sentence with a subject and a verb* (not merely a topic).

2. A thesis statement must be *an idea that you can explain or defend* (not simply a statement of fact).

Writing Exercise 6

IDENTIFY A TOPIC, FACT, OR THESIS

Which of the following are merely topics or facts, and which are statements that you could explain or defend in an essay? In front of each one that is just a topic or a fact, write **TOPIC** or **FACT.** In front of each one that could be a thesis statement, write **THESIS.** Check your answers.

   1. _____ Gasoline prices are rising again.

   2. _____ Animals that seem to be able to predict earthquakes.

   3. _____ On July 20, 1969, Neil Armstrong planted an American flag on the moon.

   4. _____ Plagiarism is a misunderstood "crime."

   5. _____ Computer-generated movie characters can affect us in the same ways as "real-life" characters.

   6. _____ Voice-recognition technology may eventually weaken people's reading and writing skills.

   7. _____ Home schooling advantages and disadvantages.

   8. _____ Kobe Bryant's score of 60 points in his final game before retiring from the L.A. Lakers.

   9. _____ Traveling to different countries makes people more open-minded.

   10. _____ Vegetarians can suffer from health problems related to their diets.

Writing Exercise 7

WRITE A THESIS STATEMENT

Use your free-writing or clustering results from Writing Exercises 4 and 5 and write at least one thesis statement based on your interests. Be sure that the thesis you write is phrased as a complete thought that can be defended or explained in an essay.

Organizing an Essay

Once you have written a good thesis and explored your topic through discussion with others or by free writing and clustering, you are ready to **organize** your essay.

First, you need an introductory paragraph. It should catch the reader's interest, provide necessary background information, and either include or suggest your thesis statement. (See Sections 30 and 32 for two examples of student writers' introductory paragraphs.) In your introductory paragraph, you may also list supporting points, but a more effective way is to let them unfold paragraph by paragraph rather than to give them all away in the beginning of the essay. Even if your supporting points don't appear in your introduction, your reader will easily spot them later if your paper is clearly organized.

Your second paragraph will present your *first* supporting point—everything about it and nothing more.

Your next paragraph will be about your *second* supporting point—all about it and nothing more.

Each additional paragraph will develop *another* supporting point.

Finally, you'll need a concluding paragraph. In a short paper, it isn't necessary to restate your points. Your conclusion may be brief; even a single sentence to round out the paper may do the job. Remember that the main purpose of a concluding paragraph is to bring the paper to a close by sharing your final thoughts on the subject. (See Sections 30 and 32 for two examples of successful concluding paragraphs.)

Learning to write a brief organized essay of this kind will help you distinguish between the parts of an essay. Then when you're ready to write a longer paper, you'll be able to organize it clearly and be more creative in its design and content.

Topic Sentences

A **topic sentence** does for a paragraph what a thesis statement does for an essay—it states the main idea. Like thesis statements, topic sentences must be phrased as complete thoughts to be proven or developed through the presentation of details. But the topic sentence introduces an idea or subtopic that is the right size to cover in a paragraph. The topic sentence doesn't have to be the first sentence in a paragraph. It may come at the end or even in the middle, but putting it first is most common.

Each body paragraph should contain only one main idea, and no detail or example should be in a paragraph if it doesn't support the topic sentence or help to transition from one paragraph to another. (See Sections 30 and 32 for more examples of effective body paragraphs within essays and of paragraphs alone.)

Organizing Body Paragraphs (or Single Paragraphs)

A single paragraph or a body paragraph within an essay is organized in the same way as an entire essay, only on a smaller scale. Here's the way you learned to organize an essay:

Thesis: stated or suggested in introductory paragraph

First supporting paragraph

Second supporting paragraph

Additional supporting paragraphs

Concluding paragraph

And here's the way to organize a paragraph:

Topic sentence

First supporting detail or example

Second supporting detail or example

Additional supporting details or examples

Concluding or transitional sentence

You should have several details to support each topic sentence. If you find that you have little to say after writing the topic sentence, ask yourself what details or examples will make your reader believe that the topic sentence is true for you.

Transitional Expressions

Transitional expressions within a paragraph and between paragraphs help the reader move from one detail or supporting point in an essay to the next. When first learning to organize an essay, beginning writers may start each body paragraph and every new example with a transitional expression (*first, for example, next*). These common transitions are useful and clear, but they can sound mechanical. To improve the flow of your ideas and the strength of your written voice, try to replace some of these transitions with specific phrases (*at the start of the meeting* or *in many people's minds*) or with dependent clauses (*when drivers use cell phones* or *as I approached the intersection*).

Here are some transitions that show sequence:

Previously	Next	One (example, point . . .)
Later	Then	Another (example, point . . .)
Eventually	Finally	

Here are a few to show addition:

Also	First
Furthermore	Second
In addition	Third . . .

Here are several that show comparison or contrast:

Similarly	In the same way	In comparison
However	On the other hand	In contrast

Here are those that show consequence:

Therefore	Consequently	In conclusion
As a result	In other words	

Writing Exercise 8
ADD TRANSITIONAL EXPRESSIONS

Place appropriate expressions from the lists above into the blanks in the following paragraph to make the transitions clear. Then try to replace one or two with specific transitional phrases or clauses to improve the flow of ideas and to add interest. Compare your choices with the ones suggested in the answers.

_____, I used to plan my long road trips by going through the following routine._____, I made sure that I had a map of the highways so that if I got lost along the way, I wouldn't panic. _____, even if I did have a map to the city of my destination, I would call the hotel for specific driving directions from the highway._____way that I planned ahead was to check my car's tires and have its engine serviced, if necessary. _____, I never forgot to bring my cell phone because I had learned how important they are on long drives. _____, before I left my house on the day of the trip, I checked the Highway Patrol updates to see if there were any road closures on my route. This routine always worked for me;_____, I can give it up now that I have a car with its own navigation system. I just need to figure out how it works!

Writing Exercise 9
WRITE A PARAGRAPH THAT INCLUDES TRANSITIONS

To practice using transitions, write a paragraph about the steps you take to get ready to sit down and write a paper. Feel free to use the paragraph in Writing Exercise 8 as a model. Where do you go? What materials do you gather? How do you get in the right frame of mind to write? Report the steps in order, one by one, using transitional expressions wherever you see fit. Sometimes it's helpful to add humor to a process-based paragraph or essay to liven up the steps involved in an ordinary process and connect with the reader.

35. SUPPORTING WITH DETAILS

Now you're ready to **support** your main idea with subtopics and specific details. That is, you'll think of ways to prove that your thesis is true. How could you convince your reader that buying and selling on eBay can teach valuable lessons about business and geography? Try adding the word "because" to the end of your thesis to generate at least three more specific statements. You might come up with something like the following:

> I've learned a lot about business and geography by buying and selling on eBay. (because)

or

> Buyers and sellers learn a lot about business and geography through their transactions on eBay. (because)

1. Honesty and fairness are very important when dealing with others on eBay.

2. Active eBay members must keep accurate records and be very organized.

3. Buyers and sellers learn about shipping methods and policies around the world.

NOTE 35.A—Imagining the word *because* at the end of your thesis will help you find subtopics that are clear and parallel in their level and presentation of ideas.

Types of Support

The subtopics developing a thesis and the details presented in a paragraph are not always *reasons* (like the ones outlined in the **analysis** of buying and selling on eBay, for instance). Supporting points may take many forms based on the purpose of the essay or paragraph. Other kinds of support include the following:

> *examples* (in an **illustration**)
>
> *meanings* (in a **definition**)
>
> *steps* or *stages* (in a "how-to" paper or **process analysis**)
>
> *types* or *kinds* (in a **classification**)
>
> *personal experiences* (in any kind of writing)
>
> *facts, statistics,* and *expert opinions* (in an **argument**)
>
> *causes* and/or *effects* (in a **causal analysis**)
>
> *similarities* and/or *differences* (in a **comparison-contrast**)

Whatever form they take, supporting points should develop the main idea expressed in the thesis statement of the essay or the topic sentence of the paragraph and help prove it to be true.

A Sample Final Draft

Here is the final draft of a first-person student essay about a challenging assignment for college students. Notice how the body paragraphs map out the writer's personal experience (using *I, me, my, we*) as she struggles through the process of learning to draw a self-portrait. This essay could also have presented the same stages from a third-person point of view, using *they* or *them*. The result would be more of an observation of the process that all art students go through when drawing self-portraits.

Drawing a Blank

On the day my drawing class started to learn about self-portraits last year, each of us had to bring a mirror to class. In backpacks and purses were make-up mirrors, dressing table mirrors—large and small mirrors of every shape and kind. I was nervous about drawing a self-portrait, so I brought only a tiny plastic pocket mirror. That way if I didn't do a good job, it would be my mirror's fault. I discovered that drawing a self-portrait involves observing myself from the outside and the inside.

I had never done well on human figure drawing. First our teacher, Ms. Newman, demonstrated the proportion of a human figure; she explained that a human body measures about seven times a human head. She used a tiny piece of chalk to draw on the board while she was talking. Then she showed how to sketch the face, from eyebrows to eyes, nose, mouth, and ears. After her lecture, she told us to begin drawing our self-portraits.

We all set up our mirrors. The ceiling danced with the reflections they made as we got to work. I looked down at my little square of scratched-up plastic and started to draw gingerly on my paper. I tried to put the eyes, nose, and mouth I had seen on the paper. When I finished, I wondered, "Who the heck is this?" The drawing didn't look anything like me. I was frustrated and sank down in my chair. After a minute, I told myself, "Try again." I drew another one, and it was a little better. But I could not really call it a self-portrait because it didn't look exactly like me.

I asked Ms. Newman for help. She glanced at my previous attempts and said, "A good self-portrait doesn't just look like you, it also shows your personality and your feeling." She did not see either of these in my other drawings. So I tried again. I borrowed my friend's big glass mirror and stared into it; I was not only looking at my face, but also deep inside my face. This time, I freely sketched the shape of my face. Then I roughly placed my eyebrows, eyes, nose, mouth, and ears. I looked into the mirror again and drew the expression I saw there.

When my portrait was finished, I wondered at the amazing work I had done. Even though it did not perfectly look like me, it really showed my personality and emotions through the contrast of light and dark. When Ms. Newman saw it, she applauded. Not only did I get an A on this project; it also became one of the strongest pieces in my portfolio. I realized that few things can be done successfully the first time. If I had given up after my first try, I would never have captured the real me.

(Note: See Section 40 for a rough draft of this essay, before its final revisions.)
Learning to support your main ideas with vivid details is perhaps the most important goal you can accomplish in this course. Many writing problems are not really writing problems but *thinking* problems. Whether you're writing a research paper or merely an answer to a test question, if you take enough time to think, you'll be able to discover a clear thesis statement and support it with paragraphs full of meaningful details.

Writing Exercise 10

WRITE AN ESSAY ON ONE OF YOUR INTERESTS

Return to the thesis statement you wrote about one of your interests for Writing Exercise 6 in Section 34. Now write a short but thoughtful essay about your interest, explaining its allure and exploring the benefits and drawbacks of pursuing it. Don't forget to include details from any free writing or clustering you have done on the topic and to use meaningful transitional expressions.

36. Choosing and Using Quotations

Including quotations from another writer can add dimension and depth to your paragraphs and essays. Try to think of a reading as a friendly resource, inviting you to quote from it in order to present ideas beyond your own. Remember, you're in control of what any other writer "says" in your writing by choosing what to quote and where to include quotations in your paper.

Choosing Quotations

Imagine you've been asked to read a short selection and write a response that answers the following question: "Which is more important for success, talent or hard work?" You should have no trouble using the previously discussed methods to organize your ideas about talent vs. hard work and support them with details and observations of your own. But the assignment also requires that you include quotations from the reading prompt in your response.

Let's look at the sample reading below. It's about how hard work may have contributed as much to Mozart's music as his legendary talent did. As you read this brief excerpt from Geoff Colvin's book *Talent Is Overrated,* try to spot phrases or statements that you think would be particularly quotable in a paper about talent vs. hard work. Also notice that Colvin includes a quotation to support his own ideas:

> Mozart is the ultimate example of the divine-spark theory of greatness. Composing music at age five, giving public performances as a pianist and violinist at age eight, going on to produce hundreds of works, some of which are widely regarded as ethereally great and treasures of Western culture, all in the brief time before his death at age thirty-five—if that isn't talent, and on a mammoth scale, nothing is. . . .
>
> Mozart's method of composing was not quite the wonder it was long thought to be. For nearly two hundred years many people have believed that he had a miraculous ability to compose entire major pieces in his head, after which writing them down was mere clerical work. That view was based on a famous letter in which he says as much: "the whole, though it be long, stands almost finished and complete in my mind . . . the committing to paper is done quickly enough . . . and it rarely differs on paper from what it was in my imagination."
>
> That report certainly does portray a superhuman performer. The trouble is, this letter is a forgery, as many scholars later established. Mozart did not conceive whole works in his mind, perfect and complete. Surviving manuscripts show that Mozart was constantly revising, reworking, crossing out and rewriting whole sections, jotting down fragments and putting them aside for months or years. Though it makes the results no less magnificent, he wrote music the way ordinary humans do.

One way to begin quoting effectively is to highlight the details or phrasing that you respond to the most in a reading. Be choosy. Just as you would choose ring tones or clothes to reflect your personality, you can pick particular quotations from readings to enhance the effect of your writing. Remember that quotations must reproduce the original's exact wording, so transcribe them very carefully and place them within quotation marks. (See Section 28.)

Let's say you've chosen these four sentences to quote from in your essay:

"Mozart is the ultimate example of the divine-spark theory of greatness."

"For nearly two hundred years many people have believed that he had a miraculous ability to compose entire major pieces in his head, after which writing them down was mere clerical work."

"Surviving manuscripts show that Mozart was constantly revising, reworking, crossing out and rewriting whole sections, jotting down fragments and putting them aside for months or years."

"Though it makes the results no less magnificent, he wrote music the way ordinary humans do."

Using Quotations

The next step is to cut the quotations down to a manageable size so they won't overpower your ideas.

"Mozart is the ultimate example ~~of the divine-spark theory~~ of greatness."

"For nearly two hundred years many people have believed that he had a miraculous ability to compose entire major pieces in his head~~, after whichwriting them down was mere clerical work~~."

"~~Surviving manuscripts show that Mozart was~~ constantly revising, reworking, crossing out and rewriting whole sections, jotting down fragments and putting them aside for months or years."

"~~Though~~ it makes the results no less magnificent, ~~he~~ wrote music the way ordinary humans do."

Read on to see how these shortened quotations can be included in the paper using signal phrases and proper punctuation to let the reader know where you've left out or changed wording from the original.

Signal Phrases and Punctuation

A quotation by itself—even if it's a complete statement such as "I have a dream"—cannot function as a sentence in your paper without a signal phrase. The job of a signal phrase is to identify the writer or source of the quotation and provide a subject and a verb to anchor the quotation within your paper. The italicized subject and verb in the following sentence make up its signal phrase:

> In his famous speech, *Martin Luther King, Jr. declares,* "I have a dream."

A **signal phrase** should include the writer's name or other identification and a strong verb like the ones listed below. Avoid relying on the verb *says* or *writes* when so many more interesting verbs like the following are available:

explains	suggests	argues	feels
points out	asserts	illustrates	adds
believes	thinks	notes	insists
claims	observes	declares	reports
acknowledges	admits	states	concludes

A signal phrase can be placed *at the beginning, in the middle,* or *at the end* of the quotation to add variety to your sentences. Use commas to set off signal phrases and an **ellipsis** (. . .) to show where you have cut words from full-length quoted sentences. No ellipsis is necessary when quoting only phrases from the original. If an ellipsis ends the sentence, the period makes a total of four dots:

Signal phrase at the beginning of the quotation (a comma follows the signal phrase):

> **Geoff Colvin believes**, "Mozart is the ultimate example of . . . greatness."

Signal phrase in the middle of the quotation (commas surround the signal phrase):

> "For nearly two hundred years," **Colvin explains**, "many people have believed that he had a miraculous ability to compose entire major pieces in his head. . . ."

Signal phrase at the end of the quotation (a comma comes before the signal phrase):

> Mozart worked very hard, "constantly revising, reworking, crossing out and rewriting whole sections, jotting down fragments and putting them aside for months or years," **Colvin adds**.

You may have noticed that the previous examples use an ellipsis when words have been left out of the *middle* or the *end* of a shortened quote, but not the *beginning* of one. When leaving off the first words of a quotation, maintain the small letter that the quoted part begins with to show that the opening words have been cut.

When a quotation is introduced by "that," the signal phrase does *not* require a comma. Note that any change made to a quote should be placed within **brackets** [ ]:

> **Colvin feels *that*** "it makes [Mozart's] results no less magnificent. . . ."

Once you've identified the single source writer's name in previous sentences, you can include *brief* quotations without a signal phrase:

> As a music major myself, I'm glad to know that Mozart "wrote music the way ordinary humans do."

To read a sample paragraph that includes all of the quotations from Colvin's excerpt, see Section 37.

TABLE 36.A GUIDELINES FOR INCLUDING QUOTATIONS

1. Choose a sentence that you would like to quote from a reading.
2. Consider shortening the phrasing of the original sentence for clarity.
3. Put quotation marks around the other writer's words.
4. Write a signal phrase to identify the writer or source of the quotation.
5. Use a comma (or commas) to set off the signal phrase in your sentence.
6. No comma is necessary if the word "that" introduces the quotation.
7. Use brackets [ ] to identify a change made within a quotation.
8. Use an ellipsis . . . in place of words cut from the middle or end of a quoted sentence (but not when quoting just a phrase).

These methods for including quotations are not difficult to learn; with practice, they will become second nature. Understanding how to include quotations from a single source effectively will help when you need to quote from multiple readings and to document them using the Modern Language Association (MLA) format.

Writing Exercise 11

WRITE SENTENCES USING SIGNAL PHRASES AND QUOTATIONS

Return to Dominique Browning's essay "Wandering Home" in Section 31, and choose five sentences that you like. Then practice quoting parts of them in sentences of your own using signal phrases. As you write your sentences, be sure to follow the "Guidelines for Including Quotations" in Table 36.A.

37. Writing in Response to a Reading

Many of your future assignments will ask you to respond to one or more readings. Think of reading-response assignments as opportunities to strengthen your position as a writer. Always participate fully with a reading by highlighting quotable sentences and noting similar observations or contrasting experiences of your own.

Read the following paragraph-length response to the reading about Mozart in Section 36. Note how the writer includes quotations from Colvin's excerpt, using well-punctuated signal phrases, to enhance her own ideas and experiences.

A Sample Paragraph Response Using Quotations

I always thought that talent was more important than hard work. I never tried anything for too long if I didn't have the ability to do it easily. For instance, I started learning the violin but gave it up within two weeks because it didn't feel natural to me. After reading Geoff Colvin's information about Mozart, I wish I had tried harder. Many people think of Mozart when the word *talent* comes up. Colvin believes, "Mozart is the ultimate example of . . . greatness." Without even studying Mozart's life, everyone seems to know about his gifts. "For nearly two hundred years," Colvin explains, "many people have believed that he had a miraculous ability to compose entire major pieces in his head. . . ." However, Mozart worked very hard, "constantly revising, reworking, crossing out and rewriting whole sections, jotting down fragments and putting them aside for months or years," Colvin adds. I never pictured Mozart doing so much hard work. Colvin feels that "it makes [Mozart's] results no less magnificent. . . ." I agree with him. As a music major myself, I'm glad to know that Mozart "wrote music the way ordinary humans do." Next semester, I might give the violin one more try.

In-class (or timed) writing assignments often include *prompts,* thought-provoking readings that "prompt" writers to generate their own ideas while providing quotable content to use as support. Here's an example of an assignment that asked students to read the following prompt, an excerpt from the book *Manwatching,* and respond to Desmond Morris's observations about "Personal Space."

Sample Reading Prompt 1

If a man enters a waiting room and sits at one end of a long row of empty chairs, it is possible to predict where the next man to enter will seat himself. He will not sit next to the first man, nor will he sit at the far end, right away from him. He will choose a position about halfway between these two points. The next man to enter will take the largest gap left, and sit roughly in the middle of that, and so on, until eventually that latest newcomer will be forced to select a seat that places him right next to one of the already seatedmen. . . . This is a reflection of the fact that we all carry with us, everywhere we go, a portable territory called a Personal Space. If people move inside this space, we feel threatened. If they keep too far outside it, we feel rejected.

After reading this prompt, one student wrote the following in-class essay. The directions asked her to summarize Morris's concept of "Personal Space," quote from the excerpt to include Morris's voice, and respond to his ideas with insights and examples of her own.

A Sample Essay Response Using Quotations

Space Games

The idea of "Personal Space" suggested by Desmond Morris is that everyone likes to have choices. They like to be able to select the amount of space they want or in some cases need. Morris shares his perception that people pick their places in a waiting room based on their comfort zones, so to speak. The example he gives is much like anything else in life where people have to share space. The thought that choices about personal space are "possible to predict," but usually unnoticed, is interesting and a little peculiar.

Riding in someone else's car, standing in line at the bank, even putting food on our plates—all of these say the same thing about us. We want choices. If someone sits in the wrong spot or stands too close, we can feel claustrophobic or "threatened," as Morris points out. If another person is distant or sits "too far" away, we might "feel rejected." People lead their lives on choice to mold their lives into what they dream. With personal space, it's a choice of how close and how far.

My personal space is definitely variable. I have
found that there are some days when my personal space
doesn't matter. Other people can get as close as they
want, or stay as far as the eye can see, and it wouldn't
make me feel any different. Then there are days when
I need two empty seats worth of space on both sides. When
I get a ride to school, I hold my belongings close to me.
With people who, on a scale of 1 to 10 (1 being stranger
and 10 being relative), range from 1 to 3, my belongings
don't leave my lap. With people who range from 4 to 7,
I may place my stuff on the seat next to me. And with
those from 8 to 10, I just throw my stuff on the floor.

I never gave personal space much thought before
reading Morris's paragraph, but I pay close attention
to everything around me, especially the reactions and
expressions on people's faces. Life makes more sense
when I see the examples of everyone else's. I definitely
recognize the look of someone whose personal space has
been invaded. I remember one moment on the train the
other day when a little boy got tired and dozed off with
his head against the woman next to him, not his mother.
The woman kept looking down at the child until it was
clear that he meant no harm. She had no choice but to
readjust her space to include the sleepy little boy until
his stop came.

My feelings and other people's reactions support
Morris's idea that "we all carry with us, everywhere we
go, a portable territory called a Personal Space." We
protect this territory whenever we have a choice, but it
is adjustable, so the more conscious of it we are, the
better.

Clearly, even though it was written under the pressure of time, the student
participated fully with Morris's reading, which prompted her to think about the
unconscious habits that we all have when negotiating for our "Personal Space." The
result is a successful in-class essay.

TIPS FOR IN-CLASS WRITING

In-class (or timed) writing is a special skill that reveals how you think and write under pressure. Keep the following five areas in mind when writing an in-class essay or a timed essay online:

1. **Topic or Prompt Analysis:** *Really think* about the topic or prompt before starting to write; highlight key (or quotable) parts and briefly map out your own ideas and details in response. Then start your paper with a direct response to the topic (or reading prompt) and an idea/thesis of your own that relates to it.

2. **Organization:** In-class essays don't need long introductions because they are prompted by a reading or question that both the writer and reader already know. Begin your response immediately and follow the order of tasks shown by key verbs in the question (summarize, explain, illustrate, describe . . .). Start a new paragraph at each natural break in the topic, in your ideas, or in any extended areas of support. Conclude with your *final* insights about the topic or prompt, not just a review of the same general points. Finally, choose a unique phrase that previews your paper's focus, and use it as a title.

3. **Detail:** To find real and meaningful details, think of your own experiences and observations as diamonds in a mine. Go on an inward exploration to discover your unique ideas, as well as the best parts of the prompt. All you need to do is gather sparkling thoughts, well-chosen quotations from the prompt, and examples of your own that *you* want to present to the reader. Map them out on paper; then write the essay in sentences with strong punctuation.

4. **Word Use, Sentence Structure, and Punctuation:** Use Standard English spelling, sentence structure, punctuation, and capitalization. Avoid slang expressions like "guy" or "gonna" and short-cuts like "&," "u," "w/," "etc." Remember, proofreading is more important than finishing every point you plan to make.

5. **Presentation:** *Relax* as much as possible so that your handwriting and written "voice" are clear and confident. If you make a mistake, don't scratch it out or frantically apply correction tape to it. Cross it out with *one* line; then include your correction above it. Self-editing is the sign of a strong writer, so let the reader see any changes you've made.

To see these tips at work, review the sample in-class essays in Sections 32, 37, and 38.

> Essentially, the family is a breeding unit and the family territory is a breeding ground. At the center of this space, there is the nest—the bedroom—where, tucked up in bed, we feel at our most territorially secure. In the typical house, the bedroom is upstairs, where a safe nest should be. This puts it farther away from the entrance hall, the area where contact is made, intermittently, with the outside world. The less private reception rooms, where intruders are allowed access, are the next line of defense. Beyond them, outside the walls of the building, there is often a symbolic remnant of the ancient feeding grounds—a garden. Its symbolism often extends to the plants and animals it contains, which cease to be nutritional and become merely decorative—flowers and pets.

Writing Exercise 12

WRITE A PARAGRAPH OR ESSAY IN RESPONSE TO A READING

Using the sample paragraph and essay responses in this section as models, write a paragraph or essay response to Reading Prompt 2, Desmond Morris's excerpt about "Family Territory." First, summarize Morris's concept of "Family Territory," quote from the excerpt to include Morris's voice, and respond to his ideas with insights and examples of your own. Refer to the "Guidelines for Including Quotations" in Table 36.A whenever necessary.

38. WRITING AN ARGUMENT

Writing assignments often ask you to take a stand on an issue or to share an opinion and prove that it is valid. Such writing is called **argumentation**, but it doesn't involve "fighting" or "arguing" in the sense that these words might be used in everyday life. In fact, intense emotions can weaken an argument if they are not balanced by logic and fairness. The purpose of a written argument is to convince the reader that your idea or position on a topic is valid and possibly to agree with it.

Taking a Stand and Proving Your Point

A strong written argument fulfills three basic requirements. First, it takes a clear stand in relation to an idea, an issue, or a controversial topic. Second, it provides logical and relevant support for the writer's position. And third, it discusses the issue or topic in a fair-minded way, taking other points of view into account. Let's look at some examples by both professional and student writers.

As an in-class assignment, students were asked to write a short essay in response to the following excerpts from Leon Botstein's book *Jefferson's Children: Education and the Promise of American Culture*. In Chapter III, "Replacing the

American High School," Botstein argues that young people in America should enter the "real world" two years earlier than they do now. Here are the excerpts that the students read from Botstein's book:

> The American high school is obsolete. It can no longer fulfill the expectations we legitimately place on it. It offers an inadequate solution to the problem of how best to motivate and educate American adolescents. . . .
>
> The key reason for reducing the total number of years in school before college is educational. Children and young adults can begin learning sooner and more quickly. Since they mature earlier, they need to be released from the obligations of compulsory education at an earlier age. The high school diploma as we define it, which is now given to Americans at age eighteen, could be awarded at age sixteen. . . .
>
> Those interested in going to college will be able to exercise greater choice in the new system. For those who stay at home, the community college system is the most likely option. Already these institutions are dedicated to repairing the damage done in high school or doing what ought to have been done. The basic organization of the community college is more respectful of the incipient adult. Classes are selected and scheduled by the individual. There is a campus. The day is divided so that night classes are an option. The classes are run by faculty with better training in the subject matter. The presumption of the classroom is not rote fulfillment of state requirements, but rather teaching in response to the ambitions of students to learn and get ahead. Community colleges have large numbers of older students, well beyond the so-called traditional college age. As teachers know, nothing better serves the swaggering sixteen- and seventeen-year-old more obsessed with style and the peer group than being in classes with students in their late twenties and early thirties, for whom school has become truly voluntary and serious.

A Sample Argument

As you might imagine, Botstein's idea to shorten high school and send sixteen-year-olds directly to college drew mixed reactions from student writers. In the short essay that follows, one student argues that the last two years of high school are extremely important based on her own high school experiences:

```
                    College at 16? I Think Not!


        I strongly disagree with Leon Botstein's idea to
    eliminate the American high school. I don't believe that
    all teenagers mature early enough to attend college at
    sixteen. Yes, there is a small percentage (that could be
```

counted on the fingers of my left hand) who could indeed go off to college and do very well at sixteen years of age, but is it really worth letting the other ninety-five percent go, too?

When I think of my high school experience and the kids who attended with me, I think of just that—kids. Most of the students at my high school sought pleasure in spitting over the third floor balcony onto the lunch crowd below. Half of the population of my school had not learned how to throw their trash into the trashcan five feet away from them. Most weren't mature enough to leave high school at eighteen, let alone sixteen.

How would my life have been without high school? Well, that would have been interesting, and Botstein's ideas do make me wonder if I might have accomplished more sooner. But I believe that if I had gone off to college at sixteen, I would have lost more than I gained. I learned a lot from my high school experience, not from the mandatory classes that were required for graduation, but from the classes that I chose to take and that I participated in with my teenage peers.

It may sound strange to say so, but my dance and drama classes taught me a lot of very important life skills. I learned responsibility by multitasking to be able to fit weekend rehearsals and practices into my full load of regular classes, homework, and after-school activities. I learned that it is possible to get out of bed before ten o'clock on Saturday because 3 a.m. roll calls, teamwork, dedication, and competition can take you anywhere you want to go.

Without my valuable high school experiences, I know I wouldn't be the well-rounded person I am today. If I had to compete with Botstein's thirty-year-old community college students and meet them at 3 a.m. on Saturdays for dance rehearsals as my introduction to responsibility, the effects would not have been the same. In high school, we matured together, and that was important.

This student's in-class essay fulfills the three requirements of a strong written argument (see Table 38.A) by clearly stating her position in her opening sentences, by describing her own vivid high school experiences to support her position, and by fairly acknowledging that some people in high school would be better off in college and even wondering what would have happened if she had graduated earlier.

Obviously, the student's paper would have been longer and more developed if it had been an out-of-class essay with a two- or three-week deadline. Then this student could have responded to Botstein's whole book and included factual support with her personal experiences. She could have interviewed fellow students and included their comments. She might have found an expert who shares her opinion about high school and written her essay as a comparison–contrast of Botstein's and the other expert's opinions.

TABLE 38.A THREE REQUIREMENTS OF A STRONG WRITTEN ARGUMENT

1. Takes a clear stand in relation to an idea, an issue, or a controversial topic.
2. Provides logical and relevant support (personal experience, opinions of experts, facts and statistics, results of interviews).
3. Discusses the idea, issue, or topic in a fair-minded way, allowing for other points of view.

Writing Exercise 13

WRITE AN ARGUMENT ABOUT GRADES

Read and carefully consider the following paragraph proposing a few changes in education:

> Education at all levels should be changed so that it is completely grade-free and noncompetitive. All letter grades should be eliminated and replaced by a pass/fail system, and scores of any kind should be provided as information only, not for the purpose of ranking. Students should also receive credit for self-study and Internet-gained knowledge and skills. Attendance and completion of assignments should be the only requirements for moving ahead in a course of study. In addition, students should be allowed to repeat courses, even after successfully completing all of the assignments, if they so choose. Students should take charge of their own educations and learn at their own pace.

Do you agree or disagree with this hypothetical proposal to eliminate grades and give students total flexibility in their studies? Take care to consider the issue from all angles. How would such profound changes affect students, teachers, parents, school officials, and the public? Then use what you've learned about argumentation to write a brief essay in which you take a stand on one side of this issue or the other. Refer to the student sample "College at Sixteen? I Think Not!" as a model for using relevant experiences and observations to prove your point, and remember to be fair-minded in your presentation.

39. Writing Summaries

One of the best ways to learn to read carefully and write concisely is to write summaries. A summary is a brief piece of writing (a paragraph, usually) that presents the main ideas of a reading—a book chapter, an article, a speech, or a long essay—in your own words. It does not call for any reactions, opinions, or experiences of your own for support. Summaries contain only the most important points of the original and leave everything else out. Writing summaries strengthens your reading and writing skills. You have to understand the essence of a reading, gather its supporting points, and rephrase them in your *own* words (without including quotations from the original). Here's a tip: put the original away while you make a list of its four or five "big ideas." Then you can write sentences that express those ideas and combine them in paragraph form.

A summary, by definition, should always be shorter than the original. Writing something *short* sounds easy, but actually it isn't. Rephrasing the main ideas of a reading in a short paragraph is a time-consuming task—not to be undertaken in the last hour before class. However, if you practice writing summaries conscientiously, you will improve as a reader and will be able to write concise, clear, smooth paragraphs. These skills will then carry over into your reading and writing for other courses.

A Sample Reading

Read the following excerpt from the book *Bollywood Crafts—20 Projects Inspired by Popular Indian Cinema*. It will be followed by a sample summary.

Bollywood Film Facts

Bollywood is the biggest film industry in the world. Approximately one thousand films are made in India under the "Bollywood" umbrella each year (that is double the amount of Hollywood films) and over 12 million Indians watch a Bollywood film every day. The films are also popular throughout the Middle East, Russia and Africa, and, increasingly, Western audiences are surrendering to the charms of Indian cinema.

Bollywood is also referred to as Hindi cinema—there are 22 official languages spoken in India; however, the major movies are made in Hindi as it is the country's dominant language, though films in other languages, such as Tamil and Urdu, are also made. Although the main hub of production companies are based in Mumbai (Bombay), films are shot in locations all over the country and recent films have even been set abroad [in England, Europe, Australia, and America].

Like mainstream Hollywood movies, Bollywood films also fall into specific genres, such as action or romance, but most are multi-genre, family movies. In India, going to the movies is a family event, and often several generations watch a film together. This means the content has to appeal to all. It also means filmmakers have to be creative in their approach to telling narratives. How they express emotions is a key element. Emotions are represented not just through acting, but also through the use of spectacle—songs and dance.

The key to a successful [Bollywood] movie is to have a popular soundtrack, and for the choreography that accompanies it to be equally impressive. Song sequences usually start in the middle of a dialogue and are a break from the reality of the storyline. Characters are transported to different locations and their costumes become very significant; a leading lady can go through several costume changes per dance scene, which makes for compelling viewing! When you're watching a song from a film, it's best to ignore the subtitles and instead let yourself be entertained by the visuals. The choreography is a mixture of Indian dancing styles with global influences such as MTV. Extras play a key role in bringing the dances to life, and as a viewer, I often want to get up and join in!

Some Bollywood films are inspired by Hollywood tales, but most are original ideas, often based on moral or family dilemmas. Like Hollywood, the star system is an important part of Bollywood and the biggest actors and actresses are celebrities in their own right. Unlike Hollywood, however, Indian actors often work on several films at one time, even switching between movie sets in the same day. And while Hollywood left behind its musicals in the 1950s, Bollywood films always contain a performance element. Actors have to demonstrate impeccable dancing skills as well as acting ability.

If you have yet to watch a Bollywood movie, don't worry! They are far more accessible than you may think, with cinemas and rental stores responding to audience demands by showing and stocking new movies. Don't be alarmed by the length; Bollywood movies are longer than other films to allow for the songs, but there is always an interval [intermission].

Bollywood films are an exciting and original contribution to the filmmaking world and, as the popularity of Bollywood continues to spread around the globe, Indian filmmakers are getting more progressive with their plots, special effects and visuals. This means that films will develop stylistically even further and continue to get better—something I'm really looking forward to!

Source: From *Bollywood Crafts—20 Projects Inspired by Popular Indian Cinema*, by Momtaz Begum-Hossain, a freelance crafts maker and customized clothing designer (*www.momtazbh.co.uk*). Reprinted by permission of the author.

A good summary begins with a statement of the reading's "biggest" idea, written in your own words. An effective summary does not just translate or re-order the words of the original. Some single words from the original—"India," "Hollywood," and "Bollywood," in this case—may be used in a summary when they lack a substitute. However, as the writer of an effective summary, you must find new ways to phrase the original reading's ideas, present them in a condensed form, and reveal your understanding of the original in the process.

A Sample Summary

> In "Bollywood Film Facts," Momtaz Begum-Hossain explains that India has its own version of Hollywood—called Bollywood—that produces movies that are growing in popularity worldwide. Bollywood releases twice as many movies a year as Hollywood does. Unlike Hollywood movies, Bollywood movies can include different languages besides their main language, Hindi. These films also include more music and dancing than Hollywood movies do. Elaborate, well-performed songs are essential and unique to Bollywood films. Therefore, movie stars in India have to act well and dance well, too. Indian movies are longer than Hollywood movies and might require subtitles, but they continue to attract new audiences because of their high entertainment value and universal appeal.

Writing Exercise 14
WRITE A SUMMARY OF A READING

Write a summary of the following excerpt (with minor omissions) from the book *13: The Story of the World's Most Notorious Superstition* by Nathaniel Lachenmeyer. Note that the word *triskaidekaphobe* refers to a person who firmly believes in superstitions about the number 13. After reading the excerpt carefully, follow the instructions below to write a practice summary:

13 AND THE UNITED STATES

There is no evidence that unlucky 13 reached the United States before the nineteenth century. In fact, one of the principal arguments skeptics in the United States use to prove triskaidekaphobes wrong is the prominent, benevolent role 13 has played in the nation's history. It is true that the full title of the Declaration of Independence is The Declaration of Independence of the Thirteen Colonies, and that for the first fifteen years of its existence, the United States was the "thirteen united States of America." In the late eighteenth century, the number 13 symbolized the new nation's independence and unity. Every Fourth of July there was a 13-gun salute in honor of the 13 states. When George Washington's birthday began to be celebrated around the country in the 1780s, it, too, was accompanied by a 13-gun salute. The 13-gun salute was lost to history as new states were added. In 1841, the U.S. Navy finally fixed the number at 21, giving us a tradition that survives to this day.

Thirteen remained a benevolent number and a positive symbol of the birth of the nation beyond 1791—but not for very long. The nineteenth century brought with it a strange new idea—the number 13 was unlucky, and not just unlucky—mortally unlucky. Thirteen's sudden reversal of fortune in the United States is proof that cultural beliefs do not always evolve slowly, directed by significant historical forces; often, they can and do turn on a dime. . . .

By the 1930s, Friday the 13th was the most popular superstition in the country. A 1933 study in the *Journal of Abnormal Psychology* found that 95 percent of seniors and 91 percent of freshmen at seven midwestern colleges believed that "Friday the 13th always brings bad luck." The Friday the 13th superstition became so popular that it even infringed upon that hallowed ground of reason and rationality—the law. On Thursday, October 12, 1939, the town board of French Lick, Indiana, decreed that beginning at midnight and continuing for twenty-four hours, all the black cats in town had to wear bells, so residents could avoid them on the fateful day. An article in that day's *Indianapolis News* explained, "The board thinks there's enough bad luck in the world right now without black cats adding their share on Friday the 13th." The board assigned the town marshal with the task of belling the cats. The timing of the decree, five weeks after the start of World War II, lends support to the popular theory that superstitions become more pronounced during times of uncertainty. There is no information on when the tradition ended—whether, for example, it survived the war. It did continue at least through November 13,1942; the *New York Times* picked up the story, calling the decree "a war measure to alleviate mental strain upon the populace."

A good way to begin the summary of a reading is to identify the biggest idea that the author wants to get across to the reader. Write your own sentence expressing the main idea of the excerpt now.

You may have written a sentence like this:

> America has a complex relationship with the number 13.

Next, it's important to add the author's name and the reading's title to identify what you are summarizing:

> In "13 and the United States," Nathaniel Lachenmeyer explains how historical factors have affected the way Americans feel about the number 13.

Now that you have a first sentence, summarize the rest of the reading by rephrasing only its "big ideas." Be sure to use your *own* words. Since the excerpt is already relatively short, you may be able to summarize it in as few as four or five sentences. It's not difficult if you remember to put the reading aside and write as if you're telling a friend the essay's main ideas in your own way.

The first draft of your summary may be too long. Cut it down by including only the essential points and omitting any of its details or examples. Stay within a limit of 100–120 words. Once you have written the best summary you can, consider the five questions listed in the Summary Checklist (Table 39.A) and revise your paragraph until the answer to each question is "Yes."

TABLE 39.A SUMMARY CHECKLIST

Consider these questions while working on the final draft of your summary:

1. Have you included all of the writer's main ideas *without* adding your own reactions or opinions?
2. Have you written the summary in your own words *without* using any quotations?
3. Have you left out all of the writer's examples and supporting details?
4. Does your summary read smoothly?
5. Would someone who had not read the original get a clear overview of it from your summary?

40. REVISING, PROOFREADING, AND PRESENTING YOUR WORK

Great writers don't just sit down and write a final draft. They write and **revise**. You may have heard the expression, "Easy writing makes hard reading." True, it is *easier* to turn in a piece of writing as soon as you finish the first draft. But your reader (and eventually you) might be disappointed by the results. Think of revision as a necessary step in your writing, as a welcome opportunity to make changes—both large and small—that will enhance your writing's overall effect

Whenever possible, write a paper several days before it is due. Let it sit for a while. When you reread it, you'll see many ways to improve the organization, add more details, and clarify phrasing. After revising the paper, put it away for another day, and try again to improve it. Save all of your drafts along the way to see the progress you've made or possibly to find text deleted in an early draft that fits in again after revision.

Don't call any paper finished until you have worked through it several times. Revising is one of the best ways to improve your writing.

A Sample Rough Draft

Take a look at an early draft of the student essay you read in Section 35 about learning to draw a self-portrait. Notice that the student has revised her rough draft by crossing out weak parts, correcting word forms, and adding new phrasing or reminders for later improvement.

Drawing a Blank

~~If at First You Don't Succeed . . . . Try, Try Again~~

On the day ~~that~~ my drawing class started to learn about self portraits last year, each of us had to bring a mirror to class. *In backpacks and purses* ~~There~~ were make-up mirrors, dressing table mirrors—large and small mirrors of every shape and kind. I was nervous about drawing a self portrait, so I brought *only* a tiny plastic pocket mirror. That way if I didn't do a good job, it would be my mirror's fault. *Add a thesis*

I had never done well on human figure drawing. ~~Anyway,~~ *First* *, Ms. Newman, demonstrated* our teacher ~~showed us how to do~~ the proportion of a human figure; *she explained that* ~~something like~~ a human body measures about seven times a human head. She used a tiny piece of chalk to draw on the board while she was talking. Then she ~~also~~ showed how to sketch ~~out~~ the face, from eyebrows to eyes, nose, mouth and ears. After ~~all that~~ *her lecture*, she ~~led~~ *told* us to ~~start~~ *begin* ~~our~~ drawing *our self-portraits*

We all set up our mirrors, and the ceiling danced with the reflections they made as we got to work. I looked down at my little square of scratched-up plastic and started to draw gingerly on my paper. I tried to put the eyes, nose, and mouth I had seen on the paper. When I finished, I wondered, "Who the heck is this?" The drawing didn't look anything like me. I was frustrated and sank down in my chair. After a minute, I told myself, "Try again." I drew another one, and it was a little better. But I could not really call it a self-portrait because it did not look exactly like me.

I asked Ms. Newman for help. She glanced at my previous attempts and said, "A good self-portrait doesn't just look like you, it also shows your personality and your feelings." in my other drawings. So I tried again. I borrowed my friend's big glass mirror and stared into it; I was not only looking at my face, but also deep inside my face. This time, I freely sketched the shape of my face. Then, I roughly placed my eyebrows, eyes, nose, mouth, and ears. I looked into the mirror, again and drew the expression I saw there.

When my portrait was finished, I wondered at the amazing work I had done. Even though it did not perfectly look like me, it really showed my personality and emotions through the contrast of light and dark. When Ms. Newman saw it, she applauded. Not only did I get an A on this project; it also became one of the strongest pieces in my portfolio. I realized that few things can be done successfully the first time. If I had given up after my first try, I would never have captured the real me.

Can you see why each change was made? Analyzing the reasons for the changes will help you improve your own revision skills.

Writing Exercise 15

REVISE A NEW PIECE OF WRITING

The old test of optimism and pessimism is to look at a glass filled to the middle. An optimist, or positive thinker, sees it as "half *full.*" But a pessimist, or negative thinker, considers it "half *empty.*" Is it better to be an optimist or a pessimist? What are the consequences of focusing on the bright side or on the dark side? Do you think Ernest Cline focuses on the bright or the dark side in his excerpt about our attraction to video games in the "Sentence Structure Practice" at the end of Section 24? Think about these questions, do some free writing or clustering about them, come up with a thesis statement, and organize your results into the structure of a brief essay.

Write a rough draft of the paper and set it aside. A day or two later, revisit your paper to see what improvements you can make to your rough draft. Use the following checklist (Table 40.a) to help guide you through this or any other revision.

TABLE 40.A   REVISION CHECKLIST

Here's a checklist of revision questions. If the answer to any of these questions is no, revise that part of your paper until you're satisfied that the answer is yes.

1. Does the introductory paragraph identify the topic and any readings clearly and include a main idea (thesis statement) that the paper will explain or defend?
2. Do all of the body paragraphs develop and support the thesis statement?
3. Does each body paragraph begin with a topic sentence to identify its focus on one part or point relating to the thesis?
4. Do the body paragraphs contain relevant details, smooth transitions, and correct quotations (if the paper responds to a reading)?
5. Does the concluding paragraph bring your (the writer's) thoughts or argument to a smooth, convincing close?
6. Does your (the writer's) voice come through, and are other points of view included for fairness?
7. Do the sentences read smoothly and appear to be correct?
8. Are words well chosen and are spelling and punctuation consistent and correct?

Exchanging Papers (Peer Evaluations)

The preceding checklist can also be used if you exchange papers with another student. Since you both have written a response to the same assignment, you will understand what the other writer has been going through and learn from the differences between the two papers.

Proofreading Aloud

Finally, you should read your finished paper *aloud*. If you read it silently, your eyes will see what you *think* is there, but you are sure to miss some errors. Read your paper aloud slowly, pointing to—and listening carefully to—each word as you read it. When you *hear* your sentences, you will notice missing words and find errors in spelling and punctuation. Reading a paper to yourself this way may take fifteen minutes to half an hour, but it will be time well spent. You can also ask a friend or relative to read your paper to you. This method can be fun as well as helpful. If you don't like the way something sounds, don't be afraid to change it! Make it a rule to read each of your papers *aloud* before handing it in.

PRESENTING YOUR WORK

Part of the success of a paper could depend on how it looks. The same paper written sloppily or typed neatly might even receive a completely different grade. It is human nature to respond positively to an object created and presented with care. Here are some general guidelines to follow when **presenting your written work.**

Paper Formats

Following instructions and standard **formats** is essential. Your paper should be typed, double-spaced, or written neatly in ink on 8 1/2-by-11-inch paper. A 1-inch margin should be left around the text on all sides for your instructor's comments. The beginning of each paragraph should be indented.

Most instructors specify a particular format for presenting your name and the course material on your papers. Always follow such instructions and other formats carefully in preparation for following more complicated formats in the future.

Titles

A strong **title** makes an important first impression. Look at the following pairs—each with a generic title on the left and a unique title on the right. In just a few well-chosen words, each title on the right prepares the reader for the topic *and* tone of the essay.

Immigration in America	American Beauty: Diversity
An Embarrassing Experience	Gone in a Flush!
Process Analysis Essay	Got Silk?

Just as you're more likely to pick up a book or see a movie with a special title, so your readers will want to read your paper if its title distinguishes it as something special. To present your own titles correctly, use the following guidelines:

1. Capitalize only the first, the last, and the important words within a title. Don't capitalize articles (*a, an,* or *the*), prepositions (*to, at, in, around* . . .), or the connecting words (*and, or, but* . . .) in the middle of a title. (See Section 29.)

   A Night on Eagle Rock   To the Limit of Endurance and Beyond

2. Don't use quotation marks unless your title includes a quotation or the title of an article, a poem, a song, or other short work. (See Section 28.)

   Mozart's "Divine" Talent   The Call of "The Raven"

3. Don't underline or use italics in your title unless it includes the title of a book, movie, magazine, or other long work. (See Section 28.)

   Promises in <u>The Pact</u>   *Avatar* Will Never Sink *Titanic*

Remember that "Haste is the assassin of elegance." Instead of rushing to finish a paper and turn it in, take the time to give your writing the polish that it deserves.

Answers

PART ONE PREVIEW TEST: WORD USE

Answers for the preview and progress tests include references to relevant sections.

1. affects (This "*a*" spelling means that it *alters* the car's potential—see Section 1.)

2. complimented (This "*i*" spelling means a *nice* comment—see Section 1.)

3. past (This spelling of *past* means that the ambulance sped *by* us—see Section 2.)

4. quite (This "*ite*" spelling means that they can be *very* dangerous—see Section 2.)

5. preposition ("*On*" shows the *position* of the keys in relation to the dashboard—see Section 3.)

6. conjunction ("*So*" joins the two clauses in the sentence. It is one of seven easy-to-remember conjunctions called *fanboys*—see Section 3.)

7. adjective ("*Identical*" describes the noun *twins*—see Section 4.)

8. well (The adverb "*well*" works with the verb to tell *how* they *did*—see Section 4.)

9. bad (The adjective form *bad* works with the linking verb *felt* in the same way that *happy*, not *happily*, would—see Section 4.)

10. It's (This form *with* an apostrophe means "*It has* been raining"—see Sections 1 and 5.)

11. Who's (This form *with* an apostrophe means "*Who is* the creator"—see Sections 2 and 5.)

12. party's (This form with the '*s* after *party* means the success belongs to every single surprise *party*—see Section 6.)

13. teenagers' (This possessive form with the ' after *teenagers* means the expectations belong to all of the *teenagers*. If all of the expectations belong to only one *teenager*, the answer could also be *teenager's*—see Section 6.)

14. eye-catching (A *hyphen* joins these two words to become one adjective—see our new Section 7 on "Consulting a Dictionary.")

15. Internet (Internet is capitalized unless the writing is informal—see our new Section 7 on "Consulting a Dictionary.")

SECTION 1: WORDS OFTEN CONFUSED (SET 1)

EXERCISE 1.1

1. choose

2. it's, affects

3. an, except, due

4. accept

5. a, compliment, it's

6. already, feel

7. Here

8. course, conscious

9. effect, break

10. do

EXERCISE 1.2

1. an, new

2. It's, due

3. choose, an

4. a, its

5. already

6. complement

7. choose

8. It's, know, accept

9. hear, do

10. an, it's

EXERCISE 1.3

1. It's, new

2. have, accepted

3. feel, an

4. chose

5. already, fourth

6. fill, except, have

7. hear, an

8. advice

9. course, effects

10. complemented

EXERCISE 1.4

1. clothes, an

2. Due, a

3. accept

4. course, are, all ready

5. coarse, new

6. conscious

7. an

8. break, feel

9. have, already

10. It's, no

EXERCISE 1.5

1. are

2. our

3. accept

4. It's

5. New, forth

6. effects

7. know, fill

8. It's, feel

9. effect

10. fill, an

EXERCISE 1.6 PROOFREADING PRACTICE

In the middle of a debate in my speech class last week, I suddenly became very self-~~conscience~~ *conscious*. I could ~~fill~~ *feel* my heart beating faster, and I didn't ~~no~~ *know* what to do. I looked around to see if my nerves were having ~~a~~ *an* ~~affect~~ *effect* on the audience. Of ~~coarse~~ *course*, they could ~~here~~ *hear* my voice trembling. The topic that we were debating was whether to eliminate letter grades in college, and everyone else was doing really well. But for some reason, my face turned red, and I would ~~of~~ *have* left the room if I could. After the debate, my classmates gave me lots of ~~complements~~ *compliments*, but I ~~new~~ *knew* that they were just trying to be nice.

SECTION 2: WORDS OFTEN CONFUSED (SET 2)

EXERCISE 2.1

1. your

2. you're, than

3. whether

4. piece, women

5. They're, their

6. principle, their

7. to, than

8. principal, their

9. to, then

10. they're, through

EXERCISE 2.2

1. through

2. You're

3. past, there

4. there, peace, quiet, there

5. their, they're

6. there, lose, their, right

7. who's, to

8. then

9. past

10. Whether, you're, quite

EXERCISE 2.3

1. There

2. through

3. to

4. They're

5. personnel

6. past, lose

7. there

8. led, through, were

9. than

10. whether

EXERCISE 2.4

1. whose

2. quite

3. than, personnel

4. whether

5. their, principle

6. led, to

7. were

8. to

9. passed

10. than, to

EXERCISE 2.5

1. were

2. weather

3. led

4. past, whether

5. passed

6. past, there

7. quiet

8. lose, two, right

9. through, past

10. piece, weather

Yesterday, we watched and discussed a short animated video in my philosophy class. The film shows office workers in a high-rise building looking down from ~~there~~ *their* windows and watching pedestrians walk ~~passed~~ *past* a small construction site on the street below, ~~wear~~ *where* a jack hammer has broken a ~~peace~~ *piece* of the sidewalk. As pedestrians walk over the ~~lose~~ *loose* brick, several of them trip and fall but are not injured. The office personnel who are watching from above find each accident funnier ~~then~~ *than* the one before until an old man with a cane approaches the dangerous site. His weak condition makes the office workers remember their ~~principals~~ *principles* of ~~write~~ *right* and wrong, and they all try ~~too~~ *to* warn the old man before he falls too. The film ends in a way that is ~~quiet~~ *quite* a surprise.

SECTION 3: THE EIGHT PARTS OF SPEECH

Note: These *exercises* include several proper nouns with two or more capitalized words working as *one noun* (ex. *London Zoo)*. Also, remember that possessive nouns and pronouns play the part of *adjectives* when they modify a noun (ex. *Graham's* idea or *her* idea).

EXERCISE 3.1

            n   v   adj   n   prep   n
1. Bette Nesmith Graham invented correction fluid in the 1950s.

   pro   adv   v   adj   n   n
2. She originally called her invention Mistake Out.

    adv   pro   v   adj   n   prep   n
3. Later, she changed its name to Liquid Paper.

    adv   n   v   prep n   conj pro adv   v   n
4. Originally, Graham worked as a typist, and she often made mistakes.

    pro   v   adj   n   prep n   conj   v   adj   n   prep pro
5. She brought white paint to work and covered her typos with it.

    adv   pro   v   n   prep adj   adj   n
6. Soon everyone wanted a bottle of Graham's correction paint.

    pro   v   n   prep adj   n   conj   v   pro prep adj   n
7. She mixed the product in her kitchen and bottled it like fingernail polish.

     adv   n   v   n   pro v   n   prep n
8. Single-handedly, Graham developed a product that made millions of dollars. (Note: *That* is a relative pronoun standing for "product.")

    adj n   n   adv   v   prep adj   n

9. Her son, Michael Nesmith, also benefited from her success.

    pro v   n   prep   n   adj   n   prep   n

10. He was a member of The Monkees, a popular band in the 1960s.

EXERCISE 3.2

        n   v   adj   n   n   prep n

1. Clyde Tombaugh discovered the ninth "planet," Pluto, in 1930.

     n   v prep n   prep   n prep n

2. Tombaugh died in 1997 at the age of 90.

     n   v   adj   n   prep   n   adj   n   pro v

3. Scientists loaded Tombaugh's ashes onto New Horizons, a space probe that was

     v   prep   n   prep n

launched in January of 2006. (Note: *That* is a relative pronoun standing for "probe.")

      n   v   prep n   prep n

4. New Horizons arrived near Pluto in 2015.

   prep   n   prep   n   n   v   n   prep   n prep

5. After the launch of New Horizons, astronomers deleted Pluto from the list of

    adj   n

real planets.

    pro   v   conj adj   n   v   v   adj adj   n

6. They determined that real planets must control their own orbits. (Note: In this sentence, *that* acts as a conjunction joining two clauses.)

     n v   adj n   prep   n   prep adj   n

7. Pluto is an icy ball under the influence of Neptune's orbit.

       n   v   n prep   adj   n   prep adj   n

8. Astronomers put Pluto into the new category of "dwarf planet."

    conj   pro   v   n   adj   n   prep adj   n   v   prep n

9. When they demoted Pluto, the official number of real planets changed to eight.

   interj. conj adj   n   prep adj   n   v   v   adj   n   prep n adv

10. Yes, but recent evidence of a new planet may bring that number to nine again.

EXERCISE 3.3

    prep   n   prep n   n   v   adj   n
1. In the summer of 2005, London Zoo opened a temporary exhibit.

       n   prep   n   v   adj   n
2. The title of the exhibit was "The Human Zoo."

    adj   n   v   adj   adj   n
3. Zoo officials selected eight human volunteers.

    adv pro   v   n   prep   n prep adj   n
4. Then they put the humans on display for several days.

     n   prep n   v   v   adv   prep   n
5. Dozens of people had applied online for the project.

        n   v   adj   n   conj adj   n
6. The exhibit showcased three males and five females.

    pro   v   prep adj adj   n   pro   v   adj   n   conj adj   n
7. They dressed in fake fig leaves that covered their shorts and bikini tops.

    prep adj adj   n   conj   adj   n   n   v   adv
8. With its rocky ledges and cave-like structures, the enclosure had previously

    v   n
housed bears.

    adj   n   v   v   n   conj   v   n prep   n
9. The eight humans talked, played games, and received a lot of attention.

     prep   n   n   v   n   prep   adj   n   n   conj
10. Outside the exhibit, the zoo posted signs about human diet, habitat, and

      n
behavior.

EXERCISE 3.4

    interj   n   v   adj   n   prep adj   n
1. Wow, pigeons have a built-in compass in their brains!

    adj   n   v   pro prep   adj   n   conj pro v
2. This compass points them in the right direction as they fly.

    adv   adj   n   prep n   v   n   prep adj   n
3. Recently, pigeon experts in England conducted a study of these birds.

        n   v   n   prep adj   n   prep adj   n

4. The study tracked the flights of certain pigeons for two years.

           n   v   adv   adj

5. The results were very surprising.

     adj   n   adv   v   adj adj   n

6. Modern pigeons usually ignored their inner compasses.

   pro   v   prep adj   n   adv

7. They navigated by other methods instead.

         n   adv   v   adv conj   v   adj   n

8. The pigeons simply looked down and followed human highways.

   pro   v   n   prep   adj   n conj v   adj   n   adv

9. They remembered roads from previous flights and took the same roads home

   adv

again.

      n   adv   v   adj   n   n   conj   n   conj pro v

10. The pigeons even traced the roads' turns, curves, and roundabouts as they flew.

EXERCISE 3.5

    adj   n   v   adj   n conj   adj   n

1. Some people collect rare coins and paper money.

     adj   adj   n v adv   adj

2. The Del Monte twenty-dollar bill is very famous.

     n   v   n   conj pro   v   adj   n

3. The mint made a mistake when it printed this bill.

    n   prep   n   adv   v   pro prep   n   prep

4. A sticker from a banana accidentally attached itself to the paper during the

   adj   n

printing process.

    adj   adj conj adj   n   v   n prep   n

5. The round green and red sticker became a part of the bill.

   adj   n   adv   v prep adj   n

6. Such mistakes usually lead to a bill's destruction.

      adj   adj   n   adv   v   n   prep   adj   n
7. This flawed note, however, left the mint with the normal twenties.

         n   adv   v   adj adj   n
8. Experts immediately authenticated its rare status.

          n   adv v prep n prep   n
9. The bill first sold on eBay for $10,000.

      adv   n   prep   n   v   n   prep adj   adj   n
10. Eventually, a couple from Texas paid $25,000 for this one-of-a-kind note.

EXERCISE 3.6 PARAGRAPH PRACTICE

                                    adj   n
Baseball Hat

    adj   adj   n   prep   adj   n   v   adv   v   prep
This billed cap with a dome-shaped crown is sometimes constructed with an

   adj   n conj n   prep n prep   adj   n   n   adv   v adj n
adjustable band or elastic in back for a customized fit. The hat obviously got its name

  prep   n   prep   n   conj pro v adv   adv   v   adj   n
from the sport of baseball, but it did *not* originally have a shade-creating bill. The

    adj   n   v   adv   v   prep   n conj   n   v   adj   adj   n
bill-less kind was first worn around 1860, and the hat underwent its design change

  adv prep adj   n   prep   n   adj   n   v   adj   prep
later in the early 1900s. In the 1920s, the billed-style hat became popular among the

    n   conj   n   v   adj   adj   n   prep   n   n
masses, as fans emulated their favorite players like superstar Babe Ruth.

SECTION 4: ADJECTIVES AND ADVERBS

EXERCISE 4.1

1. adjective adding "which one" to the noun *leader*

2. adverb adding "how" to the verb *works*

3. adverb adding "how" to the verb *work*

4. adverb adding "in what way" to the verb *is working*

5. adjective adding "how many" to the noun *person*

6. adjective adding "what kind" to the noun *manager*

7. adjective adding "which one" to the noun *goal*

8. adverb adding "where" to the verb form *pulling*

9. adverb adding "in what way" to the adjective *responsible*

10. adverb adding "when" to the clause *that's just not possible*

EXERCISE 4.2

1. adjective adding to the noun *coupon*

2. adverb adding to the adjective *one*

3. adjective adding to the pronoun *I*

4. adverb adding to the verb *sells*

5. adjective adding to the noun *software*

6. adjective adding to the noun *hardware*

7. adjective adding to the noun *Spanish*

8. adjective adding to the noun *students*

9. adjective adding to the noun *child*

10. adjective adding to the pronoun *she*

EXERCISE 4.3

1. close	**5.** bad	**8.** very happy
2. closely	**6.** badly	**9.** good
3. close	**7.** very happily	**10.** well
4. badly		

EXERCISE 4.4

1. the smallest	**5.** newer	**9.** better
2. a small	**6.** newer	**10.** more important
3. smaller	**7.** better	
4. the newest	**8.** the best	

EXERCISE 4.5

(Notice that *online* is used as both an adjective and an adverb in this exercise.)

        adj   adv

1. I took a helpful class online in the spring.

     adj   adj

2. An Internet specialist taught me research skills.

adv   adj   adj
3. I discovered very useful tools for Web research.

adv   adj   adj
4. The instructor clearly explained various kinds of online resources.

adj   adj   adj
5. She gave me several optional topics for each assignment.

adv   adj adj   adj
6. I especially enjoyed the articles from my two projects about world music.

adv   adv   adj
7. Now I fully understand the benefits of online classes.

adj   adj   adj adj
8. They are fun and rewarding because students work at their own pace.

adv   adv   adj   adj
9. I am definitely less confused about online sources.

adv   adv
10. I can do research online and enjoy the process completely.

EXERCISE 4.6 PROOFREADING PRACTICE

I didn't do very ~~good~~ *well* during my first semester at community college. I feel ~~badly~~ *bad* whenever I think of it. I skipped classes and turned in sloppy work. My counselor warned me about my negative attitude, but I was ~~real~~ *really* stubborn. I dropped out for a year and a half. Now that I have come back to college, I am even ~~stubborner~~ *more stubborn* than before. I go to every class and always do my best. Today, a college degree is ~~only~~ my *only* goal.

SECTION 5: CONTRACTIONS

EXERCISE 5.1

1. that's

2. It's

3. someone's

4. person's

5. no contractions

6. there's, they'll, they're

7. they've

8. no contractions (The word *its* is a possessive pronoun that acts as an adjective; it does not mean *it* is or *it* has.)

9. They're

10. no contractions

EXERCISE 5.2

1. aren't

2. no contractions

3. weren't

4. no contractions

5. there's

6. no contractions

7. They've

8. it's

9. no contractions

10. It's

EXERCISE 5.3

1. What's

2. You're, you're

3. no contractions (The word *its* is a possessive pronoun that acts as an **a**djective; it does not mean *it is* or *it has*.)

4. it's, it's, it's (The third *its* in the sentence is a possessive pronoun that acts as an adjective; it does not mean *it is* or *it has*.)

5. there's

6. don't, they're

7. There's

8. doesn't, won't

9. It's, isn't

10. they'll, won't

EXERCISE 5.4

1. wasn't

2. I'll

3. isn't

4. It's, It's, I'm

5. you've

6. don't, don't

7. there's

8. you'll

9. haven't

10. we'd

EXERCISE 5.5

1. I'm, she's

2. We've, we've

3. aren't

4. they're

5. they're

6. that's

7. We've, can't, doesn't

8. we'd

9. that's, it's, they're

10. isn't

EXERCISE 5.6 PARAGRAPH PRACTICE

~~I have~~ *I've* had the same group of friends since I was in junior high school. Now that ~~we are~~ *we're* all in college, my friends ~~do not~~ *don't* spend as much time on schoolwork as I do. Whenever ~~I am~~ *I'm* studying for an exam or working on a project, they call and ask if ~~I would~~ *I'd* like to see a movie or go to a game. ~~It is~~ *It's* the worst in the summer. ~~I have~~ *I've* been enrolling in summer school classes for the past two years so that ~~I will~~ *I'll* be ready to transfer soon. However, none of my friends has taken a class during the summer. At the rate ~~they are~~ *they're* going, my friends ~~will not~~ *won't* ever transfer.

SECTION 6: POSSESSIVES

EXERCISE 6.1

1. people's
2. building's
3. St. Michael's
4. neighborhood's
5. victim's
6. study's, residents'
7. rescuers'
8. someone's
9. Scientists'
10. people's

EXERCISE 6.2

1. Monet's
2. London's
3. fog's
4. weather's
5. no possessives
6. no possessives
7. People's (Note: The word *its* is a possessive pronoun that acts as an adjective. It does not require an apostrophe.)
8. no possessives
9. artist's
10. "Monet's London."

EXERCISE 6.3

1. Manning's
2. critic's, Columbia Pictures'
3. Manning's, *Knight's*
4. writer's
5. Manning's
6. studio's
7. Manning's
8. studio's
9. no possessives
10. films', critic's

EXERCISE 6.4

1. car's
2. passengers'

3. tires'

4. road's

5. No apostrophe is needed. *Its* is a possessive pronoun that acts as an adjective.

6. suspension's

7. father's, salesperson's

8. No additional apostrophe is needed. *Its* is a possessive pronoun that acts as an adjective.

9. No additional apostrophe is needed.

10. else's

EXERCISE 6.5

1. Sloane's	**5.** cloud's	**8.** artist's
2. people's	**6.** no possessives	**9.** no possessives
3. clouds'	**7.** Sloane's	**10.** cloudscape's
4. cloud's		

EXERCISE 6.6 PARAGRAPH PRACTICE

   I consider my friend Alexis to be one of the smartest people I know. Alexis is a twenty-five-year-old film student at a nearby university. She's presently in her senior year, but *that is* just the beginning for Alexis. She plans to take full advantage of her *university's* resources to learn what she needs before starting her own filmmaking career. She has access to her fellow *students'* talents, her different *teachers'* experiences, and the film *school's* state-of-the-art equipment and industry contacts. *I've* always been impressed by *Alexis'* (or *Alexis's*) self-confidence, and it *has* inspired me to make a plan of my own for the future.

SECTION 7: CONSULTING A DICTIONARY

Consult a dictionary for the answers to Exercises 7.1–7.6.

PART ONE PROGRESS TEST: WORD USE

1. a (The "*u*" in "*unique*" sounds like "*you*"—see Section 1.)
2. advise (The "*s*" spelling means an *action* by someone "*wise*"—see Section 1.)
3. have (*Have* completes the verb *could have dressed*—see Section 1.)
4. principle (This spelling ending in "*le*" means that it's a *rule*—see Section 2.)
5. verb ("*Took*" shows an *action*—see Section 3.)
6. pronoun ("*Someone*" stands for an unknown person—see Section 3.)
7. adverb ("*Inside*" works with the *verb* to show *where* we *moved*—see Section 4.)

8. **adjective** (The word *"early"* works with the *noun "students"* to tell *which ones* received extra credit—see Section 4.)

9. **better** (*"Better"* creates a comparison by joining with the *verb "did"*—see Section 4.)

10. **they're** (This form *with* an apostrophe means "before *they are* needed"—see Sections 2 and 5.)

11. **whose** (This form *without* an apostrophe is a possessive pronoun that acts as an adjective—see Sections 2 and 5.)

12. **their** (This form *without* an apostrophe is a possessive pronoun that acts as an adjective—see Sections 2 and 5.)

13. **children's** (This form *with* the *'s* after *children* means that the clothes belong to *children*, a word that does not end in *s*. Note that *adults'* has the apostrophe *after the s* because the clothes belong to *adults*, a word that does end in *s*—see Section 6.)

14. **judgment** (Dictionaries list *judgment* as the preferred spelling in American English—see Section 7.)

15. **self-made** (Dictionaries specify that a hyphen joins these two words when they are used as one adjective—see Section 7.)

PART ONE PARAGRAPH PRACTICE: WORD USE

On a recent expedition in Siberia, scientists made an ~~un-expected~~ *unexpected* discovery. They found a pair of baby lion cubs that have been frozen for over 10,000 years. ~~Whats~~ *What's* amazing about ~~they're~~ *their* discovery is the condition of the two ~~cub's~~ *cubs*. The little lions look as if they were frozen yesterday. Thousands of years in ice have had almost no ~~affect~~ *effect* on the ~~cub's~~ *cubs'* fur and physical features. ~~Its~~ *It's* clear that the cubs were about two weeks old when they died, since they did not *even* have their baby teeth ~~even~~ yet. The cubs belonged to a species that is now extinct—the cave lions of Siberia. By studying these ~~perfect~~ *perfectly* preserved lion cubs, scientists can learn more about how the cave lion species lived and how these two ~~tiniest~~ *tiny* cubs died.

SENTENCE STRUCTURE

PART TWO PREVIEW TEST: SENTENCE STRUCTURE

1. **A. is correct.** (The other sentence contains a *dangling modifier, "Taking a family cruise to Alaska"*—see Section 19).

2. **B. is correct.** (The other sentence contains a *misused pronoun*, "luckier than *me*"—see Section 23).

3. **A. is correct.** (The other sentence contains *faulty parallel structure,* "but never *weekends*"—see Section 22).

4. **B. is correct.** (The other word group is a *dependent clause fragment,* "*As* the teacher. . ."—see Sections 10 and 11).

5. **A. is correct.** (The other sentence contains two verbs that unnecessarily *shift in time,* "*wandered* in if they *don't*"—see Section 17).

6. **B. is correct.** (The other sentence is *wordy* and uses *clichéd expressions,* "*In today's society . . . mind their own business*"—see Section 21).

7. **B. is correct.** (The other sentence includes a *misused pronoun,* "gave my friend and *I* an extension"—see Section 23).

8. **B. is correct.** (The other sentence contains a *wordy expression,* "*free gift*"—see Section 21).

9. **B. is correct.** (The other is a *run-on sentence,* "*essay is* . . . and *it has*"—see Section 12).

10. **A. is correct.** (The other sentence contains a *pronoun agreement error,* "*everyone . . . their* faces"—see Section 23).

11. **B. is correct.** (The other sentence contains a *pronoun agreement error,* "*furniture . . . them*"—see Section 23).

12. **A. is correct.** (The other word group is a *phrase fragment* without a subject or a verb, "*From . . . of . . . to . . . of . . .*"—see Section 11).

13. **B. is correct.** (The other word group is a *phrase fragment* without a subject or a verb, "*Walking around . . . before . . .*"—see Section 11).

14. **B. is correct.** The other word group is a *dependent clause fragment* (my twin cousins *who* are . . ."—see Sections 10 and 11).

15. **B. is correct.** The other sentence contains awkward, wordy phrasing ("*whole meal . . . single specific . . . dishes themselves don't always . . .*"—see Section 21).

SECTION 8: LOCATING PREPOSITIONAL PHRASES

EXERCISE 8.1

1. Viganella is a tiny village (at the bottom) (of the Alps) (in Italy).

2. Due (to its physical position) (between the mountains), the town (of Viganella) suffered (from an unusual problem).

3. The sun's rays never reached the village (from the middle) (of November) (to the first week) (in February).

4. The mountains kept the little town (in shadow) (without any direct sunlight) (for several months) each year.

5. Then Giacomo Bonzani found a high-tech solution (to Viganella's dreary situation).

6. (In 2006), engineers installed a huge mirror thousands (of feet) (above Viganella) (on the side) (of one) (of the mountains) (around it).

7. A computer (at the mirror's location) keeps track (of the sun's movements).

8. The computer's software rotates the mirror (into the perfect position) to reflect sunlight (into the village square). [Note: "To reflect sunlight" is a verbal, not a prepositional phrase. See Section 18.]

9. The mirror began its work (in December) (of 2006).

10. Now the sun "shines" (on the town) (of Viganella) (during all months) (of the year).

EXERCISE 8.2

1. One fact (about William Shakespeare and his work) always surprises people.

2. There are no copies (of his original manuscripts).

3. No museum or library has even one page (from a Shakespeare play) (in Shakespeare's own handwriting).

4. Museums and libraries have copies (of the First Folio) instead.

5. (After Shakespeare's death) (in 1616), actors (from his company) gathered the texts (of his plays) and published them (as one book), the First Folio, (in 1623).

6. They printed approximately 750 copies (at the time).

7. Currently, there are 230 known copies (of the First Folio) (in the world).

8. Many owners (of the Folio) remain anonymous (by choice).

9. One woman inherited her copy (of the Folio) (from a distant relative).

10. Another copy (of the First Folio) recently sold (for five million dollars).

EXERCISE 8.3

1. Most (of us) remember playing (with Frisbees) (in our front yards) (in the early evenings) and (at parks or beaches) (on weekend afternoons).

2. Fred Morrison invented the original flat Frisbee (for the Wham-O toy company) (in the 1950s).

3. Ed Headrick, designer (of the professional Frisbee), passed away (at his home) (in California) (in August) (of 2002).

4. Working (at Wham-O) (in the 1960s), Headrick improved the performance (of the existing Frisbee) (with the addition) (of ridges) (in the surface) (of the disc).

5. Headrick's improvements led (to increased sales) (of his "professional model" Frisbee) and (to the popularity) (of Frisbee tournaments).

6. (After Headrick's redesign), Wham-O sold 100 million (of the flying discs).

7. Headrick also invented the game (of disc golf).

8. (Like regular golf) but (with discs), the game takes place (on special disc golf courses) (like the first one) (at Oak Grove Park) (in California).

9. (Before his death), Headrick asked (for his ashes) to be formed (into memorial flying discs) (for select family and friends). [*To be formed* is a verbal. See Section 18.]

10. Donations (from sales) (of the remaining memorial discs) went (toward the establishment) (of a museum) (on the history) (of the Frisbee and disc golf).

EXERCISE 8.4

1. Roald Dahl is the author (of *Charlie and the Chocolate Factory*).

2. (In his youth), Dahl had two memorable experiences (with sweets).

3. One (of them) involved the owner (of a candy store).

4. Dahl and his young friends had a bad relationship (with this particular woman).

5. (On one visit) (to her store), Dahl put a dead mouse (into one) (of the candy jars) (behind her back).

6. The woman later went (to his school) and demanded his punishment.

7. He and his friends received several lashes (from a cane) (in her presence).

8. (During his later childhood years), Dahl became a taste-tester (for the Cadbury chocolate company).

9. Cadbury sent him and other schoolchildren boxes (of sweets) to evaluate. [*To evaluate* is a verbal, not a prepositional phrase. See Section 18.]

10. Dahl tried each candy and made a list (of his reactions and recommendations).

EXERCISE 8.5

1. (At 2 a.m.) (on the second Sunday) (in March), something happens (to nearly everyone) (in America): Daylight Saving Time.

2. But few people are awake (at two) (in the morning).

3. So we set the hands or digits (of our clocks) ahead one hour (on Saturday night) (in preparation) (for it).

4. And (before bed) (on the first Saturday) (in November), we turn them back again.

5. (For days) (after both events), I have trouble (with my sleep patterns and my mood).

6. (In spring), the feeling is one (of loss).

7. That Saturday-night sleep (into Sunday) is one hour shorter than usual.

8. But (in fall), I gain a false sense (of security) (about time).

9. That endless Sunday morning quickly melts (into the start) (of a hectic week) (like the other fifty-one) (in the year).

10. All (of this upheaval) is due (to the Uniform Time Act) (of 1966).

EXERCISE 8.6 PARAGRAPH PRACTICE

I put the red paperclip (on the desk) and took a picture (of it). I walked (to the door) and pulled the handle. The door swung open. I lifted my right foot (into the air). As my right foot came forward (to the threshold) (of the doorframe), the phone rang. My foot hung (in the air), just short (of the outside hallway). The phone rang again. I spun around slowly, almost (in slow motion). I slowly slunk away (from the door) and lifted the phone (from the receiver). [Note that this writer also uses several single-word adverbs to show position—*open, forward, around,* and *away*.]

SECTION 9: FINDING SUBJECTS AND VERBS

EXERCISE 9.1

1. Many people know the name (of Uggie, the dog actor).

2. Uggie became famous (in the Oscar-winning silent movie *The Artist*).

3. His big break came (after ten years) (of work) (in other films and projects).

4. (With his role) (in *The Artist*), Uggie showcased the skills and expressions (of Jack Russell terriers) and made them very popular.

5. Originally, Uggie's trainer rescued him (from an animal shelter).

6. (In June 2012), Uggie retired (from his long acting career) due (to a physical setback).

7. (Before his retirement), this famous little dog left his mark (on Hollywood)—literally.

8. (On June 25, 2012), Uggie put his paw prints (in cement) (at Grauman's Chinese Theater).

9. Crowds (of fans) gathered (on Hollywood Blvd.) (in honor) (of Uggie's work) (in films).

10. They were the first canine footprints (in the history) (of this famous landmark).

EXERCISE 9.2

1. (In 1940), four teenagers took a walk and discovered something marvelous.

2. They entered an underground cavern (in Lascaux, France), and found vivid images (of animals) (on its walls).

3. There <u>were</u> <u>horses</u>, <u>deer</u>, <u>bulls</u>, <u>cats</u>, and <u>oxen</u>.

4. The prehistoric <u>artists</u> also <u>left</u> tracings (of their handprints) (on the walls).

5. <u>Scientists</u> <u>dated</u> the paintings and engravings (at approximately 17,000 years) old.

6. (After its discovery), the Lascaux <u>cave</u> <u>became</u> a popular tourist attraction.

7. Twelve hundred <u>people</u> <u>visited</u> the site daily.

8. These <u>visitors</u> <u>had</u> a negative impact (on the cave's prehistoric artwork).

9. <u>They</u> <u>breathed</u> carbon dioxide (into the cave) and <u>increased</u> its humidity.

10. French <u>officials</u> <u>closed</u> the Lascaux cave (to the public) (in 1963).

EXERCISE 9.3

1. <u>Harold Lloyd</u> <u>became</u> a star (of comic films) (during the silent era) (of Hollywood).

2. <u>Lloyd</u> <u>worked</u> (in Hollywood) (at the same time) (as Charlie Chaplin and Buster Keaton).

3. The <u>name</u> (of Harold Lloyd's character) (in many) (of his films) <u>was</u> also Harold.

4. One <u>accessory</u> <u>distinguished</u> Harold (from other silent-film characters)—a pair (of perfectly round eyeglasses).

5. The <u>glasses</u> <u>had</u> no lenses but <u>fit</u> his face and <u>gave</u> him a distinct personality.

6. A <u>suit</u> and a straw <u>hat</u> <u>completed</u> Harold's simple yet memorable costume.

7. (Unlike Chaplin and Keaton's clownish characters), <u>Harold</u> <u>looked</u> (like a normal young man) out (for adventure)—anything (from good fun) (to a great fight).

8. (As Harold), <u>Lloyd</u> <u>performed</u> incredible stunts (in spite) (of an injury) (from an accident) (with a prop bomb) early (in his career).

9. <u>He</u> <u>lost</u> part (of his hand) and <u>covered</u> it (in his films) (with a special glove).

10. (In his most famous film, *Safety Last!*), <u>Harold</u> <u>climbed</u> (outside a tall building) and <u>dangled</u> dangerously (from the hands) (of its clock).

EXERCISE 9.4

1. There <u>are</u> many world-famous <u>trees</u> (in California).

2. (Among them) <u>are</u> the oldest <u>trees</u> (on the planet).

3. These <u>trees</u> <u>live</u> somewhere (in Inyo National Forest).

4. One (of these ancient trees) <u>is</u> a bristlecone pine.

5. <u>Scientists</u> <u>call</u> it the Methuselah Tree.

6. They <u>place</u> its age (at five thousand years).

7. The <u>soil</u> and <u>temperatures</u> (around it) <u>seem</u> too poor (for a tree's health).

8. But the <u>Methuselah Tree</u> and its <u>neighbors</u> obviously <u>thrive</u> (in such conditions).

9. Due (to its importance), the Methuselah Tree's exact <u>location</u> <u>is</u> a secret.

10. Such important natural <u>specimens</u> <u>need</u> protection.

EXERCISE 9.5

1. Ancient <u>Egyptians</u> <u>worshipped</u> cats (of all sizes).

2. <u>Archeologists</u> <u>find</u> many mummies (of cats) (in Egyptian tombs).

3. <u>Carvings</u> (in the tombs) <u>reveal</u> a strong belief (in the god-like powers) (of large cats).

4. <u>Scientists</u> always <u>look</u> (for new evidence) (of ancient beliefs).

5. <u>Archaeologists</u> recently <u>discovered</u> the mummy (of a lion) (in a tomb in Saqqara, Egypt).

6. <u>It</u> <u>is</u> the first discovery (of a lion skeleton) (in an Egyptian tomb).

7. There <u>were</u> no <u>bandages</u> (around the lion).

8. But there <u>were</u> other <u>signs</u> (of mummification).

9. The <u>lion</u> <u>rested</u> (in the tomb) (of King Tutankhamen's nurse).

10. <u>Archaeologists</u> now <u>have</u> real evidence (of lion worship) (in Egypt).

EXERCISE 9.6 PARAGRAPH PRACTICE

(On March 30, 1858), <u>Hymen Lipman</u> (of Philadelphia) <u>patented</u> the first pencil (with an attached eraser). The eraser-tipped <u>pencil</u> <u>is</u> something (of an American phenomenton). Most European <u>pencils</u> <u>are</u> still eraserless. The humble <u>pencil</u> <u>has</u> a long history. <u>It</u> <u>goes</u> back (to the Roman stylus), a pointed piece (of lead). <u>We</u> still <u>call</u> the business end (of the pencil) the "lead." However, <u>it</u> <u>is</u> really nontoxic graphite.

Mass-production (of the pencil) <u>began</u> (in Nuremburg, Germany), (in 1662) and later <u>flourished</u> (as a result) (of the Industrial Revolution) (of the 19th century). <u>Henry David Thoreau</u> and his father <u>made</u> the hardest, blackest pencils (in the United States). <u>Thomas Edison</u> <u>was</u> fond (of short pencils) and <u>kept</u> them (in his vest pocket), ready (for ideas). <u>John Steinbeck</u> <u>loved</u> the pencil and <u>started</u> every day (with 24 fresh, sharp ones). <u>He</u> <u>used</u> 300 pencils to write *East* (of Eden) and <u>needed</u> 60 a day (for *The Grapes of Wrath*). ["To write" is a verbal. See Section 18.]

There <u>are</u> many more interesting <u>facts</u> (about pencils). A single <u>pencil</u> <u>can</u> <u>draw</u> a line 35 miles long or <u>write</u> (around 45,000 words). And if <u>you</u> <u>make</u> a mistake, thanks (to Hymen Lipman), <u>you</u> <u>have</u> an eraser handy.

SECTION 10: UNDERSTANDING DEPENDENT CLAUSES

EXERCISE 10.1

1. Edgar and Nina Otto, who live in Florida, were the winning bidders in an unusual auction in 2008.

2. Whoever placed the highest bid won the opportunity of a lifetime: a chance to clone their dog. [Note: The dependent clause acts as the subject of the sentence.]

3. The company that held the auction and provided the service was BioArts International.

4. The Ottos wanted to clone Sir Lancelot, a yellow Labrador that died in 2008.

5. The price that they paid exceeded $150,000.

6. Once the auction ended, the scientists at BioArts went to work.

7. They used the DNA that the Ottos saved from Sir Lancelot to produce a genetic match.

8. The complex process, which took place in South Korea, yielded an adorable puppy.

9. The puppy looked so much like Sir Lancelot that the company named him Encore Lancelot, Lancey for short.

10. At the first meeting with their new dog in January of 2009, the Ottos were overjoyed that Lancey walked with crossed feet, just like Sir Lancelot.

EXERCISE 10.2

1. When I was on vacation in New York City, I loved the look of the Empire State Building at night.

2. I thought that the colored lights at the top of this landmark were just decorative.

3. I did not know that their patterns also have meaning.

4. While I waited at the airport, I read about the patterns.

5. Some of the light combinations reveal connections that are obvious.

6. For instance, if the occasion is St. Patrick's Day, the top of the building glows with green lights.

7. When the holiday involves a celebration of America, the three levels of lights shine red, white, and blue.

8. There are other combinations that are less well known.

9. Red-black-green is a pattern that signals Martin Luther King, Jr. Day.

10. Whenever I visit the city again, I'll know that the lights on the Empire State Building have meaning.

EXERCISE 10.3

1. When people visit Google's homepage on one evening in March each year, they are often surprised.

2. They notice immediately that the whole page is black instead of white.

3. After they look into it further, they discover the reason for the temporary color change.

4. The black page signifies that Google is a participant in Earth Hour.

5. In 2008, Google joined countless cities, companies, and individuals who turn their lights off for one hour in an international effort to encourage energy conservation.

6. People around the globe cut their electricity and live in the dark as soon as clocks strike the appointed hour in their locations.

7. When the hour is up, they turn the electricity back on.

8. Earth Hour is an idea that began in Australia.

9. In 2007, the first Earth Hour that the Australians celebrated occurred between 7:30 and 8:30 p.m. on March 31.

10. Even though some people dismiss Earth Hour as a minor event, others believe in its power as a symbol of environmental awareness.

EXERCISE 10.4

1. On June 8, 1924, George Mallory and Andrew Irvine disappeared as they climbed to the top of Mount Everest.

2. Earlier, when a reporter asked Mallory why he climbed Everest, his response became legendary.

3. "Because it is there," Mallory replied.

4. No living person knows whether the two British men reached the summit of Everest before they died.

5. Nine years after Mallory and Irvine disappeared, English climbers found Irvine's ice ax.

6. In 1975, a Chinese climber spotted a body that was frozen in deep snow on the side of the mountain.

7. He kept the news secret for several years but finally told a fellow climber on the day before he died himself in an avalanche on Everest.

8. In May 1999, a team of mountaineers searched the area that the Chinese man described and found George Mallory's frozen body still intact after seventy-five years.

9. After they took DNA samples for identification, the mountaineers buried the famous climber on the mountainside where he fell.

10. The question remains whether Mallory was on his way up or down when he met his fate.

EXERCISE 10.5

1. I just read an article with a list of "What Doctors Wish [that] You Knew."

2. One fact is that red and blue fruits are the healthiest.

3. Patients who have doctor's appointments after lunchtime spend less time in the waiting room.

4. Drivers who apply more sunscreen to their left sides get less skin cancer.

5. People who take ten deep breaths in the morning and evening feel less stress.

6. A clock that is visible from the bed makes insomnia worse.

7. People often suffer from weekend headaches because they get up too late.

8. They withdraw from caffeine by skipping the coffee that they usually drink on workdays.

9. Doctors suggest that people maintain weekday hours on weekends.

10. I am glad that I found this list.

EXERCISE 10.6 PARAGRAPH PRACTICE

We have numbered the dependent clauses in the excerpt to show where one ends and another begins.

Parenting Babies

We are most prone to rely on stereotypes (1) when our children are babies. It is difficult to pay attention to their unique qualities (2) when they just lie there, cry, and drool. They don't show much interest in toys yet. They are primarily interested in milk and our dangling car keys. So we fill in the missing information about their personality and interests with stereotypes about (3) what they should like. We don't know much about them as individuals, but we do know their gender. So we let gender drive a lot of our own behavior.

Not surprisingly, (4) when researchers examined the rooms of infant boys and girls, they found differences in (5) what babies are exposed to right from the start. Boys had more "toys of the world," like cars, trains, and machines; girls had more "toys of the home," like dolls and housekeeping toys. Right from the start, parents are shaping (6) whether their children will gravitate toward trucks or dolls (7) once they become mobile.

Parents also differ in (8) how they interact with their babies. Mothers talk more, interact more, and are more sensitive to the smiles of girl babies than boy babies. Baby boys are handled more roughly than baby girls. This is even true (9) when the baby is a stranger in a research study and the researchers alternate (10) whether they call the baby a boy or a girl. The "boy" gets handled like a boy, even (11) when she is secretly a girl.

SECTION 11: CORRECTING FRAGMENTS

EXERCISE 11.1

Possible revisions to make the fragments into sentences are *italicized*.

1. Correct

2. Improvements in fabric coatings *are* making it possible.

3. Clothes *are* treated with certain chemicals.

4. Correct

5. *They have already been tested* by the military for soldiers' uniforms.

6. Correct

7. Correct

8. *They* helped cure soldiers' skin problems, too.

9. Correct

10. *It could also* be used for hospital bedding, kitchen linens, and sport-related clothing.

EXERCISE 11.2

Possible revisions to make the fragments into sentences are *italicized*.

1. Correct

2. *It is* good at holding objects together firmly.

3. *Campers use it to* patch holes in backpacks and tents.

4. Correct

5. Books *have been* written about the unique uses for it.

6. *The makers of Duck Brand duct tape hold a yearly contest.*

7. Correct

8. Strips of duct tape *form* tuxedos, cummerbunds, gowns, hats, and corsages.

9. A $5,000 prize *goes* to the couple with the best use of duct tape and another $5,000 *goes* to their high school.

10. Correct

EXERCISE 11.3

Answers may vary, but here are some possible revisions.

1. A worker at the Smithsonian discovered an important historical object on a shelf in one of the museum's storage rooms.

2. Made of cardboard and covered with short, smooth fur, it was a tall black top hat.

3. The hat didn't look like anything special—more like an old costume or prop.

4. It was special, however, having been worn by Abraham Lincoln on the night of his assassination.

5. Once found and identified, Lincoln's hat traveled with the 150th anniversary exhibition, called "America's Smithsonian."

6. For such a priceless object to be able to travel around the country safely, experts needed to build a unique display case for Lincoln's top hat.

7. The design allowed visitors to view the famous stovepipe hat without damaging it with their breath or hands.

8. The hat traveled in a sealed box that was designed against even earthquakes.

9. Keeping the hat earthquake-proof was an important concern because it would be on display in California for part of the time.

10. Among the millions of objects in the archives of the Smithsonian, President Lincoln's hat is one of the most impressive.

EXERCISE 11.4

Answers may vary, but here are some possible revisions.

1. When Nathan King turned twelve, he had a heart-stopping experience.

2. Nathan was tossing a football against his bedroom wall, which made the ball ricochet and land on his bed.

3. In a diving motion, Nathan fell on his bed to catch the ball as it landed.

4. After he caught the ball, Nathan felt a strange sensation in his chest.

5. To his surprise, he looked down and saw the eraser end of a no. 2 pencil that had pierced his chest and entered his heart.

6. Nathan immediately shouted for his mother, who luckily was in the house at the time.

7. Because Nathan's mom is a nurse, she knew not to remove the pencil.

8. If she had pulled the pencil out of her son's chest, he would have died.

9. After Nathan was taken to a hospital equipped for open-heart surgery, he had the pencil carefully removed.

10. Fate may be partly responsible for Nathan's happy birthday story since it turned out to be his heart surgeon's birthday too.

EXERCISE 11.5

Answers may vary, but here are some possible revisions. (Changes and additions are in *italics*.)

1. One of the people sitting next to me on the train *sneezed four times in a row*.

2. Taking good pictures with my cell phone camera *is easy*.

3. Before the paint was dry in the classrooms, *the new semester began*.

4. The judge's question and the answer it received *surprised everyone*.

5. Because there were fewer students in the program this year, *it ran smoothly*.

6. *His speech lasted* for over an hour.

7. Whenever the teacher reminds us about the midterm exam, *we get nervous*.

8. If we move to Kentucky and stay for two years, *we will save money*.

9. *Please notify us* as soon as the order form reaches the warehouse.

10. Buildings with odd shapes always interest me.

EXERCISE 11.6 PROOFREADING PRACTICE

Answers may vary, but here is one revision to eliminate the seven fragments. Areas of revision are in *italics*.

On June 15, 2012, Nik Wallenda made *history by being* the first person to walk on a tightrope from the U.S. to Canada directly above the raging falls of Niagara Gorge. His trip on the high wire that misty evening took 30 minutes. *It was* a nail-biting half hour that one major network, ABC, televised live. To be on the safe side, the network made sure that Wallenda attached himself to a safety cable in case he fell off the wire on live TV. Nik Wallenda comes from a long line of daredevil *performers, the famous family* known as the Flying Wallendas. Nik represents the seventh generation of people willing to risk their lives in the name of entertainment. Before attempting his spectacular walk across Niagara Falls, Wallenda fought hard to get permission from both U.S. and Canadian *officials so that* he was not arrested—as previous stunt performers have been—when he reached the other side. Instead of handcuffs waiting for him on the Canadian bank of the *falls, Nik Wallenda* heard the cheers of 100,000 supporters welcoming him back to earth.

A year later, Wallenda also succeeded in crossing a gorge near the Grand *Canyon, this time without a safety cable*. His tightrope *was* 1,500 feet above the canyon floor. Winds were so strong that he had to stop twice in the middle of the crossing and crouch down to maintain his position on the wire.

SECTION 12: CORRECTING RUN-ON SENTENCES

EXERCISE 12.1

1. Mary Mallon is a famous name in American history, but she is not famous for something good.

2. Most people know Mary Mallon by another name, and that is "Typhoid Mary."

3. The sentence is correct.

4. The sentence is correct.

5. Mary Mallon was the first famous case of a healthy carrier of disease, but she never believed the accusations against her.

6. Mallon, an Irish immigrant, was a cook; she was also an infectious carrier of typhoid.

7. By the time the authorities discovered Mallon's problem, she had made many people ill. A few of her "victims" actually died from the disease.

8. A health specialist approached Mallon and asked her for a blood sample; she was outraged and attacked him with a long cooking fork.

9. Eventually, the authorities dragged Mallon into a hospital for testing, but she fought them hysterically the entire time.

10. The lab tests proved Mallon's infectious status, and health officials forced Mary Mallon to live on an island by herself for twenty-six years.

EXERCISE 12.2

Your answers may differ depending on how you chose to separate the two clauses.

1. I just read an article about prehistoric rodents, and I was surprised by their size.

2. Scientists recently discovered the remains of a rat-like creature called *Phoberomys;* it was as big as a buffalo.

3. *Phoberomys* sat back on its large rear feet and fed itself with its smaller front feet in just the way rats and mice do now.

4. This supersized rodent lived in South America, but luckily that was nearly ten million years ago.

5. At that time, South America was a separate continent; it had no cows or horses to graze on its open land.

6. South America and North America were separated by the sea, so there were also no large cats around to hunt and kill other large animals.

7. Scientists believe that *Phoberomys* thrived and grew large because of the lack of predators and competitors for food.

8. The *Phoberomys'* carefree lifestyle eventually disappeared, for the watery separation between North and South America slowly became a land route.

9. The big carnivores of North America could travel down the new land route, and the big rodents were defenseless against them.

10. The rodents who survived were the smaller ones who could escape underground, and that is the reason we have no buffalo-sized rats today.

EXERCISE 12.3

Your answers may differ since various words can be used to begin dependent clauses.

1. In September of 2006, Pablo Wendel was a German student of art who felt a special connection with a particular group of ancient sculptures.

2. When Pablo acted on this feeling, he won his "fifteen minutes of fame."

3. The sentence is correct.

4. The sentence is correct.

5. He made a special clay-covered costume that was complete with armor and a helmet.

6. Pablo took this outfit and a pedestal with him to the museum, which is located in Xian, China.

7. The sentence is correct.

8. The sentence is correct.

9. Pablo, in disguise, stood among his fellow "soldiers" and didn't move until eventually someone saw him.

10. Although the museum guards took Pablo's clay costume, they let him go with just a warning.

EXERCISE 12.4

Your answers may differ since various words can be used to begin dependent clauses.

1. Since I've been reading about sleep in my psychology class, I know a lot more about it.

2. Sleep has four stages, which we usually go through many times during the night.

3. The first stage of sleep begins as our muscles relax and mental activity slows down.

4. The sentence is correct.

5. Stage two takes us deeper than stage one so that we are no longer aware of our surroundings.

6. The sentence is correct.

7. Next is stage three, in which we become more and more relaxed and are very hard to awaken.

8. Stage four is so deep that we don't even hear loud noises.

9. The most active type of sleep is called REM (rapid eye movement) sleep because our eyes move back and forth quickly behind our eyelids.

10. Although REM sleep is only about as deep as stage one, we do all our dreaming during the REM stage.

EXERCISE 12.5

Your answers may differ depending on how you chose to separate the clauses.

1. White buffalos are very rare, and they are extremely important in Native American folklore.

2. Many American Indian tribes feel a strong attachment to white buffalos because they are viewed as omens of peace and prosperity.

3. One farm in Wisconsin is famous as a source of white buffalos. Three of them have been born on this farm since 1994.

4. The owners of the farm are Valerie and Dave Heider, and they are as surprised as anyone about the unusual births.

5. The Heiders' first white buffalo was a female calf who was named Miracle.

6. After Miracle became a local attraction, visitors to the Heider farm raised tourism in the area by twenty-two percent in 1995.

7. A second white calf was born on the farm in 1996; however, it died after a few days.

8. Miracle survived until 2004; she lived for ten years.

9. In September of 2006, the Heider farm yielded a third white buffalo calf, but it was a boy.

10. The odds against one white buffalo being born are high; the odds against three being born in the same place are astronomical.

EXERCISE 12.6 PROOFREADING PRACTICE

Your revisions may differ depending on how you chose to correct the errors.

With the focus on cleanliness lately in advertising for soaps and household cleaning products, people are surprised to hear that we may be too clean for our own good. This phenomenon is called the "hygiene hypothesis," and recent studies support its validity. For instance, one study shows the benefit of living with two or more pets. Babies may grow up with healthier immune systems and be less allergic if they live with a dog and a cat or two dogs or two cats. The old thinking was that young children would become more allergic living with many pets, but they don't. Somehow the exposure to pets and all their "dirty" habits gives youngsters much-needed defenses. There may be as much as a seventy-five percent lower allergy risk, according to this study.

SECTION 13: IDENTIFYING VERB PHRASES

EXERCISE 13.1

1. Scientists of all kinds have been learning a lot lately.

2. Those who study traffic safety have recently discovered a puzzling truth.

3. People drive more safely when they encounter fewer traffic signs and traffic lights.

4. The reason behind the "Shared Space" theory is easy to explain.

5. Drivers will regulate their speed and pay closer attention to other drivers when they are not told to do so by signs and lights.

6. Traffic signs and signals give drivers a false sense of security that often leads to recklessness.

7. When no signs or signals exist, drivers think about their own safety and drive more cautiously.

8. Many towns in Europe and America have already taken steps to test the truth of this theory.

9. In some cases, all lights, signs, and barriers have been removed so that all drivers and pedestrians must negotiate with each other to proceed through the town.

10. These changes have usually resulted in lower speeds, fewer accidents, and shorter travel times.

EXERCISE 13.2

1. Have you ever felt a craving for art?

2. Have you said to yourself, "I need a new painting, or I will lose my mind"?

3. If you do find yourself in this situation, you can get instant satisfaction.

4. I am referring to Art-o-Mat machines, of course.

5. These vending machines dispense small pieces of modern art.

6. You insert five dollars, pull a knob on a refurbished cigarette dispenser, and out comes an original art piece.

7. The artists themselves <u>get</u> fifty percent of the selling price.

8. Art-o-Mat machines <u>can be found</u> at locations across the country.

9. Art-o-Mats are currently <u>dispensing</u> tiny paintings, photographs, and sculptures in twenty-eight states and in Canada and Austria.

10. The machines <u>have sold</u> the works of hundreds of contemporary artists.

EXERCISE 13.3

1. During my last semester of high school, our English teacher <u>assigned</u> a special paper.

2. He said that he <u>was becoming</u> depressed by all the bad news out there, so each of us <u>was asked</u> to find a piece of good news and <u>write</u> a short research paper about it.

3. I must <u>admit</u> that I <u>had</u> no idea how hard that assignment <u>would be</u>.

4. Finally, I <u>found</u> an article while I <u>was reading</u> my favorite magazine.

5. The title of the article <u>was</u> a pun; it <u>was called</u> "Grin Reaper."

6. I <u>knew</u> instantly that it <u>must be</u> just the kind of news my teacher <u>wanted</u>.

7. The article <u>explained</u> that one woman, Pam Johnson, <u>had started</u> a club that she named The Secret Society of Happy People.

8. She <u>had</u> even <u>chosen</u> August 8 as "Admit You're Happy Day" and <u>had</u> already <u>convinced</u> more than fifteen state governors to recognize the holiday.

9. The club and the holiday <u>were created</u> to support people who <u>are</u> happy so that the unhappy, negative people around <u>will</u> not <u>bring</u> the happy people down.

10. As I <u>was writing</u> my essay, I <u>visited</u> the Society of Happy People web site, *www.sohp.com,* and <u>signed</u> my teacher up for their newsletter.

EXERCISE 13.4

1. I have always <u>wondered</u> how an Etch A Sketch <u>works</u>.

2. This flat TV-shaped toy <u>has been</u> popular since it first <u>arrived</u> in the 1960s.

3. Now I <u>have learned</u> the secrets inside this popular toy.

4. An Etch A Sketch <u>is filled</u> with a combination of metal powder and tiny plastic particles.

5. This mixture <u>clings</u> to the inside of the Etch A Sketch screen.

6. When the pointer that <u>is connected</u> to the two knobs <u>moves</u>, the tip of it "draws" lines in the powder on the back of the screen.

7. The powder at the bottom of the Etch A Sketch <u>does</u> not <u>fill</u> in these lines because it <u>is</u> too far away.

8. But if the Etch A Sketch <u>is turned</u> upside down, the powder <u>clings</u> to the whole underside surface of the screen and "<u>erases</u>" the image again.

9. Although the basic Etch A Sketch <u>has</u> not <u>changed</u> since I <u>was</u> a kid, it now <u>comes</u> in several different sizes.

10. Best of all, these great drawing devices <u>have</u> never <u>needed</u> batteries, and I <u>hope</u> that they never <u>will</u> [need batteries].

EXERCISE 13.5

1. Scientists successfully <u>cloned</u> a dog for the first time in 2005.

2. Cloning experts <u>had been attempting</u> to clone a dog for many years.

3. They <u>had had</u> success with horses, cats, and even rats before they <u>could clone</u> a dog.

4. The scientists who eventually <u>succeeded were</u> from Seoul National University in South Korea.

5. They <u>named</u> the cloned dog Snuppy as a tribute to the university where the accomplishment <u>was made</u>, and they <u>pronounced</u> the name "Snoopy."

6. Of course, Snuppy <u>could thank</u> his "parent" dog, a three-year-old Afghan hound, for all of his great physical features.

7. Both dogs <u>had</u> long glossy black fur that <u>was accentuated</u> by identical brown markings on their paws, tails, chests, and eyebrows.

8. Unfortunately, the cloning procedure <u>does</u> not <u>guarantee</u> that the clone of a dog <u>will share</u> the unique features of the original dog's personality.

9. Nevertheless, now that dog cloning <u>has been achieved</u>, many people <u>have shown</u> an interest in cloning their own dogs.

10. Although some people <u>may</u> not <u>be</u> happy with just a physical copy of a beloved pet, for others, a copy <u>is</u> better than nothing.

[The word forms "cloning," "to clone," and "cloned" in "the *cloned* dog" are not acting as real verbs, but as *verbals*. To learn more, see Section 18.]

EXERCISE 13.6 PARAGRAPH PRACTICE

The <u>success</u> (of some recent Korean start-ups) <u>suggests</u> that Korean culture <u>is</u> <u>becoming</u> increasingly more tolerant (of Korean Americans). <u>Daniel Shin</u>, a Korean American (from McLean, Virginia), (with a Wharton Business degree), <u>moved</u> (to Korea) (in 2010) to found Ticketmonster, a website <u>that</u> <u>offers</u> discounts (on various products), similar (to Groupon). Just twenty months (after its founding), according (to *Inc.* magazine), Ticketmonster had seven hundred employees and $25 million per month (in revenue). (In 2011), Shin sold Ticketmonster (to the Internet coupon site LivingSocial) (for a reported $380 million). (At the time), Shin was twenty-six years old.

Shin had the foresight to see an industry gap (in Korea) and jump in (with Ticketmonster). But he did butt heads (with more conservative Korean business types). Shin told *Inc.* magazine that [one] executive . . . said [that] he would disown a son (of his) who dropped a successful corporate life to embark (on a start-up).

SECTION 14: USING STANDARD ENGLISH VERBS

EXERCISE 14.1

1. end, ended
2. does, did
3. am, was
4. votes, voted
5. have, had
6. shop, shopped
7. are, were
8. pick, picked
9. do, did
10. have, had

EXERCISE 14.2

1. is, was
2. do, did
3. have, had
4. asks, asked
5. have, had
6. learn, learned
7. are, were
8. does, did
9. plays, played
10. am, was

EXERCISE 14.3

1. started, like
2. offers
3. are, have
4. finished, needed
5. run, do
6. advise, comfort
7. enjoy, are
8. completed, expected
9. have
10. thank

EXERCISE 14.4

1. have
2. play
3. plays
4. play
5. practices, do
6. is, wins
7. am, is, am
8. remind
9. follows
10. have, am, is

EXERCISE 14.5

1. gave
2. handed
3. had
4. showed

5. was
6. imagined
7. filled

8. did
9. looked
10. received

EXERCISE 14.6 PROOFREADING PRACTICE

Yesterday, when I ~~walk~~ *walked* on campus to go to my classroom, I ~~notice~~ *noticed* a problem that needs to be fixed. Every morning, there is a long line of students in their cars waiting to enter the parking lots because the light at the corner ~~do~~ *does* not change fast enough. It ~~change~~ *changes* too slowly, so cars start to stack up on the side streets. Anybody who ~~walk~~ *walks* to school is affected, too. Drivers get desperate when they are stuck in traffic. Many of them don't watch where they're going and almost run over people who ~~is~~ *are* walking in the crosswalks and driveways.

SECTION 15: USING REGULAR AND IRREGULAR VERBS

EXERCISE 15.1

1. eat
2. eat
3. eating
4. eaten

5. ate
6. eats
7. eaten (past participle as adjective)

8. eating
9. ate
10. eat

EXERCISE 15.2

1. drive, driven
2. thinking, thought
3. take, takes
4. told, telling

5. wrote, written
6. knew, know
7. teach, taught

8. torn (past participle as adjective), tear
9. ridden, rode
10. made, make

EXERCISE 15.3

1. took, supposed
2. did, earned
3. called, told, feel
4. thought, was

5. leaving, drove, saw
6. felt, knew, tell
7. tried, went
8. been, undo

9. wishes, take
10. used, called, does

EXERCISE 15.4

1. use, puts

2. does, do

3. transfers, spend

4. is, like, choose

5. does, wants

6. trusts, is

7. imagine, made

8. talking, asked, worries

9. looked, said, lived, understand

10. wonder, is

EXERCISE 15.5

1. lying, fell

2. was, done

3. wearing, shielded

4. lain, woke, realized, happened

5. felt, started

6. passed, turned, began

7. describe, experienced

8. was, felt, saw

9. looked, taped, was, protected, wearing

10. had, felt

EXERCISE 15.6 PROOFREADING PRACTICE

                irr.   irr.   reg.   irr.
They <u>say</u> that cats <u>choose</u> you, not the other way around. I <u>realized</u> that Bob <u>had</u>

        irr.   reg.   irr.
<u>chosen</u> me when he <u>followed</u> me to the bus stop one day. We <u>were</u> far from home, so

            reg.   reg.
when I <u>shooed</u> him away and <u>watched</u> him disappear into the busy crowds,

        reg.   irr.   irr.   reg.
I <u>imagined</u> that <u>was</u> the last I <u>would see</u> of him. But as the bus <u>pulled</u> away, he

        reg.   reg.   reg.
<u>appeared</u> out of nowhere, <u>leaped</u> on board in a blur of ginger, and <u>plonked</u>

                                            irr.   irr.
himself down on the seat next to me. And that <u>had been</u> that.

SECTION 16: MAINTAINING SUBJECT-VERB AGREEMENT

EXERCISE 16.1
1. affects
2. go
3. have
4. were
5. were
6. were
7. was
8. describe
9. were
10. was

EXERCISE 16.2
1. gives
2. sounds, begins, is
3. connects
4. says, means
5. forecasts
6. are, mean
7. are, foretell
8. means
9. are
10. seem

EXERCISE 16.3
1. are, involve
2. suffer
3. are
4. come, lead
5. start, works, plays
6. starts
7. are
8. cause
9. is
10. warn

EXERCISE 16.4
1. is, portray
2. is
3. include, spark, are
4. give
5. rank
6. have
7. get, has, is, is
8. signifies, are
9. is, make
10. has

EXERCISE 16.5
1. is, call
2. is, are, has
3. is, are, is
4. have, is
5. are, are
6. experiences, has
7. are, functions
8. determine
9. seems
10. affect, tend

EXERCISE 16.6 PROOFREADING EXERCISE

Unfortunately, tension between members of the public ~~are~~ *is* common these days. When two people at a movie theater ~~irritates~~ *irritate* each other or have a disagreement, the whole audience ~~suffer~~ *suffers*. Everyone who is sitting around the troublemakers ~~want~~ *wants* to move immediately to another section. However, if anyone ~~get~~ *gets* up to sit somewhere else, then everyone else ~~start~~ *starts* to get nervous. So most people just ~~waits~~ *wait* until one of two fighting people ~~calm~~ *calms* down. After that, the members of the audience ~~forgets~~ *forget* about the disturbance and enjoy the rest of the movie. The same pattern ~~repeat~~ *repeats* itself in stadiums and ballparks, too.

SECTION 17: AVOIDING SHIFTS IN TIME

EXERCISE 17.1

Back in the early 1900s, Sears Roebuck sold houses through the mail. In the famous Sears catalog, these mail-order houses ~~are~~ *were* listed along with the rest of the products. The house kits arrived in thousands of pieces, and people ~~can~~ *could* put them together themselves, or they ~~hire~~ *hired* a builder to help them. In 1919, one company, Standard Oil, placed an order for an entire town's worth of homes for its employees. The house kits even ~~include~~ *included* the paint that the homeowners ~~use~~ *used* to paint the houses when they ~~finish~~ *finished*. The ability to order a whole house from the Sears catalog ended in 1940, but thousands of these houses are still standing in communities across America.

EXERCISE 17.2
The paragraph is correct.

EXERCISE 17.3

Plastic surgery helps many people look better and feel better about themselves. Of course, there ~~were~~ *are* stories of unnecessary surgeries and even heartbreaking mistakes. People make their own decisions about whether plastic surgery ~~was~~ *is* right for them. Dogs, however, can't communicate what they ~~wanted~~ *want*. Nevertheless, some people ~~took~~ *take* their dogs in for cosmetic surgeries, such as tummy tucks and face-lifts. Just like humans, dogs sometimes ~~needed~~ *need* surgery to correct painful or unhealthy conditions. A dog with a low-hanging tummy ~~could~~ *can* get an infection from scratches that *are* caused by rocks on the ground. And another dog may need a face-lift to help it stay clean when it ~~ate~~ *eats*. Animal lovers ~~were~~ *are* worried that some canine plastic surgeries ~~were~~ *are* done without good reasons.

SECTION 18: RECOGNIZING VERBAL PHRASES

EXERCISE 18.1

1. Mark Twain lived [to become one of the most [admired] Americans of his time].

2. [Traveling across the U.S. and to countries around the world], Twain formed [unwavering] opinions, both favorable and unfavorable, of the people and places he visited.

3. Twain began [to write his autobiography] in the last years before he died in 1910.

4. [Hoping [to be honest and thorough]], he decided [to dictate his thoughts] as they struck him.

5. However, he <u>knew</u> that it <u>might be</u> impossible [to be as honest] as he <u>wanted</u> [to be].

6. [Being truthful] <u>meant</u> [including statements that <u>could hurt</u> or <u>upset</u> the people] that he <u>knew</u>, and he <u>knew</u> almost everyone.

7. Twain <u>thought</u> of a way [to avoid [causing that potential pain or embarrassment]].

8. He <u>decided</u> not [to publish his autobiography until 100 years after his death].

9. In that way, Twain <u>did</u> not <u>need</u> [to hold back any of his strong opinions].

10. In 2010, the first volume of *The Autobiography of Mark Twain* <u>was</u> finally <u>released</u>, [making it one of the most [anticipated] books of all time].

EXERCISE 18.2

1. The idea of [home-schooling children] <u>has become</u> more popular recently.

2. Some families <u>decide</u> [to teach children at home] instead of [enrolling them in schools with other students].

3. Many school districts <u>have</u> special independent-study "schools," [offering such families the structure and materials] that they need [to provide an appropriate curriculum] [to study at home].

4. There are many different reasons for [choosing home-schooling and independent-study programs].

5. For instance, child actors and potential Olympic athletes often must study independently [to fit school into their busy schedules].

6. The independent-study format allows parents and special teachers [to instruct young actors [filming] and young athletes [training]] around the world.

7. [Home-schooling] can also benefit gifted children and students with long-[lasting] medical issues.

8. Independent-study programs help students from kindergarten through high school [to do all of their [reading], [writing], and [studying] on their own].

9. Students do meet with independent-study school teachers regularly [to turn in homework and receive new assignments].

10. These teachers ensure students' progress by [checking the completion of assignments] and [clarifying any points of confusion].

EXERCISE 18.3

1. Philippe Halsman <u>was</u> a well-[known] portrait photographer [working in the twentieth century].

2. Halsman's photographs <u>were</u> good enough [to appear on the cover of *Life* magazine 101 times].

3. [Capturing the essence of famous people on film] <u>was</u> Halsman's specialty.

4. The list of celebrities that Halsman <u>was asked</u> [to photograph] <u>included</u> Marilyn Monroe, Albert Einstein, and Winston Churchill.

5. Halsman <u>found</u> that [taking good pictures of such powerful people] <u>was</u> not easy.

6. He often <u>tried</u> [to find new ways] [to loosen them up].

7. In 1952, Halsman <u>asked</u> one of his elite clients [to jump in the air] while [being photographed].

8. Halsman <u>loved</u> the results, and he <u>started</u> a series of [jumping] pictures.

9. Who <u>doesn't</u> <u>like</u> [to see famous people like Richard Nixon] [jumping up like a little boy in a photograph]?

10. Halsman <u>gathered</u> the best of the [jumping] photographs in a book [called *Philippe Halsman's Jump Book*].

EXERCISE 18.4

1. Some travelers <u>want</u> [to know how [to behave in other countries]].

2. *Behave Yourself!* <u>is</u> a book [written [to help such people]].

3. It <u>outlines</u> what [to do] and what not [to do] in countries around the world.

4. In Austria, for example, [cutting your food with a fork] <u>is</u> more polite than [cutting it with a knife].

5. In Egypt, [nodding the head upward]—not [shaking the head from side to side]—<u>means</u> "no."

6. In the Netherlands, [complimenting people about their clothes] <u>is</u> not a good idea.

7. An Italian diner <u>will fold</u> lettuce into a bite-size piece with the fork and knife instead of [cutting it].

8. A common mistake that people <u>make</u> in many countries <u>is</u> [to stand with their hands on their hips].

9. This posture and [pointing at anything with the fingers] <u>are thought</u> [to be very rude] and even [threatening].

10. Travelers <u>should study</u> any country before [visiting it] in order [to avoid [confusing] or [offending] anyone].

EXERCISE 18.5

1. John Steinbeck, author of *The Grapes of Wrath,* <u>was</u> the first native of California [to receive the Nobel Prize for literature].

2. [Calling his hometown of Salinas "Lettuceberg,"] Steinbeck's [writing] <u>made</u> the area famous.

3. At the time, not everyone <u>liked</u> the attention [brought by his portrayals of life in *Cannery Row* and other works].

4. Steinbeck's father <u>was</u> the treasurer of Monterey County for ten years, [working also for the Spreckels company].

5. John Steinbeck <u>tried</u> [to find satisfaction in his birthplace], [enrolling in and quitting his studies at Stanford University many times].

6. Finally, Steinbeck <u>moved</u> to New York, [distancing himself from his California roots].

7. Steinbeck <u>won</u> the Nobel Prize in 1962, [revealing the literary world's esteem for his work].

8. Not [writing anything of the caliber of the Salinas stories] while [living in New York], Steinbeck <u>did return</u> to California before he <u>died</u> in 1968.

9. In 1972, the Salinas library <u>changed</u> its name, [to be known thereafter as the John Steinbeck Library].

10. The house Steinbeck <u>was born</u> in <u>became</u> a restaurant and then a full-[fledged] museum [chronicling the life of Salinas' most [celebrated] citizen].

EXERCISE 18.6 PARAGRAPH EXERCISE

As even-[tempered] as it <u>turned</u> out [to be], Earth <u>started</u> off 4.6 billion years ago as a red-[faced] and hellish infant. The universe <u>had been</u> unfolding for about 10 billion years. A new star, the sun, <u>had</u> just <u>been born</u>. Its afterbirth—cold gas and dust and heavier minerals and [flaming] rocks—<u>was flying</u> about, [beginning [to orbit]]. The heavy debris <u>gravitated</u> to the sun, where temperatures <u>were</u> well [suited] for rock and metal [to condense]. That is why the four planets closest in, [known as the terrestrials], are all <u>made</u> of essentially the same stuff.

For its first half-billion years, Earth <u>was</u> a [molten] inferno some 8,000 degrees Celcius—hotter than today's sun. Scientists <u>call</u> this violent era the Hadean, from the Greek word *Hades,* or hell. Time and again, the young Earth <u>built</u> up a crust, only [to see it [incinerated]] by storms of [flaming] meteors . . . .

Only when air <u>cools</u> do water molecules <u>begin</u> [to stick together], [latching on to gritty particles]. When billions of them <u>have condensed</u>, they <u>form</u> tiny liquid droplets. Billions of droplets, in turn, <u>become</u> clouds in the sky. This <u>is</u> the beauty of water vapor: It <u>falls</u> back to Earth as rain. . . .

About half a billion years after it <u>started</u>, the blitzkrieg <u>began</u> [to wind down]. As the last [flaming] chunks <u>fell</u> to the surface or <u>hurtled</u> away, the planet finally <u>had</u> a chance [to cool]. The water vapor <u>could condense</u>.

At long last, it <u>began</u> [to rain].

EXERCISE 18.7 SENTENCE WRITING

Your sentences may vary from the following examples, but make sure that your verbals are not actually the main verbs of your clauses. You should be able to double underline your real verbs, as we have done here.

1. [Thinking of a good title] <u>takes</u> time.

2. We <u>spent</u> the morning [folding laundry].

3. I <u>enjoy</u> [skiing], but golf relaxes me.

4. I <u>was taught</u> that [marking up a book] <u>is</u> wrong.

5. I <u>would love</u> [to take you to school].

6. I <u>need</u> [to get a good grade on the next quiz].

7. Yesterday, I <u>started</u> [to paste my old photos in a scrapbook].

8. He <u>doesn't have</u> any desire [to exercise].

9. The school <u>canceled</u> the [planned] [parking] lot next to the library.

10. [Given to me as a gift], my dog <u>has become</u> my best friend.

SECTIOIN 19: CORRECTING MISPLACED OR DANGLING MODIFIERS

Answers may vary. Corrections are in *italics.*

EXERCISE 19.1

1. *While I was walking to my car,* I noticed an iPad on the ground.

2. The sentence is correct.

3. People will wait for hours to ride the new roller coaster *that's full of 360-degree loops.*

4. The flight attendant helped a six-year-old boy *find his seat.*

5. The sentence is correct.

6. We have found several travel bargains *by shopping on the Internet.*

7. Angelica finally spotted her lost keys *that were hidden by the long curtains.*

8. *After she got help from a specialist,* her knee began to improve.

9. The sentence is correct. *or* With a low-cost data plan, I can't use my phone *to go online very often.*

10. Students couldn't read the bulletin board *because it had faded from direct sunlight.*

EXERCISE 19.2

1. The sentence is correct.

2. *Before we could ask for an extension,* the teacher gave us a few extra days to turn in our papers.

3. *Looking through their binoculars,* they spotted a hawk and its babies.

4. The sentence is correct.

5. I called the doctor *while I was on the roof.*

6. The sentence is correct.

7. *After it screeched to a stop,* I got on the bus and grabbed a seat.

8. I can't eat a hamburger *without pickles.*

9. The sentence is correct.

10. We had to write a paragraph *in our notebooks, and the topic was the weather.*

EXERCISE 19.3

1. They finally found their lost credit card *that had been lying under the table for a week.*

2. *Walking down the hall, she located the door to the auditorium.*

3. The sentence is correct.

4. *My doctor told me to drink extra water after taking an aspirin.*

5. The sentence is correct.

6. Our mail carrier *tripped on a crack in the sidewalk and fell.*

7. *Since we argued nonstop,* the road trip was not as much fun as we hoped it would be.

8. The sentence is correct.

9. The sentence is correct.

10. The students immediately liked their substitute teacher, *who smiled nicely at everyone.*

EXERCISE 19.4

1. The sentence is correct.

2. Filled with the perfect amount of air, *the new tires made my car handle really well on the road.*

3. After three weeks of waiting, *I finally received the textbooks that I bought online.*

4. He cooked all of his meals *while he was wearing* his slippers.

5. The sentence is correct.

6. *As we drove past the park,* a ball bounced into the street between two parked cars.

7. *I didn't even want the tiny pieces of that torn quiz paper near me.*

8. The sentence is correct.

9. The sentence is correct.

10. I saw an army of ants walking in the cracks of the sidewalk.

1. *Because I felt the thrill of a day at the amusement park,* my blisters didn't bother me.

2. My friends and I saw the new tearjerker, *which is full of touching scenes.*

3. The sentence is correct.

4. Practicing for an hour a day, *she improved her piano playing.*

5. The sentence is correct.

6. *While she was sitting on a bench all day,* an idea came to her.

7. They discovered a new outlet mall *on the road to their cousins' house.*

8. *From his parents,* he felt the pressure of trying to get a good job.

9. The sentence is correct.

10. The sentence is correct.

EXERCISE 19.6 PROOFREADING PRACTICE

Corrections are *italicized.* Yours may differ slightly.

I love parades, so last year my family and I traveled to Pasadena, California, to see one of the biggest parades of all—the Tournament of Roses Parade on New Year's Day. It turned out to be even more wonderful than I expected.

Although we arrived one day early, the city was already crowded with people. *By nightfall*, lots of families were setting up campsites on Colorado Boulevard. We didn't want to miss one float in the parade, so we found our own spot and made ourselves at home. When the parade began, I had as much fun watching the spectators as the parade itself. I saw children *sitting on their fathers'* shoulders and pointing at the breathtaking horses and floats. *The floats were decorated completely with flowers or plant material.* I couldn't believe how beautiful they were and how good they smelled.

The crowd appreciated all the sights and sounds of the parade. Everyone especially enjoyed hearing the school bands, *marching and playing their instruments with perfect precision.* They must have practiced for the whole year to be that good.

My experience didn't end with the parade, however. After the last float had passed by, I found a twenty-dollar bill as *I walked down Colorado Boulevard. I framed it as a souvenir of my trip to the Rose Parade, and now it hangs on my wall at home.*

SECTION 20: FOLLOWING SENTENCE PATTERNS

EXERCISE 20.1

       S   LV   Desc

1. Sleep is an important part (of life).

             S   S   AV   Obj

2. Animals and humans use sleep (as a vacation) (for their brains and bodies).

           S   AV   Obj

3. Some facts (about sleep) might surprise people.

          S   AV   Obj   S   AV

4. Large animals require less sleep than small animals do.

            S   AV

5. A typical cat will sleep (for twelve hours) (in a day).

              S   AV

6. An ordinary elephant will sleep (for only three hours).

         S   AV   Obj   Obj

7. Smaller animals use their brains and bodies (at higher rates).

            S   AV   Obj

8. Therefore, they need many hours (of sleep).

         S   LV Desc

9. The reverse is true (for large animals).

      S   AV

10. Humans fall (between cats and elephants) (for their sleep requirements).

EXERCISE 20.2

         S   LV   Desc

1. Erasto Mpemba is a big name (in science).

                S   AV   Obj

2. (In the early 1960s), he observed an odd phenomenon.

            S   LV   Desc

3. (At the time), he was a high school student (in Tanzania).

          S   AV   Obj
4. Mpemba made ice cream (for a school project).

          S   AV   Obj   AV Obj
5. He boiled the milk and mixed it (with the other ice cream ingredients).

              S   AV   Obj
6. Then he put this boiling hot mixture directly (into the freezer). [*Boiling* is a verbal.]

      S   AV   Obj...   S   AV
7. He discovered *that the hot liquid froze very fast*. [Note: This *dependent clause* is the object in the sentence. It is *what* Mpemba discovered.]

          S   AV   Obj   Obj
8. Mpemba told his teachers and fellow students (about his discovery).

          S   AV
9. They laughed (at the idea) (of hot liquid) freezing quickly. [Note: *Freezing quickly* is a verbal phrase in this sentence. See Section 18 for more about verbals.]

              S   AV   Obj
10. Now all scientists call this phenomenon the "Mpemba effect."

EXERCISE 20.3

                                  S   AV   Obj
1. (In late September), the Stade de France (in Paris) hosted an unusual spectacle.

          S   AV
2. Hundreds (of actors, stunt people, and extras) reenacted the famous chariot
   Obj
   race (from the classic film *Ben-Hur*).

              S   AV   Obj   Obj
3. The same show included live gladiator fights and a galley ship assault.

          S   AV   Obj
4. Promoters also encouraged participation (from the audience).

          S   AV
5. Many (of the 60,000 audience members) attended (in traditional Roman costumes).

          S   AV   Obj
6. The stadium sold toga-like robes (in advance) (along with the tickets).

                     S   LV   Desc

7. Obviously, the live chariot <u>race</u> <u>was</u> the highlight (of the show).

         S   AV

8. <u>Participants</u> (in the dangerous race) <u>rehearsed</u> (for nine months).

              S   AV

9. The chariot <u>race</u> <u>lasted</u> (for fifteen minutes).

    S LV   Desc

10. <u>It</u> <u>was</u> the final event (of the night).

EXERCISE 20.4

       S   LV   Desc

1. <u>Horatio Greenough</u> <u>was</u> a sculptor (in the 1800s).

       S   AV   Obj

2. <u>Greenough</u> <u>created</u> a controversial statue (of George Washington).

        S   LV   Desc   S   LV   Desc

3. The <u>statue</u> <u>weighed</u> twelve tons, but its <u>weight</u> <u>was</u> not the reason (for the controversy).

                 S   AV   Obj

4. The controversial <u>aspect</u> (of the statue) <u>involved</u> Washington's clothes.

         S   AV   Obj

5. The <u>statue</u> <u>portrayed</u> Washington (in a toga-like garment).

         S   S   S   LV Desc   Desc

6. His <u>stomach</u>, <u>chest</u>, and <u>arms</u> <u>were</u> bare and very muscular.

        S   AV

7. One <u>part</u> (of the toga) <u>draped</u> (over the statue's raised right arm).

                S   AV

8. The bare-chested <u>statue</u> (of Washington) <u>stood</u> (in the rotunda) (of the Capitol) (for only three years).

      S   AV   Obj

9. <u>Officials</u> <u>moved</u> the statue many times.

         S   AV

10. (In 1962), <u>it</u> <u>arrived</u> (in its final home) (at the American History Museum).

EXERCISE 20.5

           S   LV   Desc   Desc   Desc

1. Charles Osgood is a writer, TV host, and radio personality.

    S LV   Desc

2. He is also the editor (of a book) (about letters).

                S LV   Desc

3. The book's title is *Funny Letters (from Famous People)*.

                 S   AV   Obj

4. (In his book), Osgood shares hilarious letters (from history).

          S   AV

5. Thomas Jefferson wrote (to an acquaintance) (about rodents) [eating his wallet].

            S   AV   Obj

6. Benjamin Franklin penned the perfect recommendation letter.

      S   AV   Obj

7. Franklin did not know the recommended fellow (at all).

      S   AV   Obj

8. Beethoven cursed his friend bitterly (in a letter) one day.

                        S   AV   Obj

9. (In a letter) the following day, Beethoven praised the same friend excessively

      AV   Obj

and asked him (for a visit).

     S   AV   Obj   AV   Obj

10. Osgood ends the book (with a letter) (by Julia Child) and includes her secrets (for a long life).

EXERCISE 20.6 PARAGRAPH EXERCISE

        S   AV   Obj   AV

Armstrong released his grip (on the handrail) (of the ladder) and stepped

                      S   AV   Obj   Obj DC...

fully (off the foot pad). Walter Cronkite proudly told his CBS audience that a

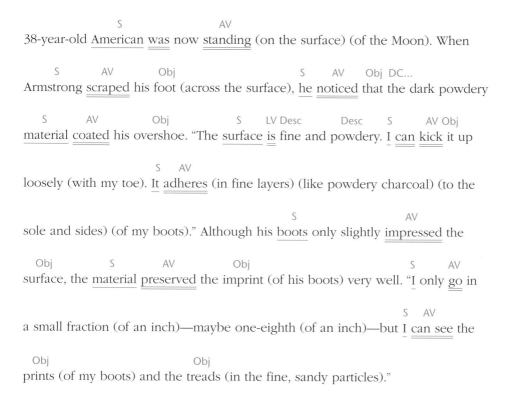

        S   AV

38-year-old American was now standing (on the surface) (of the Moon). When

       S   AV   Obj   S   AV   Obj DC...

Armstrong scraped his foot (across the surface), he noticed that the dark powdery

     S   AV   Obj   S   LV Desc   Desc   S   AV Obj

material coated his overshoe. "The surface is fine and powdery. I can kick it up

                        S   AV

loosely (with my toe). It adheres (in fine layers) (like powdery charcoal) (to the

                                            S   AV

sole and sides) (of my boots)." Although his boots only slightly impressed the

 Obj   S   AV   Obj   S   AV

surface, the material preserved the imprint (of his boots) very well. "I only go in

                                            S   AV

a small fraction (of an inch)—maybe one-eighth (of an inch)—but I can see the

 Obj   Obj

prints (of my boots) and the treads (in the fine, sandy particles)."

SECTION 21: AVOIDING CLICHÉS, AWKWARD PHRASING, AND WORDINESS

Your answers may differ from these possible revisions.

EXERCISE 21.1

    I've been trying to help my son finish his first-grade homework every night, but it isn't easy. Of course, I know that he is smart, but he doesn't always show it. I can get him to sit for a few minutes with his workbooks, but he runs off as soon as I turn around. I tell him stories of how strict teachers were about homework when I was his age. Unfortunately, my son's teacher uses stickers as motivators, and they just don't work. I really hope that my son will learn the value of keeping up in school.

EXERCISE 21.2

    Today, many shoppers buy only organic meats, fruits, and vegetables. They get excited whenever they see an organic label on a can, box, or package. I work at a busy supermarket, and I see customers with and without a lot of money buying these foods to avoid eating pesticides and hormones. Ordinary folks have started to care more about what they and their children eat. Admittedly, organic eggs do taste better, and it feels good to know that the eggs come from happy, free-ranging chickens. Of course, budget-conscious shoppers will always care more about price and will rarely buy organic foods if they cost more.

I have a friend who used to be a struggling actor, but now she has become a professional house sitter. First, she joined an organization that advertises house-sitting opportunities. My friend's first house-sitting job was in Malibu. Unbelievably, she was paid to live in a house on the beach, eat free food, and watch free movies. All she had to do was stay at the house and feed the owners' indoor cat. Now my friend is house sitting in Sedona for friends of the owners of the Malibu house. I am thinking seriously of becoming a house sitter myself.

SECTION 22: CORRECTING FOR PARALLEL STRUCTURE

Your revisions may vary.

EXERCISE 22.1

1. Preparing for emergencies involves two steps: planning for anything and gathering certain supplies.

2. The sentence is correct.

3. The sentence is correct.

4. Where would you go, and how would you get there?

5. Have you made a list of phone contacts inside and outside the area?

6. Do the adults, teenagers, and children in the family carry those phone numbers with them?

7. Are the most important supplies ready at hand, including water, food, flashlight, radio, and batteries?

8. Have you assembled your own first-aid kit or bought a ready-made one?

9. Do you stay prepared by reading, understanding, and updating your important insurance policies?

10. By planning for anything and stocking up on the right supplies, you can prepare yourself and your family for emergencies.

EXERCISE 22.2

1. Taking driving lessons was exciting but nerve-wracking.

2. At first, I learned how to start, steer, and stop the car smoothly.

3. Between driving lessons, I studied the manual, watched driving videos, and practiced emergency hand signals.

4. My instructors taught me, tested me, and encouraged me.

5. The sentence is correct.

6. Finally, my teachers decided that I had learned enough and that I was ready to take the test for my driver's license.

7. I arrived at the testing location, waited in the lobby for a few minutes, and heard someone call my name.

8. During the test, I changed lanes, made right and left turns, and parallel parked like a professional driver.

9. The man who tested me said that I knew the rules and that I must have had good teachers.

10. The sentence is correct.

EXERCISE 22.3

1. The Internet is full of information about new gadgets and technology.

2. People want to have the coolest phones, the clearest photos, and the best travel accessories.

3. The sentence is correct.

4. The ring doesn't use technology to help people do something more easily or live more comfortably.

5. Instead, it helps people avoid doing something—forgetting their anniversary.

6. The "Remember Ring" is designed for people who love gadgets but tend to forget special occasions.

7. It includes several hi-tech features: a perpetually charging battery, a clock run by a microchip, and a tiny heating element.

8. The built-in heating element activates at a preprogrammed time and reminds the wearer about an upcoming anniversary.

9. The sentence is correct.

10. The Remember Ring comes in seven styles in both white and yellow gold.

EXERCISE 22.4

1. To begin, decide which person or family you want to focus on.

2. Make a blank chart that includes spaces for all of a person's important information.

3. Then visit a relative who knows a lot of family history and hopefully saves papers and mementos.

4. Plan to spend a lot of time with any such valuable resource.

5. Gather information from and about one individual at a time.

6. Ask about every part of the person's life—marital status, children, religion, occupation, and travel.

7. Thank your resources for providing you with valuable information.

8. Visit the attics or the dusty old cupboards of anyone who has documents relating to your family.

9. Don't forget the local records office in the town where a relative grew up.

10. Purchase books that provide preprinted worksheets and family tree templates to make your family tree come together faster.

EXERCISE 22.5
Your revisions may differ.

1. The sentence is correct.

2. First, avoid getting frustrated if you have to wait a long time in the reception area or the exam room.

3. Always answer the doctor's questions first; then ask your own questions.

4. Inquire about a referral to a specialist if you think you need one.

5. Find out about other treatments besides the one the doctor first recommends.

6. Ask about any tests that the doctor orders and determine how to get in touch with the doctor about the results.

7. Take the time to ask about prescription drugs' side effects and optional medicines.

8. Try to be calm in your discussions with the doctor.

9. Finally, be prepared to wait in a long line at the pharmacy.

10. If you follow these suggestions when visiting a doctor, you will be more informed and feel more involved in your own treatment.

EXERCISE 22.6 PROOFREADING PRACTICE

The world knows relatively little about the life of William Shakespeare. Stanley Wells' book *Is It True What They Say about Shakespeare?* addresses the questions that people continue to have about the famous poet and playwright. Because of Shakespeare's talent and reputation, everyone wants to know when he was born, which schools he went to, where he traveled, who his friends or lovers were, what he looked like, as well as how and when he wrote each of his poems and plays. Wells starts with the basic question "Is it true that . . .?" Throughout the book, he identifies commonly held beliefs about Shakespeare, discusses the historical evidence, and judges each belief to be "true," "untrue," or something in between. Wells even examines the numerous theories that someone else wrote the works of Shakespeare but finds no evidence strong enough to convince him of their validity.

SECTION 23: USING PRONOUNS

EXERCISE 23.1

1. I

2. she (*does*, a missing verb)

3. she and I (or replace the pair with *we*)

4. I

5. she and I (or replace the pair with *we*), me

6. she

7. I

8. I

9. her and me (or replace the pair with *us*)

10. me, her

EXERCISE 23.2

1. its

2. its

3. its

4. their

5. his or her (One day last week, *the passengers* had to gather *their* belongings. . . .)

6. their

7. their

8. his or her, his or her (*The passengers* did their best to hide *their* annoyance . . . .)

9. him or her, his or her (As *the passengers* stepped off the bus at the end of the line, the driver thanked *them* for *their* patience and understanding.)

10. it

EXERCISE 23.3

1. me

2. he (. . . taller than *he was*.)

3. She and he (or *They* are working. . . .)

4. The dentists received gift bags full of toothbrushes and dental floss. (To avoid wordiness, we deleted the *his or her* pronouns, as well as *Each of* in the beginning.)

5. their

6. I (*I* was the person responsible . . . .)

7. The audience expressed its opinion of the performances with its applause. (To avoid wordiness, we changed the subject to *audience* and used the pronoun *its.*)

8. its

9. I (. . . better than *I do.*)

10. she

EXERCISE 23.4

1. I (. . . as *I am.*)

2. she (. . . than *she does.*)

3. she

4. their

5. its

6. Everyone must use *a* password to enter the network.

7. me (. . . or *by me.*)

8. she (*She* and Justin were the winners. . . .)

9. their

10. us (. . . judge sent *us* a message.)

EXERCISE 23.5

1. me

2. Students will buy *their* own materials for the jewelry class.

3. their

4. I

5. Due to the holiday, everyone was allowed to turn *the* essay in late.

6. she

7. he (. . . than *he is.*)

8. I

9. me

10. her

Corrections are *italicized*.

Rude drivers have one thing in common. Whether male or female, they all believe that they know how to drive better than anyone else. The other day, as my friends and ~~me~~ *I* were driving to school, we stopped at an intersection. A very old man who used a cane started to walk across ~~it~~ *the intersection* in front of my friends and ~~I~~ *me* just before the light was ready to change. So we waited. But while we waited for him, an impatient driver behind us started to honk his horn since he couldn't see ~~him~~ *the old man*. I wondered, "Does ~~he~~ *this driver* want us to hit ~~him~~ *the old man*, or what?" Finally, ~~it~~ *the intersection* was clear. ~~He~~ *The angry man* pulled his car up beside ours, opened his window, and yelled at us before he sped away. The old man reached the other side safely, but ~~he~~ *the rude driver* hardly noticed.

SECTION 24: AVOIDING SHIFTS IN PERSON

This paragraph includes only **one** shift from second person to first person:

Coats are high fashion nowadays, but did you know that most coat styles made their first appearance as military apparel? Your rain-proof multitasking trench coat? [It was] first seen on British soldiers in WWII. Your friend's cool-looking bomber jacket? It came straight from the US Air Force, which designed the garment specifically for pilots. Whether trudging through 35-degree temperatures in Virginia during the Civil War or fighting in snow-bitten Armenia in January of 1914 during WWI, soldiers have always relied on serious outerwear to get the job done, and designers have always looked to the military for ideas about how to create functional clothing. Of course, not all coat styles originated from the armed forces. ~~We~~ *You* have Native Americans to thank for the parka. Whether you're suiting up to battle the elements or adding a final touch to an outfit, take a moment to really look at—and appreciate—the history and style behind your outermost layer.

This paragraph begins with an appropriate introduction in first person (I) and then includes **many** unnecessary shifts between third person *(people, they)* and second person *(you, your)* to report the details about broom superstitions. We have revised the second-person phrasing to maintain the use of third person:

I was reading about superstitions for my psychology class, and I learned that a lot of these beliefs concern brooms and sweeping. One superstition says that, whenever ~~you~~ *people* change ~~your~~ *their* residence, ~~you~~ *they* should get a new broom. People should not take their old brooms with them because the brooms might carry any bad luck that was swept up at the old place and bring it to the new one. Also, if ~~you~~ *people* sweep dirt out an open door, *they should* make it the back door so that the bad luck will depart forever. If ~~you~~ *they* sweep dirt out the front way, the same bad luck will come right back in again. Finally, ~~I learned never to~~ *people should never* walk across a fallen broomstick unless ~~I~~ *they* never want to get married, for that is the fate for anyone who steps over a broomstick. I bet most people would be surprised by how many things can go wrong when ~~you~~ *they* pick up a broom.

EXERCISE 24.3
This paragraph is correct.

PART TWO PROGRESS TEST: SENTENCE STRUCTURE

1. **B**. **is correct**. (The other sentence contains a *misplaced modifier, "looking through my backpack"*—see Section 19).

2. **A**. **is correct**. (The other sentence contains a *misused pronoun*, "asked Jake and *I*"—see Section 23).

3. **A**. **is correct**. (The other sentence contains a *subject-verb agreement error*, "a <u>bunch</u> . . . <u>*were*</u>"—see Section 16).

4. **A**. **is correct**. (The other sentence contains a *subject-verb agreement error*, "<u>adults</u> and <u>children</u> <u>*collects*</u>"—see Section 16).

5. **B**. **is correct**. (The other sentence contains a *subject-verb agreement error*, "<u>compensation</u> . . . <u>*need*</u>"—see Section 16).

6. **A**. **is correct**. (The other sentence is *wordy* and uses *clichés, "Truth be told,"* "*team player,*" and "*loose cannon*"—see Section 21).

7. **B**. **is correct**. (The other sentence includes a *shift in person*, "most of *us* learn that *you* . . ."—see Section 24).

8. **B**. **is correct**. (The other sentence is a *fragment* that contains dependent clauses but *no independent clause*—see Sections 10 and 11).

9. **A**. **is correct**. (The other contains a *pronoun agreement error*, "a *book* . . . *them*"—see Section 23).

10. **B**. **is correct**. (The other sentence contains a *pronoun agreement error*, "*club* . . . *their* boxes"—see Section 23).

11. **B**. **is correct**. (The other sentence suffers from wordiness, "*critique* . . . *lasted* longer than a *critique* usually *does*"—see Section 21).

12. B. is correct. (The other word group is a *dependent clause fragment*, "*Although* reunions are . . ."—see Sections 10 and 11).

13. A. is correct. (The other sentence contains a *subject-verb agreement error*, "the <u>employees</u> or the <u>owner</u> *have* . . ."—see Section 16).

14. B. is correct. (The other word group contains two verbs that unnecessarily *shift in time* "must <u>*convey*</u> . . . and <u>*captures*</u>"—see Section 17).

15. B. is correct. (The other sentence contains a *subject-verb agreement error*, "hazardous <u>conditions</u> . . . *was* responsible . . ."—see Section 16).

PART TWO PARAGRAPH PRACTICE: SENTENCE STRUCTURE

1) *simple:* (Since their invention) half a century ago, video <u>games</u> <u>have come</u> [to play a vital role] (in modern human civilization). **2)** *complex:* <u>I</u> <u>think</u> that this is because we modern <u>humans</u> <u>were</u> never <u>designed</u> [to live as we <u>do</u> now]—[sitting (in traffic)], [working (in offices)], [shopping (in stores)]. **3)** *simple:* <u>We</u> <u>are</u>, (by design), hunter-gatherers. **4)** *simple:* <u>Millions</u> (of years) (of evolution) <u>have wired</u> our brains (with an inherent need) [to hunt, gather, explore, solve puzzles, form teams, and conquer challenge (after challenge)] (in order) [to survive]. **5)** *compound:* (For most people), day-to-day <u>life</u> no longer <u>requires</u> many (of those experiences or challenges), and so those primal, instinctive <u>needs</u> (inside us) <u>have</u> no natural outlet. **6)** *complex:* [To keep our minds and bodies healthy], <u>we</u> <u>simulate</u> those old ways (in the midst) (of our modern, technological lives), where <u>everything</u> (on the planet) <u>has</u> already <u>been hunted</u> and <u>gathered</u>. **7)** *complex:* Thankfully, the <u>technology</u> <u>that</u> <u>created</u> this problem also <u>gave</u> us its solution: video games.

PUNCTUATION

PART THREE PREVIEW TEST: PUNCTUATION

1. A. is correct. (The other sentence contains an unnecessary *comma* before the dependent clause at the end of a sentence—see Section 26).

2. B. is correct. (The other sentence needs a *capital letter* in *liberty*—see Section 29).

3. B. is correct. (The other sentence needs a *comma* after the year *2015*—see Section 26).

4. B. is correct. (The other sentence contains an unnecessary *colon* that does not follow a complete set-up clause—see Section 25).

5. A. is correct. (The other sentence needs to position the *question mark* inside the end *quotation mark*—see Sections 25 and 28).

6. B. is correct. (The words "And The" in the other sentence should not start with *capital letters*—see Section 29).

7. A. is correct. (The other sentence includes an unnecessary *comma* between two verbs in an infinitive phrase—see Section 26).

8. B. is correct. (In the other sentence, "Spring" incorrectly begins with a *capital letter*—see Section 29).

9. B. is correct. (The other sentence includes the error known as a *comma splice*—see Section 26).

10. B. is correct. (The other sentence needs a second *comma* to enclose the *scoopable* phrase "one of the most famous rock bands in the world"—see Section 27).

11. A. is correct. (The other sentence uses unnecessary *commas* to enclose a dependent clause that is *not scoopable*—see Section 27).

12. B. is correct. (The other sentence needs a *comma* after "South Korea"—see Section 26).

13. A. is correct. (The other sentence is an *indirect question* that requires a *period*—see Section 25).

14. A. is correct. (The other sentence needs another *comma* to separate all three items in the series "systems, products and procedures"—see Section 26).

15. B. is correct. (The other sentence needs to position the *comma inside* the quotation mark after "Hello"—see Sections 26 and 28).

SECTION 25: PERIODS, QUESTION MARKS, EXCLAMATION POINTS, SEMICOLONS, COLONS, DASHES

EXERCISE 25.1

1. Do you know how many resources go into making the jeans that we all love to wear?

2. Here are a couple of the details: the dyeing process uses about a pound of harsh chemicals and 15 dye baths to create a single pair of jeans.

3. Would you believe that it also takes 2,500 gallons of water to finish that one pair?

4. Of course, each movement of the jeans through the process requires electricity.

5. Luckily, textile scientists in Switzerland have come up with a "greener" method of jeans production.

6. The result is called Advanced Denim, and its environmental benefits are staggering!

7. The scientific and environmental communities are excited, and who wouldn't be?

8. This new denim requires only one trip through a dye vat and finishes the fabric with eco-friendly substances.

9. The Advanced Denim process uses 30 percent less energy and over 90 percent less water than traditional denim.

10. Can you imagine the positive effects it could have when multiplied by the 2 billion pairs of jeans produced each year?

EXERCISE 25.2

1. Have you noticed that light bulbs don't last as long as they used to?

2. Some seem to burn out after only a month or two.

3. Would you believe that one light bulb has lasted for 110 years?

4. Well, it's true—believe it or not! (or)

5. At a fire station in Livermore, California, the same bulb has been burning since 1901.

6. The now famous light bulb is treated like a celebrity by the firefighters.

7. They are proud of its history, and who wouldn't be?

8. The famous bulb doesn't get cleaned or covered by any type of shade; no one wants to risk damaging it or making it burn out after so many years.

9. The Livermore Light Bulb, as it's called, has even made it into the *Guinness Book of World Records* as the longest running light bulb.

10. Anyone who wants to see this famous bulb in action can visit its 24-hour webcam online.

EXERCISE 25.3

1. The sentence is correct.

2. This young woman—a very controversial figure in Washington, D.C.—began her career as a sculptor in 1863 at the age of sixteen.

3. Miss Ream was a student of the famous sculptor Clark Mills; he is perhaps best known for his statue of Andrew Jackson located across from the White House.

4. Vinnie Ream started to work with Mills in his studio in the basement of the Capitol building; soon members of Congress were volunteering to sit for Miss Ream, and she sculpted busts of them.

5. Her fame and reputation grew in the late 1860s; that's when she was awarded a ten-thousand-dollar commission to create a life-size statue of Abraham Lincoln.

6. Vinnie Ream had known Lincoln; in fact, before his assassination, President Lincoln would allow Miss Ream to sit in his office within the White House and work on a bust of him as he carried out the business of running the country.

7. The sentence is correct.

8. Vinnie Ream's relationships and the works she produced were not accepted by everyone; Ream's youth and physical beauty led to much of this harsh criticism.

9. Some people questioned her motives; others even questioned her abilities.

10. The sentence is correct.

EXERCISE 25.4

1. The sentence is correct.

2. The sentence is correct.

3. One relatively safe place is inside a building that has plumbing pipes or electrical wires; those channels can absorb the electrical energy unleashed by lightning.

4. Of course, once inside such a building, people should stay away from the end sources of plumbing and wiring: faucets, hoses, phone receivers, and computer terminals.

5. Buildings without pipes or wires are not safe shelters during lightning strikes; these might include pergolas, dugouts, and tents.

6. Outside, lightning can move over the ground; therefore, you should be aware of a position that emergency officials call the "lightning squat."

7. The sentence is correct.

8. The sentence is correct.

9. Lightning is electrical energy; consequently, it can travel far from the actual storm clouds.

10. The sentence is correct.

EXERCISE 25.5

1. What do math and origami—Japanese paper folding—have to do with each other?

2. Erik Demaine and other origami mathematicians would answer, "Everything." (or "Everything!")

3. If you have never heard of the field of origami mathematics, you're not alone.

4. Origami math is a relatively new field; back in 2003, Demaine won a "genius" award partly due to his work with origami and its applications in many fields.

5. The MacArthur Foundation awarded Demaine more than just the title "genius"; it awarded him half a million dollars. (or !)

6. At twenty, Demaine was hired as a professor by the Massachusetts Institute of Technology; he became the youngest professor MIT has ever had.

7. Erik Demaine has his father to thank for much of his education: (or ;) Martin Demaine home-schooled Erik as the two of them traveled around North America.

8. Erik was always intensely interested in academic subjects; during his travels, he and his father would consult university professors whenever Erik had questions that no one else could answer.

9. Erik Demaine continues to investigate one area in particular: the single-cut problem.

10. This problem involves folding a piece of paper—then making one cut; the result can be anything from a swan to a star, a unicorn, or any letter of the alphabet.

EXERCISE 25.6 PROOFREADING EXERCISE

Manage your ego. If you want to be recognized for designing a good or even great building, forget about what *you* want the building to be; instead ask, "What does the *building* want to be?" A design problem has to be addressed on its own terms: the needs of the client, the nature of the site, the realities of the building program, and many others. These factors point toward an inherent order that must be acknowledged before self-expression can enter the design process.

Strive to accommodate and express universal concerns in your work—the human quest for meaning and purpose, the variegated play of light and shadow on a textured wall, the interweaving of public and private relationships, the structural and aesthetic opportunities inherent in building materials—and you will find an interested audience.

SECTION 26: COMMAS USED TO SEPARATE ELEMENTS

EXERCISE 26.1

1. The young actor named Sabu began his career in 1937, and he became famous for his unique background and abilities.

2. The sentence is correct.

3. The sentence is correct.

4. In real life, Sabu understood elephants very well, for his father was an owner and trainer of elephants.

5. Sabu's first film was called *The Elephant Boy*, and it made him an instant celebrity.

6. The sentence is correct.

7. The sentence is correct.

8. The sentence is correct.

9. Sabu's version of *The Jungle Book* was made decades before Disney's animated versions, but it captured the essence of the mysterious jungle even more vividly with real actors and animals.

10. The sentence is correct.

1. I finished high school on June 23, 2015, in Amherst, Massachusetts.

2. My favorite English teacher was young, enthusiastic, and highly motivated.

3. We read essays, stories, poems, novels, and research articles in her class.

4. My group even opted to read a play, memorize all of its parts, and perform it for everyone.

5. The sentence is correct.

6. The sentence is correct.

7. We each wrote letter of complaint about a product, a service, or an experience that was unsatisfactory to us.

8. Then we sent copies of our letter to the company's business address, to our home address, and to Ms. Kern's school address.

9. Ms. Kern assured us that we would receive a response from the company if we explained our dissatisfaction clearly, asked for a reasonable solution, and used a respectful tone.

10. My company replied to my letter with a note of apology, a bumper sticker, and an impressive gift card to use at any of the company's stores.

1. As if people don't have enough to worry about, Melinda Muse wrote a book called *I'm Afraid, You're Afraid: 448 Things to Fear and Why.*

2. In her book, Muse points out the dangers of common places, objects, foods, months, days, and activities.

3. If people go to Vegas regularly, they should worry because paramedics can't reach people as quickly in large crowds or huge buildings.

4. The sentence is correct.

5. In the comfort of our homes, unwashed new clothes may transfer dangerous chemicals to people's eyes, skin, and lungs.

6. Among the foods to avoid, grapefruit juice can interfere with certain medications' effectiveness.

7. Thanks to Independence Day celebrations and outdoor picnics, July ranks highest of all the months in accidental injuries and food poisonings.

8. Being linked with more suicides and heart attacks than any other weekday, Mondays are the most dangerous days of the week.

9. Believe it or not, singing in a choir can even permanently damage people's ears.

10. After reading *I'm Afraid, You're Afraid*, it's possible to be afraid of almost everything.

EXERCISE 26.4

1. The United States introduced the Susan B. Anthony dollar in 1979, making her the first woman on a circulating coin.

2. No one deserved this honor more than Susan B. Anthony, having led the fight for women's voting rights in America.

3. The Anthony dollar quickly became unpopular, however.

4. People disliked certain features of the coin, not the person on the coin.

5. This dollar coin was too much like a quarter, nearly the same size and color with the same rough edge around it.

6. The sentence is correct.

7. In 1999, the government stopped issuing Susan B. Anthony dollars, preferring to introduce a new golden dollar coin instead.

8. The new coin portrayed the image of a famous American woman, just as the Anthony dollar did.

9. The Sacagawea "golden dollar" has suffered from its own lack of popularity, unfortunately.

10. Women haven't had much luck as images on coins, have they?

EXERCISE 26.5

1. Fish may be considered "brain food," but I've never liked it.

2. While everyone is saying how delicious a big salmon steak is or how yummy the shrimp tastes, you'll find me grimacing and munching on the bread.

3. Part of the problem with fish is the smell, but my friends who love to eat fish also love the smell of fish cooking.

4. I always thought that was strange, but it makes sense, doesn't it?

5. If someone hates the taste of onions, that person probably also hates the smell of onions cooking.

6. Come to think of it, my husband hates to eat sweets and doesn't like the smell of them either. (You could also use a comma before *either* to make it a tag.)

7. When we walk into a bakery together, he practically has to hold his nose the way I would in a fish market.

8. To me, that's odd, but my aversion to fish must seem weird to someone who loves it.

9. Our daughter adores the taste of bacon, but she hates the smell of bacon frying.

10. The sentence is correct. [Note that a *fanboys*—in this case *So*—can begin a sentence, and it does not need a comma after it.]

EXERCISE 26.6 PARAGRAPH PRACTICE

After the commas, we have identified the elements that they separate.

There I was in the pilot's seat of a small airplane. I had signed up for a course in flying at the aviation school, [*2 independent clauses (ICs) with fanboys*] but I didn't really expect to get my pilot's license. Learning the instruments took the most time. Once we began training in the cockpit, [*introductory dependent clause (DC)*] the instructor told us what to do, [*2ICs with fanboys*] and we did it. When I turned the yoke to the right, [*intro. DC*] the plane banked right. When I turned it to the left, [*intro. DC*] the plane went left. Actually, [*intro. word*] it was very similar to driving a car, [*tag contrast*] only much more fun. I'm exaggerating about it being easy, [*tag comment*] of course. My favorite type of practice involved landings, [*tag description*] bringing the plane in softly and safely. After many hours of supervised flying, [*intro. phrase*] my time to solo came, [*2ICs with fanboys*] and I was nervous but excited. [*or "I was nervous, but excited" as a tag contrast*] I covered my checklist on the ground, [*list*] took off without any problems [*list*], and landed smoothly in the middle of the runway. On a cold day in October 2014, [*intro. phrase*] I became a licensed pilot. Now I can work toward my next dream of becoming a private pilot for a rock star.

EXERCISE 26.7 SENTENCE WRITING

Here are some possible combinations. Yours may differ.

I like to watch golf and tennis, but I love to play baseball and soccer. [*2ICs with fanboys*]

Tutors do not correct students' essays, but they can explain how to clarify ideas, add stronger details, and improve organization. [*2ICs with fanboys and a list*]

When my parents were growing up in the 1960s, most cars had seatbelts, but not airbags or car seats for children. [*intro. DC and tag contrast*]

SECTION 27: COMMAS USED TO ENCLOSE ELEMENTS

For Exercises 27.1 and 27.2, correct sentences remain in the answers without commas for the sake of comparison.

Exercise 27.1

1. The first person who guessed correctly won a trip to the Grand Canyon.

2. Professor Jones, who guessed correctly, won a trip to the Grand Canyon.

3. Cookies that contain nuts may be harmful to people with allergies.

4. My cookie recipe, which does not contain nuts, is safe for people with allergies.

5. Students who take the train to school catch a shuttle from the station to campus.

6. Melissa, who takes the train to school, catches a shuttle from the station to campus.

7. The teacher explained the answer to the question that everyone missed.

8. The teacher explained the answer to question 14, which everyone missed.

9. The gorilla, an animal on many endangered species lists, has an average lifespan of 30 to 50 years.

10. Koko, the gorilla who became famous for learning to communicate through sign language, turned 45 years old in July 2016.

Exercise 27.2

1. We hope, of course, that people will honor their summons for jury duty.

2. Of course we hope that people will honor their summons for jury duty.

3. People who serve as jurors every time they're called deserve our appreciation.

4. Thelma and Trevor Martin, who serve as jurors every time they're called, deserve our appreciation.

5. We should therefore be as understanding as we can be about the slow legal process.

6. Therefore, we should be as understanding as we can be about the slow legal process.

7. A legal system that believes people are innocent until proven guilty must offer a trial-by-jury option.

8. The U.S. legal system, which believes people are innocent until proven guilty, offers a trial-by-jury option.

9. With that option, we hope that no one will receive an unfair trial.

10. With that option, no one, we hope, will receive an unfair trial.

Exercise 27.3

1. The story of Dracula, the frightening Prince Vlad Tepes, has been fascinating people across the world for hundreds of years.

2. He was held as a prisoner in Bran Castle, a medieval fortress in Transylvania in the 15th century. [This sentence needs only one comma; the end of the sentence is the end of the "scoopable."]

3. Bran Castle, also called Dracula's Castle, has become a popular tourist attraction.

4. The sentence is correct.

5. The sentence is correct.

6. The sentence is correct.

7. It was given to Marie, Queen of Romania, in 1920.

8. The sentence is correct.

9. The sentence is correct.

10. Queen Marie's grandson, Dominic von Habsburg, now owns the castle, along with his two sisters, Maria Magdalena and Elizabeth.

EXERCISE 27.4

1. Arthur S. Heineman, a California architect, designed and built the world's first motel in the 1920s.

2. He chose the perfect location, the city of San Luis Obispo, which was midway between Los Angeles and San Francisco.

3. Heineman, an insightful man of business, understood the need for inexpensive drive-in accommodations on long motor vehicle trips.

4. Hotels, which required reservations and offered only high-priced rooms within one large structure, just didn't fulfill the needs of motorists.

5. Heineman envisioned his "Motor Hotel," or Mo-Tel, as a place where the parking spaces for the cars were right next to separate bungalow-style apartments for the passengers.

6. Heineman's idea was so new that, when he put up his "Motel" sign, several residents of the area told him to fire the sign's painter, who couldn't even spell the word *hotel*.

7. The sentence is correct.

8. Heineman's Milestone Mo-Tel, the world's first motel, opened in San Luis Obispo in 1925.

9. Before Heineman's company, the Milestone Interstate Corporation, could successfully trademark the name "Mo-Tel," other builders adopted the style and made *motel* a generic term.

10. Some of the original Milestone Mo-Tel building, now called the Motel Inn, still stands on the road between L.A. and San Francisco.

EXERCISE 27.5

1. I bought a book, *The Story of the "Titanic,"* because I am interested in famous events in history.

2. This book, written by Frank O. Braynard, is a collection of postcards about the ill-fated ocean liner.

3. The book's postcards, four on each page, can be pulled apart and mailed like regular ones.

4. The sentence is correct.

5. The blank sides, where messages and addresses go, include brief captions of the images on the front of the cards. (Note: This sentence could be left without commas.)

6. The book's actual content, the part written by Braynard, offers a brief history of each image relating to the *Titanic*.

7. One of my favorite cards shows the ship's captain, Edward Smith, and its builder, Lord Pirrie, standing on the deck of the *Titanic* before it set sail.

8. Another card is a photograph of *Titanic* passengers on board the *Carpathia*, the ship that rescued many survivors.

9. There is also a picture of two small children, survivors themselves, who lost their father in the disaster but were later reunited with their mother.

10. The most interesting card, a photo of the ship's gymnasium, shows that one of the pieces of exercise equipment for the passengers was a rowing machine.

EXERCISE 27.6 PARAGRAPH PRACTICE

   Do you know, Ryan, that there is a one-unit library class that begins next week? It's called Library 1, Introduction to the Library, and my friends recommended it. The librarians who teach it will give us an orientation and a series of assignment sheets. Then, whenever we finish the assignments, we turn them in to the librarians for credit. Ms. Kim, the librarian that I spoke with, said that the course materials cover really valuable library skills. These skills, such as finding books or articles in our library and using the Internet to access other databases, are the ones universities will expect us to know. I therefore plan to take this class, and you, I hope, will take it with me.

EXERCISE 27.7 SENTENCE WRITING

Here are some possible combinations. Yours may differ.

   Persis Frank, a great boss, recognizes hard work and rewards dedicated employees. [or] Persis Frank is a great boss who recognizes hard work and rewards dedicated employees.

   She plans to buy herself an expensive watch by Tag Heuer, her favorite brand. [or] She plans to buy herself an expensive Tag Heuer watch.

Only two people, the manager and an actor, were in the store when the commercial was filmed. [or] The manager and an actor were the only people in the store when the commercial was filmed.

SECTION 27: COMMA REVIEW EXERCISE

I'm writing you this note, Melanie, to ask you to do me a favor. [5, name] Before you leave for work today, would you take the chicken out of the freezer? [3, intro.] I plan to get started on the appetizers, drinks, and desserts as soon as soon as I wake up. [2, list] I will be so busy, however, that I might forget to thaw out the chicken. [6, interrupter] It's the first time I've cooked all the food for a party by myself, and I want everything to be perfect. [1, 2ICs with fanboys] The big round baking pan, the one in the cupboard above the refrigerator, should be the best place to keep the chicken as it thaws. [7, scoopable] Wish me luck, seriously! [4, tag]

SECTION 28: QUOTATION MARKS AND ITALICS/ UNDERLINES

EXERCISE 28.1

1. A film crew was setting up in the park by my house, and I saw a sign that said, "Extras holding."

2. I found someone who didn't look too busy and asked, "Are you looking for extras?"

3. "Yes," she answered, "if you want to be in a crowd scene, just fill out the paperwork and sit over there."

4. I didn't even think twice and told her, "Sure, I'd love to be in it."

5. I found out from another extra that we were filming the pilot for a new TV comedy series along the lines of <u>Desperate Housewives</u>.

6. When I asked what I was supposed to do, he said, "They'll give you a picket sign, and you'll wave it. That's it."

7. I held my sign that said, "No more cuts to education!" and waved it when I was told to.

8. While it was happening, I kept telling myself, "You're going to be on TV—just try not to look stupid."

9. I heard someone ask, "Did anyone else hear that the title of the series is going to be <u>Tangle Square</u>?"

10. We all shook our heads; then I added, "But that's an interesting title, if it's true."

EXERCISE 28.2

1. I am reading a book called <u>Don't: A Manual of Mistakes & Improprieties More or Less Prevalent in Conduct and Speech.</u>

2. The book's contents are divided into chapters with titles such as "At Table," "In Public," and "In General."

3. In the section about table don'ts, the book offers the following warning: "Don't bend over your plate, or drop your head to get each mouthful."

4. The table advice continues by adding, "Don't bite your bread. Break it off."

5. This book offers particularly comforting advice about conducting oneself in public.

6. For instance, it states, "Don't brush against people, or elbow people, or in any way show disregard for others."

7. When meeting others on the street, the book advises, "Don't be in a haste to introduce. Be sure that it is mutually desired before presenting one person to another."

8. In the section titled "In General," there are more tips about how to get along in society, such as "Don't underrate everything that others do, and overstate your own doings."

9. The <u>Don't</u> book has this to say about books, whether borrowed or owned: "Read them, but treat them as friends that must not be abused."

10. And one can never take the following warning too much to heart: "Don't make yourself in any particular way a nuisance to your neighbors or your family."

EXERCISE 28.3

1. Emilie Buchwald once noted, "Children are made readers on the laps of their parents."

2. Have you read Mark Twain's book <u>The Adventures of Tom Sawyer?</u>

3. I took a deep breath when my counselor asked, "How many math classes have you had?"

4. "Let's start that again!" shouted the dance teacher.

5. Last night we watched the Beatles' movie <u>Help!</u> on DVD.

6. "Books," wrote Jonathan Swift, "are the children of the brain."

7. Voltaire stated in <u>A Philosophical Dictionary</u> that "Tears are the silent language of grief."

8. Why do dentists ask questions like "How are you?" as soon as they start working on your teeth?

9. "Time is the only incorruptible judge" is just one translation of Creon's line from the Greek play <u>Oedipus Rex</u>.

10. My favorite essay that we have read this semester has to be "The Pie" by Gary Soto.

EXERCISE 28.4

1. <u>Women's Wit and Wisdom</u> is the title of a book I found in the library.

2. The book includes many great insights that were written or spoken by women throughout history.

3. England's Queen Elizabeth I noted in the sixteenth century that "A clear and innocent conscience fears nothing."

4. "Nothing is so good as it seems beforehand," observed George Eliot, a female author whose real name was Mary Ann Evans.

5. Some of the women's quotations are funny; Alice Roosevelt Longworth, for instance, said, "If you don't have anything good to say about anyone, come and sit by me."

6. "If life is a bowl of cherries," asked Erma Bombeck, "what am I doing in the pits?"

7. Some of the quotations are serious, such as Gloria Steinem's statement, "The future depends on what each of us does every day."

8. Maya Lin, the woman who designed Washington D.C.'s Vietnam Veterans Memorial, reminded us that, as she put it, "War is not just a victory or a loss. . . . People die."

9. Emily Dickinson had this to say about truth: "Truth is such a rare thing, it is delightful to tell it."

10. Finally, columnist Ann Landers advised one of her readers that "The naked truth is always better than the best-dressed lie."

EXERCISE 28.5

1. In Booker T. Washington's autobiography <u>Up from Slavery</u>, he describes his early dream of going to school.

2. "I had no schooling whatever while I was a slave," he explains.

3. He continues, "I remember on several occasions I went as far as the schoolhouse door with one of my young mistresses to carry her books."

4. Washington then describes what he saw from the doorway: "several dozen boys and girls engaged in study."

5. "The picture," he adds, "made a deep impression upon me."

6. Washington cherished this glimpse of "boys and girls engaged in study."

7. It contrasted directly with his own situation: "My life had its beginning in the midst of the most miserable, desolate, and discouraging surroundings."

8. "I was born," he says, "in a typical log cabin, about fourteen by sixteen feet square."

9. He explains, "In this cabin I lived with my mother and a brother and sister till after the Civil War, when we were all declared free."

10. As a slave at the door of his young mistress's schoolhouse, Booker T. Washington remembers, "I had the feeling that to get into a schoolhouse and study in this way would be about the same as getting into paradise."

EXERCISE 28.6 PROOFREADING PRACTICE

We were allowed to choose a book to review in our journals last week. The teacher specified that it should be a short nonfiction book about something of interest to us. I found a great book to review. It's called Tattoo: Secrets of a Strange Art. Albert Parry breaks the contents down into chapters about tattoo legends, techniques, and purposes. A few of the chapter titles are "The Art and Its Masters," "The Circus," "Identification," and "Removal." The book also includes illustrations and photographs of tattoo designs and tattooed people and animals throughout history, including Miss Stella: The Tattooed Lady, The Famous Tattooed Cow, and Georgius Constantine. Parry describes Constantine's tattoos in the following way: "the most complete, elaborate, and artistic tattooing ever witnessed in America or Europe." Parry continues, "There was almost no part of his body, not a quarter-inch of the skin, free from designs." Needless to say, since I love tattoos, I loved Parry's book about them.

SECTION 29: CAPITAL LETTERS

In this section, titles of larger works are *italicized* rather than underlined.

EXERCISE 29.1

1. I have always wanted to learn another language besides English.

2. Recently, I have been watching a lot of films from India.

3. Some people call them "Bollywood movies."

4. Whatever they are called, I love to watch them.

5. One part of these movies that I love is their language: Hindi.

6. I have to use English subtitles to understand the dialogue most of the time.

7. But sometimes I can catch what's happening without the subtitles.

8. Because of my intense interest in Hindi-language films, I plan to take a Hindi class.

9. I have already bought a book that explains the Devanagari writing system.

10. Now I will enroll in a class and learn Hindi as a second language.

EXERCISE 29.2

1. When people think of jazz, they think of *Down Beat* magazine.

2. *Down Beat*'s motto may be "Jazz, Blues & Beyond," but some people think that the magazine has gone too far "beyond" by including two guitarists in the *Down Beat* Hall of Fame.

3. The two musicians in question are Jimi Hendrix and Frank Zappa.

4. Jimi Hendrix was inducted into the Hall of Fame in 1970.

5. *Down Beat* added Frank Zappa to the list in 1994.

6. Since then, readers and editors have been debating whether Hendrix and Zappa belong in the same group as Duke Ellington, John Coltrane, and Miles Davis.

7. Those who play jazz guitar have some of the strongest opinions on the subject.

8. Russell Malone, Mark Elf, and John Abercrombie all agree that Hendrix and Zappa were great guitarists but not jazz guitarists.

9. Others like Steve Tibbetts and Bill Frisell don't have any problem putting Hendrix on the list, but Tibbetts isn't so sure about including Zappa.

10. It will be interesting to see who *Down Beat*'s future inductees will be.

EXERCISE 29.3

1. Many consider *The Diary of Anne Frank* to be one of the most important books of the twentieth century.

2. Anne Frank wrote her famous diary during the Nazi occupation of Holland in World War II.

3. The building in Amsterdam where the Frank family and several others hid during the two years before their capture is now a museum and has been recently renovated.

4. Visitors to the Anne Frank House can stand before her desk and see pictures of movie stars like Greta Garbo on her wall.

5. They can climb the stairs hidden behind a bookcase that led to the annex where Anne lived with her mother, Edith; her father, Otto; and her sister, Margot.

6. One of the others hiding with the Franks was Peter van Pels, who was roughly the same age as Anne.

7. Anne writes of her relationship with Peter in her diary.

8. Visitors to the museum can enter the room where Peter gave Anne her first kiss just a few months before the Nazis discovered their hiding place in 1944.

9. Anne's family and Peter's were both sent to concentration camps in Germany.

10. Only Anne's father lived to see the Anne Frank House open as a museum for the first time on May 3, 1960.

EXERCISE 29.4

1. I recently saw the movie *V for Vendetta*, and I wanted to learn more about it.

2. I found out that it's based on an extensive series of comic books.

3. They were written by Alan Moore and illustrated by David Lloyd.

4. The original episodes of *V for Vendetta* were published in black and white within a British comic series called *Warrior*.

5. Once the series caught on in the United States, DC Comics began to publish it.

6. At that time, the creators added color to the drawings.

7. The letter V in the title *V for Vendetta* stands for the main character, a mysterious costumed figure who calls himself V.

8. However, many other connections between the letter V and the Roman numeral 5, which is written as a V, come up throughout the story.

9. V wears a mask that people in the United Kingdom refer to as a Guy Fawkes mask.

10. Guy Fawkes was an English historical figure famous for his involvement in the Gunpowder Plot, which failed on the fifth of November in 1605.

EXERCISE 29.5

1. When my art teacher asked the class to do research on Frida Kahlo, I knew that the name sounded familiar.

2. Then I remembered that the actress Salma Hayek starred in the movie *Frida*, which was about this Mexican-born artist's life.

3. Frida Kahlo's paintings are all very colorful and seem extremely personal.

4. She painted mostly self-portraits, and each one makes a unique statement.

5. One of these portraits is called *My Grandparents, My Parents, and I*.

6. Kahlo gave another one the title *The Two Fridas*.

7. But my favorite of Kahlo's works is *Self-Portrait on the Borderline between Mexico and the United States*.

8. In an article I read in *Smithsonian* magazine, Kahlo's mother explains that after Frida was severely injured in a bus accident, she started painting.

9. Kahlo's mother set up a mirror near her daughter's bed so that Frida could use herself as a model.

10. In the *Smithsonian* article from the November 2002 issue, Kahlo is quoted as saying, "I never painted dreams. I painted my own reality."

EXERCISE 29.6 PARAGRAPH PRACTICE

As Walt and I walked away from the story meeting that day, he seemed relieved that at last the *Sleeping Beauty* picture was going to get underway. "I want a moving illustration," he said. I felt his sincerity. To me his words summed it all up: to Walt nothing was impossible.

"We're in no hurry," Walt would say. "We'll take the time the picture needs."

I looked around me and counted the men I would be privileged to work with . . . men who could make the *Beauty* dream come true, for it was planned from the beginning that *Sleeping Beauty* would be a sharp departure from any picture we had made: in color, styling, rendering, and in character design and development. And it was to be in dramatic CinemaScope proportions with music from Tchaichovksy's *Sleeping Beauty* ballet recorded by the Berlin Symphony orchestra conducted by George Bruns. [Note that "orchestra" could also be capitalized.]

PART THREE PROGRESS TEST: PUNCTUATION

1. We couldn't leave San Antonio, Texas, without visiting its most famous site: the Alamo.

2. My teacher asked, "Have you seen the earliest episodes of *The Simpsons?*"

3. The Taylors remodeled their garage; now their son uses it as an apartment.

4. When Leslie, my older sister, got a speeding ticket, she went to traffic school.

5. We have refunded your money, Ms. Jones, and have sent you a confirmation.

6. The nutrition class that I need is offered in two ways: online or in person.

7. The United Parcel Service, better known as UPS, is hiring on campus today. [or] The United Parcel Service—better known as UPS—is hiring on campus today.

8. Even though I am enjoying my Latin class, I wish I had taken Chinese instead.

9. You always forget the month of my birthday: (or ;) you think it's in July.

10. Pink, normally a calming color, can have the opposite effect when it's neon.

11. "Stopping by Woods on a Snowy Evening" is a famous poem by Robert Frost.

12. Buying a new car online takes time, patience, and luck. [or !]

13. My friend read the play *The Taming of the Shrew* in her gender studies class.

14. That textbook, *The History of Textiles,* is expensive, isn't it?

15. The foreign film club (or Foreign Film Club) needs people to pass out flyers— let's volunteer!

PART THREE PARAGRAPH PRACTICE: PUNCTUATION

Most people know what "buyer's remorse" means. Buyer's remorse is the feeling of regret that immediately follows a purchase; it affects many wary shoppers, especially when they order online. When these shoppers purchase items in an actual store, they are fine. They know that if they don't like something, the store will take it right back for a refund. However, once they hit the "Place order" button on their computer or phone, they immediately begin to doubt themselves. The difference seems to involve the amount of time that it takes for an online order to arrive. That extra time gives shoppers a chance to ask themselves, "Is this item really worth the shipping costs and trouble it will take to return it?" To cure online buyers' remorse, many companies who sell primarily online offer free deliveries and returns, and they have shortened the transit time to offer same-day—or even one-hour!—deliveries on many items.

WRITING

WRITING EXERCISE 1: IDENTIFY A TOPIC, FACT, OR THESIS (SECTION 34)

1. FACT
2. TOPIC
3. FACT
4. THESIS
5. THESIS
6. THESIS
7. TOPIC
8. TOPIC
9. THESIS
10. THESIS

WRITING EXERCISE 9: WRITE A PARAGRAPH THAT INCLUDES TRANSITIONS (SECTION 34)

Previously (or *In the past*), I used to plan my long road trips by going through the following routine. *First*, I made sure that I had a map of the highways so that if I got lost along the way, I wouldn't panic. *Then*, even if I did have a map to the city of my destination, I would call the hotel for specific driving directions from the highway. *Another* way that I planned ahead was to check my car's tires and have its engine serviced, if necessary. *Also*, I never forgot to bring my cell phone because I had learned how important they are on long drives. *Finally* (or *As the final step*), before I left my house on the day of the trip, I checked the Highway Patrol updates to see if there were any road closures on my route. This routine always worked for me; *however*, I can give it up now that I have a car with its own navigation system. I just need to figure out how it works!

Index

a, an, 6
abbreviations, 54–55, 182
accept, except, 2, 6
action verbs, 148–150
adjectives, 26, 33–39
adverbs, 27, 33–39
advise, advice, 6
affect, effect, 7
all ready, already, 7
apostrophes, 40–52
are, our, 7
argument, 252–256
articles, 6, 26
awkward phrasing, 62–63, 155–159

body paragraphs, 222, 225, 238–239, 241–242
brackets, 247
brainstorming, 234
brake, break, 7

capital letters, 188, 211–216, 266
choose, chose, 8
clauses, 62–65, 79–86
  punctuation of, 80, 87–88, 95–103, 179–204
clichés, 155–159
clothes, cloths, 8
clustering, 234
coarse, course, 8
colons, 182–188
commands, 74, 90
commas, 2, 189–196, 246–247
comma splices, 189
complement, compliment, 8
compound words, 53
concise writing, 156–157
concluding paragraphs, 219, 223, 238–239
conjunctions, 27
conscious, conscience, 8
contractions, 40–45

dangling modifiers, 143–147
dashes, 182–188
dependent clauses, 79–86, 88
  punctuation of, 80, 95–103, 190, 197–204
definitions, 54
description, 231–232
dessert, desert, 8–9
dictionaries, 53–61
do, due, 9

effect, affect, 7
ellipsis, 246
essays, 219–228, 232–255
except, accept, 2, 6
exclamation points, 182–188

fanboys, 27, 87, 96–97, 182, 189–196, 211
feel, fill, 9
first person, 173–175, 220–221, 236
fourth, forth, 9
fragments, 62–63, 89–94, 102–103
free writing, 234

have, of, 9
hear, here, 10
helping verbs, 104–109, 114–124, 133

in-class writing, 248–252
independent clauses, 62–71
  punctuation of, 95–103, 179–204
interjections, 27
introductory paragraphs, 222, 225, 238
irregular verbs, 117–124
it's, its, 10
italics, 205–210

knew, new, 10
know, no, 10

labels, 55
lead, led, 16
linking verbs, 33, 72–73, 148–154
loose, lose, 16

misplaced modifiers, 143–147
Modern Language Association (MLA), 247

names of people, 55
names of places, 55–56
narration, 230–232
new, knew, 10
no, know, 10
nouns, 26, 33, 66, 72, 136, 149

of, have, 9
often-confused words, 6–25
organizing ideas, 236–240
our, are, 7

paper formats, 265
paragraphs, 219–225, 236–240
parallel structure, 160–165
parts of speech, 26–32, 54, 57
passed, past, 16
peace, piece, 17
periods, 182–188
personal, personnel, 17
phrases, 62
  prepositional, 66–71
  verb, 104–109
  verbal, 136–142
piece, peace, 17
possessives, 46–52
prepositional phrases, 66–71
prepositions, 27, 66–67
principal, principle, 17
pronoun agreement, 167–172
pronunciation, 53–54
pronouns, 26, 166–172, 220–221, 236

proofreading, 262–266
proper nouns, 26
punctuation, 169–218
  brackets, 247
  colons, 182–188
  commas, 189–196, 246–247
  dashes, 182–188
  ellipsis, 246
  exclamation points,
    182–188
  italics, 205–210
  periods, 182–188
  question marks, 182–188
  quotation marks, 205–210,
    244–245
  semicolons, 182–188
  underlines, 205–210

question marks, 182–188
quotations, 205–210,
  244–245
quotation marks, 205–210,
  244–245
quiet, quite, 17

reading prompts, 248–252
regular verbs, 116–124
responding to a reading,
  248–252
revision, 262–266
right, write, 17
run-on sentences, 62–63,
  95–101

scoopables, 197–203
second person, 173–175,
  220–221
semicolons, 182–188
sentence patterns, 148–154
sentence structure, 62–178
  awkward phrasing, 62–63,
    155–159
  clichés, 155–159
  dependent clauses, 79–86,
    89, 95–101
  fragments, 62–63, 89–94,
    102–103
  misplaced/dangling
    modifiers, 143–147
  parallel structure, 160–165
  prepositional phrases,
    66–71
  pronouns, 166–172
  regular/irregular verbs,
    116–124

run-on sentences, 62–63,
  95–101
sentence patterns, 148–154
shift in person, 173–175
shift in time, 133–135
Standard English verbs,
  110–115
subject-verb agreement,
  125–132
subjects/verbs, 72–78
verb phrases, 104–109
verbal phrases, 136–142
wordiness, 155–159
shift in person, 173–175
shift in time, 133–135
signal phrases, 245–247
spelling, 4–61
  adjectives and adverbs,
    33–39
  contractions, 40–45
  dictionaries, 53–60
  often-confused words,
    6–25
  parts of speech, 26–32, 54
  possessives, 46–52
  word use practice, 61
  word use preview test, 5
  word use progress test, 60
Standard English verbs,
  110–115
subject-verb agreement,
  125–132
subjects/verbs, 72–78
summaries, 256–261
supporting points, 241–243

than, then, 18
their, there, they're, 18
thesis statements, 236–237
third person, 173–175,
  220–221, 236
threw, through, 18
titles, 206, 265–266
too, to, two, 18–19
topic, finding a, 233–235
topic sentences, 238
transitional expressions,
  239–240
transitions, 239–240
two, too, to, 18–19

underlines, 205–210

verb phrases, 104–109
verbal phrases, 136–142

verbs, 72–78, 104–132,
  148–154
  action, 148–154
  finding, 72–78
  helping, 104–132
  irregular, 116–124
  linking, 148–154
  regular, 116–124
  shifts in time, 133–135
  Standard English forms,
    110–115
  subject-verb agreement,
    125–132
voice, 228–233

weather, whether, 19
were, wear, where, 19
who's, whose, 19
woman, women, 19
wordiness, 155–159
write, right, 17–18
writing, 219–266
  argument, 252–256
  description, 231–232
  essays, 219–228, 233–256
  finding a topic, 233–235
  first-person approach,
    220–221
  in-class essays, 248–252
  narration, 230–231
  organizing ideas, 236–240
  paragraphs, 221–225,
    238–240
  presentation, 265–266
  proofreading, 262–266
  prompts, 248–252
  quotations, 205–210,
    244–247
  responding to a reading,
    248–252
  revision, 262–266
  signal phrases, 245–247
  summaries, 256–261
  supporting with details,
    240–241
  thesis statements, 236–237
  third-person approach,
    220–221
  titles, 206, 265–266
  topic sentences, 238
  transitional expressions,
    239–240
  voice, 228–233

you're, your, 20